LIFE NATURE LIBRARY

THE
EARTH

OTHER BOOKS BY THE EDITORS OF LIFE:

Life's Picture History of World War II

Life's Picture History of Western Man

The World We Live In
   with Lincoln Barnett

The World's Great Religions

America's Arts and Skills

Picture Cook Book

The Second World War
   with Winston S. Churchill

The Wonders of Life on Earth
   with Lincoln Barnett

Life World Library

Life Pictorial Atlas of the World
   with The Editors of Rand McNally

The Epic of Man

The Life Treasury of American Folklore

Life Guide to Paris

LIFE NATURE LIBRARY

THE
EARTH

by Arthur Beiser
and The Editors of LIFE

TIME INCORPORATED
NEW YORK

A STONEHENGE BOOK

About the Author

Arthur Beiser, who was born and educated·in New York City, has made the study of the earth his career. A geophysicist, he has written 12 books and contributed dozens of articles to scientific journals. He has been an associate professor of physics at New York University, where he received his B.A., M.S. and Ph.D., and served as chief scientist on expeditions which established cosmic ray and geophysical observatories in the South Pacific, Alaska and Colorado. Now vice president of Nuclear Research Associates, Inc., Dr. Beiser is also adjunct senior research scientist in geophysics at N.Y.U. Among Dr. Beiser's books are *Our Earth; Basic Concepts of Physics; Mainstream of Physics; The Physical Universe* (with Konrad Krauskopf); *Physics for Everybody* and *The Story of Cosmic Rays* (with his wife, Germaine Beiser); and an anthology, *The World of Physics*. His textbooks are used in more than 150 American colleges and universities.

ON THE COVER: The buttes of Monument Valley in the southwestern U.S. glow in the sunset. Hard stone tops saved them from the water erosion which abraded the softer rock all around them.

Contents

PAGE

Introduction   7

1 A Small but Extraordinary Planet   9

2 Cloudy Beginnings   35

3 Anatomy of the Skies   57

4 The Emergence of the Crust   81

5 Shaping of the Landscape   105

6 The Record of the Rocks   131

7 An Uncertain Destiny   159

Appendix

   Bibliography   185

    A Geologic Tour of the U.S.   186

Credits   188

Index   189

TIME INC. BOOK DIVISION

Editor: NORMAN P. ROSS

Copy Director: WILLIAM JAY GOLD   *Art Director:* EDWARD A. HAMILTON

Chief of Research: BEATRICE T. DOBIE

•

EDITORIAL STAFF FOR "THE EARTH":

Editor, LIFE Nature Library: MAITLAND A. EDEY

Assistants to the Editor: GEORGE McCUE, JOHN MacDONALD

Copy Editor: RICHARD L. WILLIAMS

Copy Assistant: JOHN PURCELL

Designer: PAUL JENSEN

Chief Researcher: MARTHA TURNER

Researchers: JOAN ALLEN, DORIS BRY, PEGGY BUSHONG, NELSON J. DARROW,
LE CLAIR G. LAMBERT, PAULA NORWORTH, ROXANNA SAYRE, VICTOR H. WALDROP,
PHYLLIS M. WILLIAMSON

Picture Researchers: MARGARET K. GOLDSMITH, SUE E. THALBERG

Art Associate: ROBERT L. YOUNG

Art Assistants: JAMES D. SMITH, MARK A. BINN

Copy Staff: MARIAN GORDON GOLDMAN, SUZANNE SEIXAS, DOLORES A. LITTLES

•

Publisher: JEROME S. HARDY

General Manager: JOHN A. WATTERS

•

LIFE MAGAZINE

Editor
EDWARD K. THOMPSON

Managing Editor
GEORGE P. HUNT

Publisher
C. D. JACKSON

•

The text for the chapters of this book was written by Arthur Beiser. The text for the picture essays is by David Thomson, Harvey Loomis, Dale Brown and Gardner Thoenen. The following individuals and departments of LIFE Magazine were especially helpful in the production of the book: Eliot Elisofon, Fritz Goro, George Silk, Dmitri Kessel, Margaret Bourke-White, John Dominis, Carl Mydans, Andreas Feininger and Howard Sochurek, staff photographers; Thomas N. Carmichael, Chief of Regional Editors; and Doris O'Neil, Chief of the LIFE Picture Library. Assistance was also provided by Phillip W. Payne of the Time Inc. News Service, and Content Peckham, Chief of the Time Inc. Bureau of Editorial Reference.

Introduction

Serious study of the earth began with increasing world industrialization, largely through the need for more and more mineral raw materials —coal, oil, metals, building materials and water supplies. From this practical and fairly recent beginning, the earth sciences have matured into a history of the earth. This knowledge and these concepts constitute an essential part of the intellectual background of today's understanding and esthetic appreciation of nature and of man's place in it.

This book is not, nor does it pretend to be, a scientific treatise. Nevertheless, its superb photographs and stimulating text combine to make it a fine introduction to the earth and its processes for the nonprofessional person who wishes to "read this Book of Earth aright" and, in doing so, to see more clearly man's unceasing efforts to discover greater order, meaning and beauty in the chaos of detailed fact that makes up the natural world.

The story of the earth through the immensities of time is at once difficult and easy to read. No one can comprehend it fully, yet no one can fail to be rewarded for closely observing the scraps of records that lie everywhere about us. Every rock that crops out along the country roadside or in a city park and every feature of the natural landscape offer a host of clues to their origin. This erratic glacial boulder, that exposure of fossiliferous limestone, the alluvial valley of this river, that distant range of mountains—all will yield a wealth of information about various aspects of their history. To be sure, finding the answers to some questions that might be asked about their origin challenges all one's ingenuity, but the meaning of much of the evidence is readily apparent. To become aware of such questions about the way the earth was formed—and aware of the perspective of geologic time—is to add a new dimension to one's mind.

The earth sciences are astir. The techniques and concepts of geophysics, geochemistry, biochemistry and other disciplines are being brought to bear increasingly on old questions about the history of rocks and landscapes and on broader problems of the origin of life, the causes of mountains, continents and oceans, and the earth's place in the solar system and the universe. Surprising new facts and unsuspected relationships between facts are being discovered at an increasing rate. Some of the old problems are beginning to yield—at least a little. Man, with his inborn fire, his passion for meaning and order in all things, illuminates the record, and the story of the earth grows more fascinating every year.

William W. Rubey
Professor of Geology and Geophysics
University of California
Los Angeles, California

1

A Small
but Extraordinary
Planet

THIS is a journey to the earth. It begins far out in the immeasurable
universe, within a cluster of galaxies that are huddled together in what
astronomers call a "local group." One member of this cosmic family, itself
made up of countless stars, has a graceful, pinwheel-like form. This is the
Milky Way; as galaxies go, it is only of fair-to-middling size, yet its dimensions are numbing to the mind. From edge to edge across its luminescent
disk, it measures some 100,000 light-years. Its central bulge is as much as
25,000 light-years thick. And one light-year, the distance light travels in a
year at the speed of 186,234 miles a second, is a shade under six thousand
billion miles.

Some two thirds of the way from the galactic center, where the stars thin
out, there shines an ordinary, yellowish star. It has plenty of room to move
around in, for its nearest neighbor in the Milky Way galaxy lies 24 trillion
miles away—a distance of more than four light-years—and its next neighbor after that is about two light-years beyond. This lonely star that glows,
from afar, as weakly as a firefly, is our sun. Among its own attendant family of faithfully circling planets, satellites, asteroids, meteoroids and comets,

one oddly matched pair (third from the sun, in terms of distance) is the earth and its moon.

A minor planet bound to an ordinary star in the outskirts of one galaxy among billions—such is the earth. Approached in this way, from the chill reaches of infinite space, it would be all too easy to miss, a speck almost beneath notice but for one thing: of all the places that conceivably could support human life, the earth is the one and only place we know of that does. Its interior and its skin, its atmosphere and its climate and even its behavior in space—all of which, along with other attributes, will be examined in this book—form in combination a salubrious environment in which life, and especially intelligent life, flourishes. Until proven otherwise, the earth is the wonder of the universe, a unique sphere with an infinity of its own, encompassing everything from the busy world of the atom to the limitless mind and spirit of man. It may not be insignificant in the cosmic scheme of things after all.

Long before men had any real understanding of the shape or size of this planet that sustained them—much less a knowledge of its humble place in the universe—they felt in their bones that each native valley, sheltered harbor or game-rich plain they lived in was somehow central to the entire cosmic scheme of things. In ancient Greece, all the gods of the universe were thought to dwell on a medium-sized mountain, Olympus, 150 miles from Athens; China, although torn and occupied again and again by successions of barbarians, has always held firmly to the proud title of Central Nation; not many decades ago, Boston's joking claim to be the Hub of the Universe was no joke among many Bostonians. Behind each of these and a hundred similar sentiments lay a certain logic: after all, any man is central to his own circular horizon; any kingdom central to its neighbors; the orb of the earth central in human eyes to the surrounding heavens. It was a long time before anyone really pondered the size of the planet itself. The height of continental mountains and the depths of ocean trenches were—and are—remarkable enough, even though the vertical measure that separates Everest's crest from the bottom of the Mariana Trench is no more, horizontally, than a comfortable day's hike.

Babylon envisaged the earth as a hollow mountain, supported and surrounded by the sea. Inside the earth lay the dark, dusty realm of the dead. Arching over the earth was the solid firmament, across which moved the sun, moon and stars.

Egypt saw the earth as a reclining god, Keb, covered with vegetation, and the heavens as a gracefully bent goddess, held aloft by the god of the atmosphere. The sun god, shown in the two boats, sailed daily across the heavens into death's night.

T HOUGH earlier philosophers had concluded that the earth was a globe, it was not until about 250 B.C. that an Alexandrian Greek, Eratosthenes, exercised geometry on the problem of the earth's total dimension. In Syene, an Egyptain upriver town some 5,000 stadia (500 miles) south of Alexandria, there was a deep, dry well. Eratosthenes learned that at noon on the day of the summer solstice, the sun's light shone directly down the well shaft and lit up the bottom. In Alexandria on that same day, he knew, the noon sun was not vertical, but cast a measurable shadow. The sun being a sufficiently distant source of light to make all its rays virtually parallel, Eratosthenes used a simple geometric calculation to show that the difference in angle between Syene and Alexandria was about one fiftieth of a circle. So 5,000 stadia, multiplied by 50, gave Eratosthenes the first close approximation of the earth's circumference that has come down in history. Translating from stadia to miles, he apparently got a value of some 25,000 miles for circumference (the modern measure at the equator is 24,902) and 8,000 miles for diameter (the modern mean is 7,917 miles).

For such rough measurement, Eratosthenes' achievement was remarkable.

(On the basis of it, another Greek geometrician went so far as to calculate the moon's distance from the earth, also with surprisingly accurate results.) Somehow, the Alexandrian value was later ignored or lost. Thus it was that Columbus, some 1,700 years later, set off westward around the world to reach the Indies, with a far smaller earth in mind. Despite what folklore says, Columbus knew—as did any other master mariner of his day —that the earth was a sphere; what he did not know was the earth's true size, nor was Eratosthenes' rough value re-established until the global circumnavigations of the 16th Century.

TODAY, thanks especially to the refining measurements that were made in the course of the International Geophysical Year (1957-1958), we are quite sophisticated in our knowledge of the earth's dimensions. Indeed, long before the IGY, men were aware that the earth, although spherical, was no perfect sphere. Even before this fact was demonstrated by measurement, Isaac Newton had predicted it—partly on the ground that the more-than-1,000-mile-an-hour velocity of the earth's equatorial region must have some centrifugal effect, and partly on the visual evidence of Jupiter's and Saturn's bulging equators. Field work in the 18th Century confirmed Newton's prediction—at the equator the earth is 26.7 miles thicker than it is when measured from pole to pole. Even more exact measurements, based on the movements of America's IGY Vanguard I satellite, have shown that the equatorial bulge is not exactly symmetrical and that its highest points (a matter of 25 feet) lie a little to the south of the earth's equatorial mid-line.

These refinements have led some writers to abandon the classical description of the earth's shape as an "oblate (flattened) spheroid" and grope, instead, with such similes as "pear-shaped." Again, the dominance of vertical measurements over men's imaginations seems to be at work. If all our planet's dimensions were shrunk at once, so that we could inspect a manageable sphere—say five feet across—the human eye could not detect the difference, a matter of a fifth of an inch, between equatorial and polar diameters. At the same time, the earth's eye-catching verticalities would vanish. A fine coat of paint would be thicker than the continents' average height above sea level, and a light pinprick would probe this mock earth's crust more deeply than have man's most ambitious drilling schemes.

Human beings may soon attain such a scaled-down view of their planet by traveling the nearer regions of space. If so, the sheer spectacle of an earth shrunk to such a size may compensate for any disappointment over the globe's surpassing smoothness. From nearby space the earth would present a colorful, ever-changing visage. Its sunlit face would show a generally bluish appearance, while its sizable companion in space, the moon, would have a yellow cast. Color, rather than relief, would serve to distinguish the earth's continents from its oceans: the former would appear to be a delicate red-brown, the latter a pastel blue-green. A dazzling splash of light would mark the sun's reflection on any water surface.

Large events on earth would be easy to follow. The annual cycle of vegetation would be reflected in color changes on the continents, and it might be possible to trace the seasonal advance and retreat of snow cover in the high latitudes of the Northern Hemisphere. Clouds would be conspicuous, often arrayed in long lines with clear gaps between them. From the drift of

Hindu conceptions of the earth vary, but one tribe believed that the earth was held up by elephants, whose shiftings caused earthquakes. The elephants stood on a turtle, an incarnation of the god Vishnu, resting on a cobra, the symbol of water.

The Middle Ages gave rise to a disklike map of the world. The T that divided it into three continents represented the Mediterranean, Don River and Red Sea. Jerusalem lay at the center and the Garden of Eden was thought to be in Asia.

these white wisps across the surface, an observer could follow both the westward flow of the trade winds and the eastward procession of the major weather systems in the earth's middle latitudes. Other phenomena would be harder to detect. A good telescope should pick out the nighttime glow of great cities, however, and a sensitive radio receiver would reveal that at least a portion of the inhabitants' multitude of electromagnetic signals penetrates the upper zones of the earth's atmospheric blanket and passes on into space.

Other instruments would discern—as Explorer satellites disclosed—the vast, doughnut-shaped band of radiation that girdles the earth. First believed to consist of two bands and called the Van Allen belts, the zone was later renamed the magnetosphere. Up to 40,000 miles thick, it is a consequence of the earth's magnetic field, a trap imprisoning electrically charged particles from the sun and from space.

From an imaginary vantage point in space, an observer could also watch the variety of motions in which the earth is endlessly engaged. The most obvious of these is the earth's daily rotation on its own axis. This is the motion that is responsible for the alternation of day and night, which occurs as each place on the earth faces toward or away from the sun. Less obviously, the earth also revolves around the sun once a year, in a 600-million-mile sweep that takes almost exactly 365¼ days and is responsible for the succession of the seasons. The orbit around the sun is not a perfect circle, but an ellipse: the earth's average 92.9-million-mile distance from the sun varies by 3,100,000 miles during the course of a year. The variation between winter and summer, however, has nothing to do with this alternate nearness to and distance from the sun. It is during the Northern Hemisphere's winter and the Southern Hemisphere's summer, as it happens, that the earth comes closest to the sun.

The seasons on earth are caused by the 23 1/2° tilt of its axis and its revolution around the sun. When the north pole of the axis is inclined away from the sun (above), winter comes to the Northern Hemisphere. Days get shorter and the weather consequently cold. Also, the sun's rays shine at a slant on a place like New York (below), and do not concentrate the heat as they do when they fall vertically.

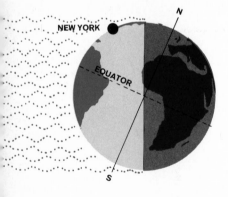

What does account for the seasons is the tilt of the earth's axis. As the earth travels around the sun in its annual journey, the North Pole points toward the sun at the summer solstice, around June 22, but away from the sun at winter solstice, around December 22 (the angle of the tilt, relative to the plane of the earth's orbit, is 23½°). The South Pole, of course, does exactly the opposite, which is why the seasons in the Southern Hemisphere are the reverse of those in the north. It is the angle at which the sun's rays strike the earth, rather than the distance they travel, that is critical in determining the earth's seasonal changes in temperature. A shaft of light that hits a surface at a right angle delivers twice as much energy per square foot as does a shaft of light hitting at an angle of 30°. In either hemisphere, it is in summer that the sun's rays come closest to striking the surface at a right angle, and in winter that they are the most oblique.

Far less apparent than the earth's tilt is the fact that the globe's elliptical path around the sun is not centered precisely in the center of the earth. This is because, in its path about the sun, the earth-moon partnership— linked together by gravitation—behaves like a dumbbell with a large ball at one end and a small one at the other. It is the center of mass of this asymmetrical dumbbell that actually traces the ellipse around the sun. Even though the earth is more than 80 times heavier than the moon, the center of mass of the earth-moon system still lies some 3,000 miles away from the exact center of the earth. Thus, as the moon circles the earth each month, the center of the earth traces an S-curve, with a range of almost 6,000 miles, along the path about the sun.

Superimposed upon this wiggle in the earth's orbit are other, far subtler ones, also due to gravitational forces—in this case, the forces exerted by the other planets. However, these deviations are insignificant in magnitude because, while all the planets are heavier than the moon—and most of them heavier by far—they are also vastly farther away.

Just as its orbital motion around the sun is imperfect, so the earth's rotation about its own axis is not altogether steady. Again, the main source of these irregularities is the moon. Its attraction for the earth's oceans causes the tides, and the weight of the tides slightly unbalances the earth's spin. At the same time, the moon's gravitational action on the earth's equatorial bulge, as the moon passes first south and then north of the equator, causes the earth's axis to wobble like an ill-spun top.

Long before men had measurements precise enough to detect the earth's equatorial bulge, this motion had been noted and measured. In 130 B.C. the Greek astronomer Hipparchus calculated that the sun completed its annual journey around the constellations of the Zodiac a little earlier each spring, reaching the point of vernal equinox a little farther to the east (about 50 seconds of arc) every year. This annual gain has been known ever since as the precession of the equinoxes. Despite the formality of the name precession, this motion is nonetheless a commonplace wobble, although so slow that it takes 25,800 years for the earth's axis to complete one. During this period the North and South Poles each trace out the base of a cone in space—with the apexes point-to-point at the earth's center—and the "North Star" changes.

Some 5,000 years ago, Egyptian astronomer-priests found that the star that lay closest to true north was Alpha Draconis, not the star in the Little Bear's tail (Alpha Ursa Minoris, or Polaris) that serves as today's North Star. At present, the axial wobble is slowly pointing the earth's North Pole ever closer toward Polaris, but 138 years from now, in A.D. 2100, the pole will begin to diverge from the Little Bear until, in the year A.D. 14,000, the new North Star will be Vega. If any mariners ply the earth's seas 12 millennia from now, they will have reason to be pleased with precession, for Vega is the brightest star in the northern sky. But by A.D. 28,000, when another cycle of precession is complete, Polaris will again take its turn as the North Star.

T HE gravitational force of the sun also plays a part in precession, and sun and moon combine to produce still a sixth motion upon the earth. Because these paramount bodies constantly change their positions with respect to the earth, the forces they apply to produce precession are not at all constant. The result is a slight "nodding" of the earth's axis, called nutation, that is superimposed on the slow wobble of precession. This nodding movement is faster but less pronounced than precession: every 18.6 years—which is the length of a full cycle of the moon's own motions—the axis of the earth completes a "nod" that measures 9.2 seconds of arc— about 1/400th of a degree.

Such an array of wobbles, nods, oscillations and whirlings might be deemed quite sufficient motions for any body. Yet the earth, as a member of the solar system, shares in two other motions as well. In the lesser of

Summer comes to the Northern Hemisphere when the earth's axis tilts toward the sun (above). The day the axis is tilted closest to it is the summer solstice. On this day, in late June, New York gets 15 hours of daylight from concentrated, more nearly vertical solar rays. But in the Southern Hemisphere it is midwinter, and the sun shines only briefly and at a low angle on places like Buenos Aires.

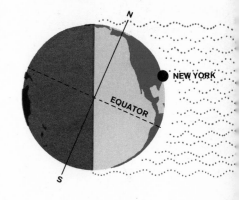

these, it follows the sun in that star's own 12-mile-per-second journey through our local star cloud in the general direction of the constellation Hercules. In the greater motion, the earth follows the sun in its major journey—a great, wheeling "annual" sweep around the hub of the Milky Way that takes 200 million years to complete—which is apparent as a seemingly straight-line motion, at a rate of 150 miles per second, toward the constellation Cygnus.

Although scientists can calculate the times and distances of such cosmic journeys, they find it hard to express their calculations in terms comprehensible by earthly standards. Of a further, final motion shared by the earth—the motion of the Milky Way with respect to the billions of sister galaxies that dot the universe—no sensible statement is yet possible. Our "home galaxy" is certainly moving, but nobody knows for sure where it is headed, or how fast.

A vantage point in nearby space would serve another useful purpose: the unusual nature of the earth's influential neighbor, the moon, would be borne home. Other satellites among the solar system's vast, gassy, outer planets rival and exceed our moon in size—Jupiter's Ganymede is three times larger—but no other body in the sun's entire family has proportionally so large a companion as does the earth. A mere frog's-jump distant from the earth by cosmic standards—at maximum distance, the moon's center is only a trifle over a quarter million miles away from the earth's center—the moon has a diameter that is more than a quarter the size of the earth's, and more than two thirds the size of Mercury's. Indeed, modern thought on the formation of the solar system regards the moon as a legitimate planet, which either took shape as a near twin from the same cosmic raw material that the earth began with or, forming elsewhere in the same general zone, was captured later by the earth to make up the present double system.

IT is impossible to consider the earth's history as a planet without giving due regard to what can be learned from a study of the moon. This lesser twin circles the earth in an elliptical orbit once each 27 1/3 days. With each such revolution, the moon also rotates on its axis exactly once, so that the earth's inhabitants never see the "back" of the moon. Actually, not only is the moon's axis inclined so that we alternately glimpse both its north polar and south polar regions, but both its shape and its motions are irregular enough so that a variety of rocking motions—called librations—have permitted earth observatories to photograph 59 per cent of the moon's total surface. Brilliantly lit by the sun during the lunar day, the earthward face of the moon is dimly illuminated during the lunar night by sunlight reflected from the earth. An ideal subject for photography as well as visual observation, the moon's visible surface has been mapped in detail—good telescopes can resolve objects as little as 5,000 feet in length—and, particularly in recent years, subjected to exhaustive scrutiny. Photographs of the far side, radioed back to earth by the Russians' Lunik rocket, showed it to be quite like the familiar near side.

The airless, waterless lunar landscape is dramatically marked by vast, dark plains (once thought to be seas and hence named *maria* by astronomers of the past), by jagged peaks that rival or surpass the greatest of the earth's mountains, and by thousands of spectacular craters, as much as

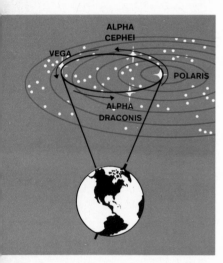

During a cycle of about 26,000 years, the axis of the earth changes with respect to the pole of the ecliptic—an imaginary pole whose axis is perpendicular to the plane of the earth's orbit. This slow rotation aims the true pole toward different points in the sky. The star map above indicates how Alpha Draconis was the North Star in 3000 B.C., and how Polaris has become the North Star today. Alpha Cephei will be the North Star in the year 7500 and Vega in the year 14000.

180 miles across. In the absence of an appreciable atmosphere with its attendant water cycle, the sort of erosion that continually softens the earth's landscape is unknown to the moon. Its sharp-edged features know no buffing but the casual effects of meteorites and the savage wrenches of alternate expansion and contraction as the boiling heat of day—200° F.—is followed by a night chill that may drop to -300° F.

What does the lunar landscape tell us about the earth's own past? Once it was believed that the vast array of craters on the moon represented a long succession of savage volcanic eruptions, such as the earth has often known. Today most students believe these surface scars to be the result of ancient meteoritic bombardment. Following this clue in recent years, the nearly vanished traces of similar, stupendous collisions on the earth have been detected. But our knowledge of the moon poses other questions than those concerning landscape. From observations that yield the moon's dimensions and its mass, we know that the moon has an average density a full third less than the density of the earth. If both bodies were formed of much the same stuff, what accounts for this discrepancy? Because we can examine and weigh the various components of the earth's crust, we know that our planet's inner portions must be a great deal denser than its surface stuff in order to make the average density work out correctly. But no one yet knows the weight of moon dust or moon rock, or how the densities of the moon's interior are apportioned.

From the pace of space-exploring programs, it seems probable that even before there are human explorers on the moon, there will be firsthand instrumental reports to study—and perhaps actual samples of moon matter in hand for terrestrial analysis. Meanwhile, other sorts of clues to the nature of extraterrestrial matter—and thus to the history of our own planet—are available. These come from studies of the chunks, lumps, fragments and specks of dust that continually rain down upon the earth from the depths of space.

Not long ago, it was believed that the brief flashes in the night sky that we know as meteor trails were somehow involved with the atmosphere, and with the weather in general (the term meteorology is a hang-over from this belief). There was logic in such a view; but it was based on the inaccurate assumption that lightning bolts—self-evidently mixed up with weather —produced something called thunderstones, actually odd rocks or, more often, the crude, unrecognized flint tools of early man. Meteor flashes, too, were sometimes accompanied by thunderous sounds and unidentifiable fragments of stone or iron. Although these occurrences were far rarer than electrical storms, it was hard to deny the obvious parallels of flashing light, noise and subsequent lump of matter. Not all meteor showers produced boloids—as the noisy, fragment-producing kind of meteorites are called—but then not all lightning is accompanied by thunder.

EVEN with today's understanding, the matter of meteors still involves complex language. Specialists are strict to distinguish between *meteoroids* (the bits of undefined matter, regardless of size or composition, that drift through space), *meteors* (the visible flashes of light produced by a meteoroid as it is heated to incandescence by its passage through the earth's atmosphere) and finally, *meteorites* (the tangible fragments, ranging from dust to sizable tonnages, that survive the fiery passage and reach the earth). These last are the only samples of extraterrestrial material that men can study pending the return of lunar and planetary expeditions. As a result, meteorites hold quite as much fascination for the students of the earth as they do for the astronomer.

Meteorites are of three general classes: irons—composed 98 per cent or more of nickel-iron; stony irons—composed roughly half-and-half of nickel-iron and of a kind of rock known as olivine; and finally, stones. The stones are further subdivided, depending on whether they contain tiny bodies (or chondrules) of the minerals olivine and pyroxene. The stones that possess them—more than 90 per cent of all known meteoritic stones—are called chondrites. The few stones that lack these minerals are known as achondrites. All these categories offer useful clues to those who try to reconstruct the history of the earth, for not only are meteorites fellow members of the solar system, but radioactive dating indicates that they are as old as the earth itself.

Quite aside from a few spectacular falls that have brought irons weighing as much as 30 tons or more smashing into the earth, a vast amount of meteoritic dust continually falls from the heavens; estimates of the annual accumulation range from a few thousand to a few million tons. This dust consists of particles ranging from a ten thousandth to a hundredth of an inch across. Meteoritic dust particles have been found around the world, and may be extracted magnetically from rain water collected at random. There is even a persuasive theory relating fluctuations in world-wide rainfall to fluctuations in the arrival of meteoritic dust.

UNFORTUNATELY the meteorites have little to tell about the meteoroids that are their presumed parents. Many meteor showers, for example, occur in streams with established orbits. (They are named after the constellation from which they appear to radiate: for example, the Perseids in early August and the Orionids in late October.) Some of these orbits are known to be the same as those of former comets—eccentric bodies that are normally the most outward inhabitants of the solar system. It is therefore plausible to suppose that all recurrent meteor showers represent the debris left in the wake of comets, past or present.

But the material of comets is notoriously insubstantial and it is doubtful if any "comet dust" ever reaches the earth's surface in the solid form of meteorites. Instead, it is the fall of sporadic meteorites that provides matter of particular interest to earth scientists. One popular theory holds that these fragments are debris left over from the disintegration of one or more planet-like bodies, perhaps former full-fledged members of the solar family. The asteroid belt, lying generally between the orbits of Mars and Jupiter, could serve as an inexhaustible source of such fragments. The stony meteorites contain some minerals akin to those in the earth's crust. The crystalline structure displayed by meteoritic iron, in turn, could well have formed during the slow cooling of molten metal under immense pressure—a situation that is most easily imagined in the environment of a planet's interior. Finally, the stony irons could fit the theoretical half-metal, half-rock specification for some planetary layer between core and crust. The meteorites that have fallen and still fall to the earth—and that in the past pockmarked the moon —offer tantalizing clues to the composition of those interior portions of our planet that lie forever beyond reach, and clues to the earth's origin as well.

A PASTEL-HUED EARTH, THINLY HALOED BY ITS ATMOSPHERE, AND A MOTTLED WHITE MOON REFLECT THE RADIANCE OF THE SUN

The Earth in Space

We live in a celestial illusion. To all appearances, our earth hangs solidly in the heavens, much as is depicted in the painting above, while the rest of the universe wheels around it. Yet we know from the subtle proofs of science that this is not true. Our world, dragging its moon along, is awhirl in space. Its complex movements and some of their consequences are shown on the following pages.

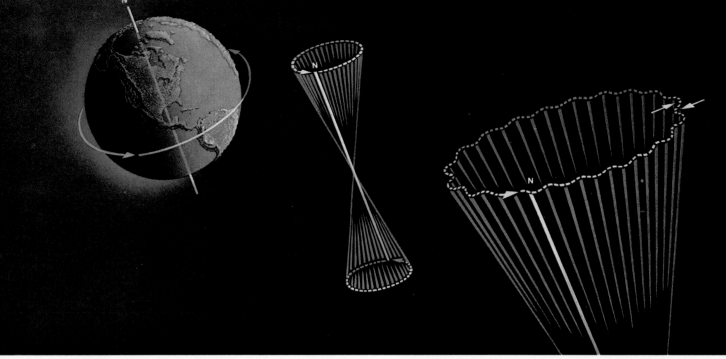

WHIRLING, WOBBLING, NODDING, the earth exhibits the three basic motions shown in the painting above. Once each 24 hours, the earth rotates on its axis (*left*), spinning from west to east on its path around the sun. Once each 26,000 years, the tilted axis of the earth swings ponderous-ly around in a tight circle to trace a double conical figure (*center*). This movement, called precession, is much like the wobbling of a top. The path of precession is not smooth since the gravitational pulls of the sun and moon create a slight back-and-forth nodding effect, or nutation (*right*).

Intricate Pathways in the Sky

The eight motions of the earth illustrated on these pages have been separated from each other for clarity. In space they go on simultaneously, one superimposed upon the other, following pathways of brain-straining complexity. (Try to move a finger as the earth's axis moves in these three drawings.) The intricate movements take place at fantastic speeds. A point on the earth's equator rotates at 1,050 miles an hour. The earth revolves around the sun at 1,100 miles a minute, and the sun moves through the galaxy at 150 miles a second. Only two of these motions have important direct effects on mankind. The rotation of the earth creates the cycle of night and day. And the revolution around the sun, taking just over 365 days, is the basis of our calendar and indirectly the cause of the changing seasons.

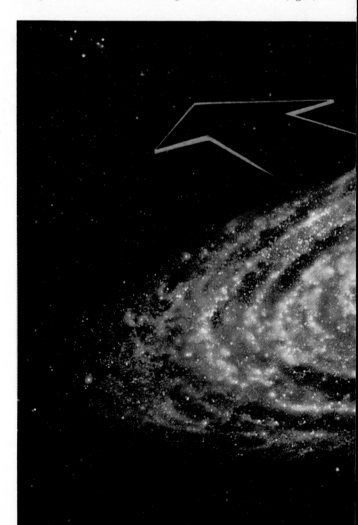

PLUNGING OUT into space with its galaxy (large arrow), the sun also circles among its neighboring stars as indicated by the smaller arrow. The sum of these two motions is the spiral at lower right.

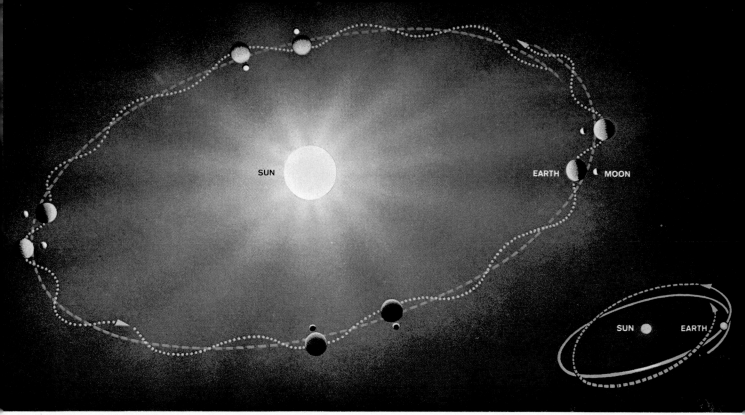

IN ERRATIC REVOLUTION, the earth and moon trace an intertwined pattern in their yearly trip around the sun. The sun's gravity acts on the earth and moon as if they were coupled into a giant dumbbell. It is the center of the dumbbell's mass, rather than the center of the earth, which moves in a smooth ellipse (broken line). The center of the earth follows a serpentine path (dotted line). The earth-moon system does not quite retrace its orbit in successive years. With each revolution, it begins a path in a position slightly counterclockwise from the previous one (lower right).

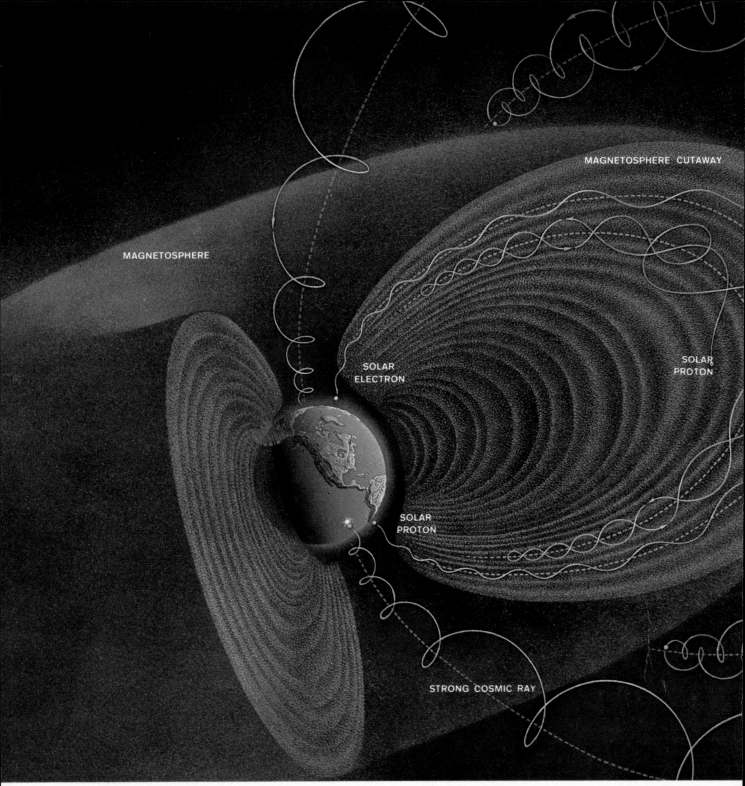

MAGNETOSPHERE CUTAWAY

MAGNETOSPHERE

SOLAR ELECTRON

SOLAR PROTON

SOLAR PROTON

STRONG COSMIC RAY

ENFOLDING THE WORLD in a tubular layer 40,000 miles thick, the magnetosphere is dangerous to space travelers, but to most of mankind it is a reassuring sign that the earth is safe from bombardment by lethal radiation. Puffs of protons and electrons from the sun constantly bump into the earth's magnetic field. Most of this radiation is trapped in

A Doughnut-Shaped Cage
of Captive Radiation

A critical and completely unexpected discovery about the earth in space astonished the scientific world in 1958. Dr. James Van Allen, head of a U.S. research team, announced that American Explorer and Pioneer satellites had found two great bands of radiation trapped high above the

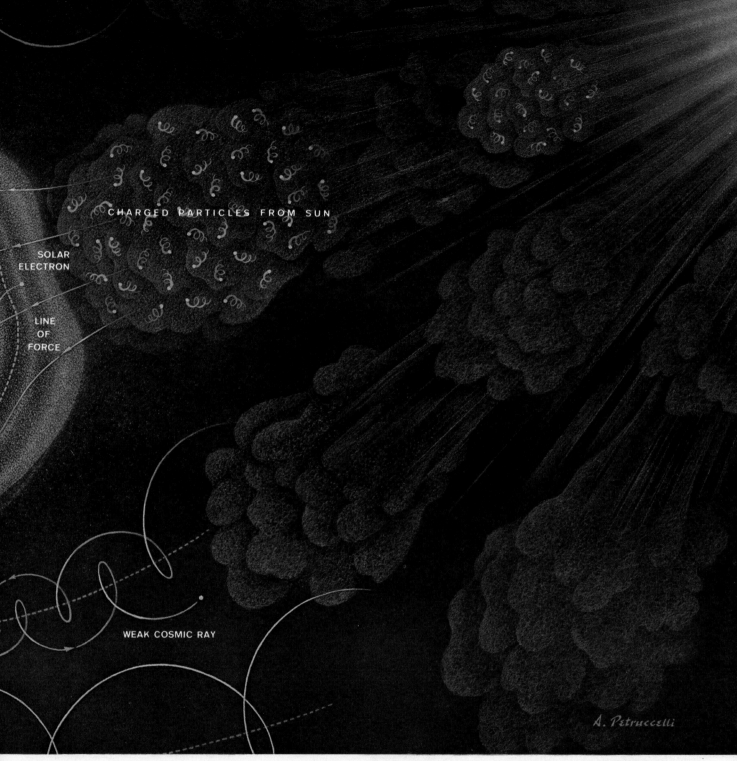

CHARGED PARTICLES FROM SUN

SOLAR
ELECTRON

LINE
OF
FORCE

WEAK COSMIC RAY

A. Petruccelli

the field, where it spirals back and forth along the lines of force without ever reaching earth. Where it actually penetrates the atmosphere, near the magnetic poles, it agitates the air molecules to create the flaming auroras. Weak cosmic rays from space are mostly deflected by the magnetosphere, but the stronger ones flash relentlessly to the earth.

surface inside the earth's magnetic field. These were named the Van Allen belts after their discoverer. Recent satellite data has shown there are not two distinct belts, but one large one starting about 600 miles up and stopping rather abruptly 40,000 miles out in space. This single doughnut-shaped band is called the magnetosphere. Sustained trips through the magnetosphere could kill a human being and all space orbits by astronauts have been below the radiation. But quick rocket flights through the band to the moon or the planets could be safely made.

The Fickle, Forceful Moon

The moon gives off no light of its own but only reflects the brilliance of the sun. As it orbits around the earth, forever showing only one side, the moon therefore has phases in which it appears as a crescent, a half moon, a gibbous—or three-quarter—moon, and finally in its full glory (explanatory drawing below).

To the ancients, the changing moon appeared to be a living thing that grew in size, dwindled and died. It seemed reasonable that its waxing and waning could affect living things on earth. Seeds were sown when the moon was waxing so they would grow strong, and trees were felled in the waning moon when they were weakest.

Such lunar effects are now all but dismissed as superstition. But the moon does exert a strong influence on the earth. Although it is only 2,160 miles in diameter and one eightieth the mass of the earth, it is so close (about 240,000 miles away) that its gravitational pull is strongly felt. The oceans are heaped into tides and even the land is affected. The North American continent may rise six inches when the moon is overhead.

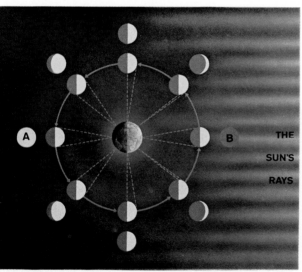

THE MOON'S PHASES are caused by differences in the amount of its sunlit surface seen from the earth (outer circle). Actually, the moon is always half dark (inner circle), but the angle of view from the earth keeps changing (dotted lines), giving a "full" moon at A, a "new" moon at B.

A LUMINOUS BALL, the moon nearing full phase rises over a Bavarian lake (*opposite*). Even in the clearest weather the full moon is only 1/450,000th as bright as the noonday sun.

A SILVER SLIVER, the crescent moon is seen in this multiple exposure as it descends over the Sahara north of Lake Chad. The white dot setting at the lower left is the planet Venus.

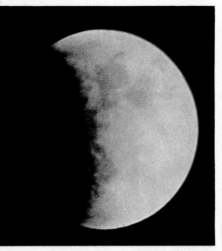

IN A LUNAR ECLIPSE, THE EARTH'S RUDDY SHADOW CROSSES THE MOON'S FACE (LEFT AND CENTER), NEARLY COVERING IT (RIGHT)

Eclipses: Shadows in the Sky

Eclipses are perhaps the most fearsome of all natural phenomena. The dependable light of the sun or moon suddenly dims or blinks out, leaving the creatures of earth uneasy in the unaccustomed darkness. As seen in the diagram below, a solar eclipse occurs when the moon passes directly between the sun and the earth, while a lunar eclipse takes place when the moon passes through the earth's shadow. Such alignments in space are not especially rare. Each year, there are at least two eclipses of the sun and there may be as many as five, although most are partial eclipses in which only a segment of the sun's face is covered. Lunar eclipses occur just as often and are seen over larger areas, although some are so faint that they can only be detected with instruments.

As a solar eclipse like the one opposite begins, a dark notch appears at the western edge of the sun, and the moon quickly bites its way deeper and deeper into the solar disk. As the face of the sun diminishes, a peculiar twilight rushes over the landscape. From start to finish an eclipse may last as much as four hours, but the dark climax seldom endures more than nine minutes.

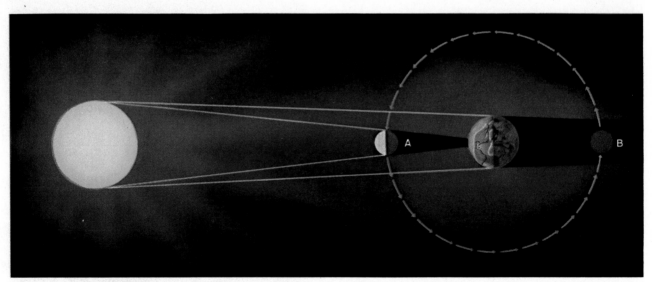

TWO KINDS OF ECLIPSES, solar and lunar, are shown above. When the moon is at position "A" in its orbit, the sun is eclipsed on those parts of the earth where the tip of the moon's conical shadow falls. When the moon is at position "B," it lies in the earth's shadow and a lunar eclipse occurs. In both cases all three bodies must be in line.

IN FIERY ECLIPSE, the sun's face is almost hidden by the dark disk of the moon. This is an annular eclipse, so called because a ring, or annulus, of sunlight is still visible around the moon's edge. In a total eclipse, when the moon is closer to the earth, the entire sun is obscured. This picture was taken in the North African desert in December 1955.

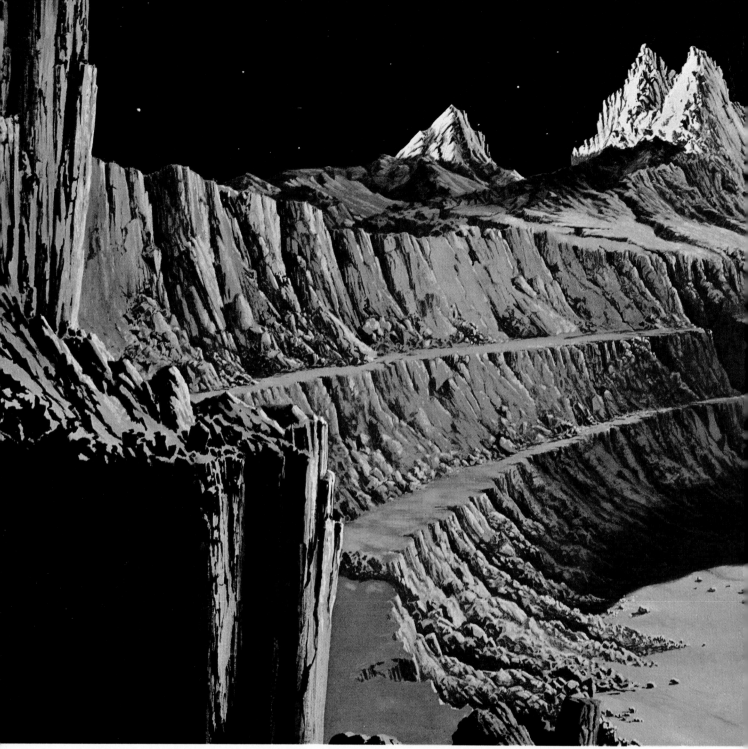

A MAMMOTH LUNAR CRATER, SHOWN IN THIS PAINTING AS IT MIGHT APPEAR TO AN EXPLORER ON THE MOON, HAS STEEP, TERRACED

The Bleak Lunar Landscape

Through the largest telescope on earth, the huge 200-inch Hale reflector at Mount Palomar, California, the moon's surface appears only 200 miles away. From such a distance objects no bigger than a city block are visible. In a telescopic view, the most striking features on the lunar surface are its craters. More than 30,000 of them, from a mile to 180 miles in diameter, have been charted. Some scientists think that they are volcanic and a Russian astronomer has reported seeing volcanic action in the crater named Alphonsus (*opposite*). A more widely accepted theory attributes the craters to a bombardment by giant meteorites some four and a half billion years ago.

26

SIDES AND SMALLER, YOUNGER CRATERS IN ITS HUGE, DUSTY FLOOR. THE SCENE IS ILLUMINATED BY GHOSTLY BLUISH EARTHLIGHT

LUNAR CLOSE-UP is one of the clearest pictures of the moon ever made. The large (90-mile) crater in the center with the small crater cone in its bottom is Ptolemaeus. The one to its left is Alphonsus.

27

The New, Two-Faced Lunar Atlas

Squinting with naked eye, peering through gradually improving telescopes, studying the streaky pictures of a rocket-borne television camera, generations of astronomers have been compiling an atlas of the moon. Although the same side of the moon always faces the earth, over half of its surface can be seen because the moon rocks slightly on its axis, permitting tantalizing peeks at the hidden side. The discernible features on the moon's near side were named long ago, generally with classic Latin appellations or after worthy scientists or philosophers. From photographs taken from a Soviet lunar satellite, most of the rest of the moon was revealed. A half dozen new names, some with the most up-to-date political overtones, were added to the lunar map.

THE FAMILIAR SIDE OF THE MOON, PHOTOGRAPHED IN SHARP DETAIL, SHOWS PEAKS AND CRATERS AS SMALL AS A QUARTER MILE ACROSS.

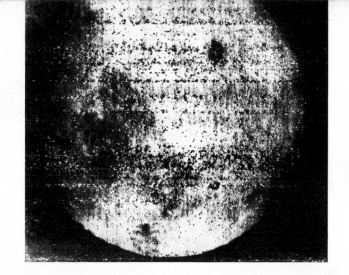

THE BACK OF THE MOON appears in a vague television image sent back by the Russian spacecraft, Lunik III, in 1959. The satellite looped the moon, then came toward earth to transmit pictures.

THE BACK SIDE OF THE MOON, RETOUCHED FROM THE ORIGINAL TELEVISED PICTURE ABOVE, REVEALS ONLY THE GROSSEST FEATURES

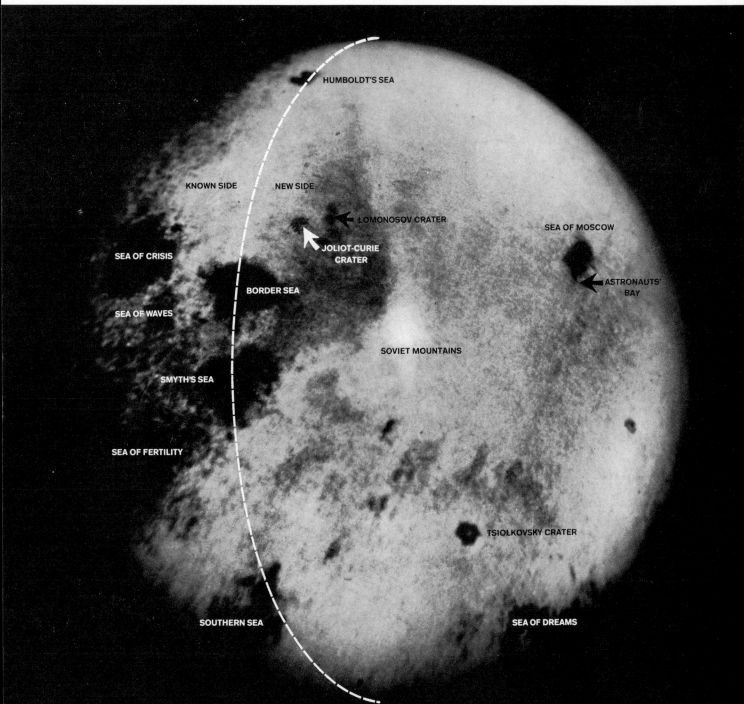

The Mysterious Meteorites

Until the first spaceman brings back rocks and dust from the moon, meteorites are the earth's only tangible samples of matter from space. Meteorites are probably fragments of a planet that exploded long ago, although some may be "planetesimals" left over from the clouds of cosmic dust out of which our solar system grew. Most of these fragments that come within the earth's gravitational pull and fall through the atmosphere are made of stone. The largest meteorites, however, like the one below, are metallic, consisting mostly of dense nickel-iron alloys. The biggest ever discovered is estimated to weigh 70 tons. Only two to eight meteorite falls of appreciable size occur each year in an area as large as the United States, but there is a constant rain of space dust, which filters down at the rate of perhaps a million tons a year.

PUZZLING PARTICLES of glass matter, australites (*top*) and tektites, may have come from ancient asteroid explosions.

THE LARGEST METEORITE ever recovered in the United States is the Willamette, found near Portland, Oregon, in 1902. It is a conical mass of nickel-iron and weighs 14 tons.

A TOUGH IRON METEORITE wore out a stack of 82 band saw blades (*opposite*) when scientists cut it in half to see the effects of its blazing plunge through the earth's atmosphere.

THREE TYPES OF METEORITES show different structures. On the left is an iron meteorite, cut, polished and etched with acid to reveal the pattern of its nickel-iron alloys. In the center is a stony meteorite section with a grainy texture similar to terrestrial rock. On the right is a stony-iron, its network of nickel-iron alloy filled with a stone called olivine.

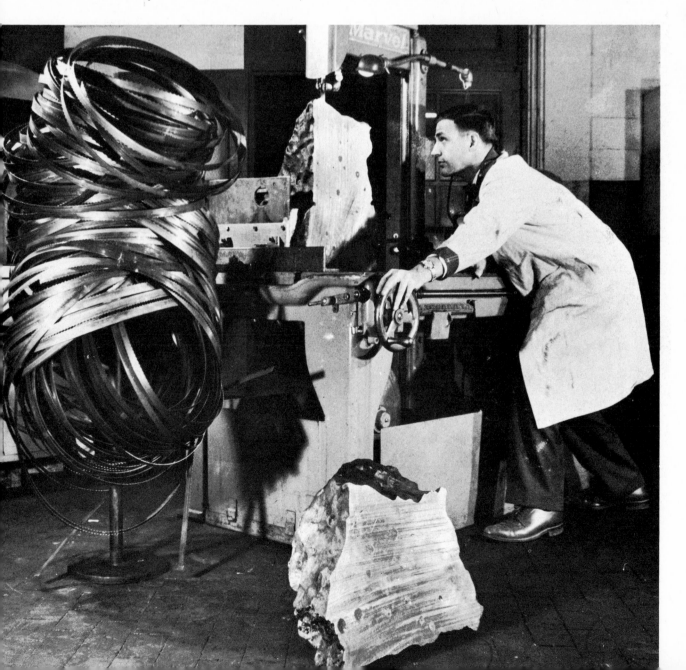

Missiles from Outer Space

Few large meteorites strike the earth. Most burn up in the atmosphere, or explode and reach the ground as fine dust. It is fortunate they do, for when a large meteorite survives its fiery flight and hits the earth it can do tremendous damage. A giant meteorite hit the Arizona desert in prehistoric times and dug a crater 4,100 feet across and 600 feet deep (*below*). A more puzzling cataclysm from space occurred in northern Siberia in 1908. There an explosion flattened the surrounding forest for a distance of 40 miles (*opposite*). It was long thought to be a meteorite blast, but Soviet scientists now believe it was caused by a comet—a mass of frozen gases—colliding with the earth.

CANYON DIABLO CRATER NEAR WINSLOW, ARIZONA, WAS BLASTED

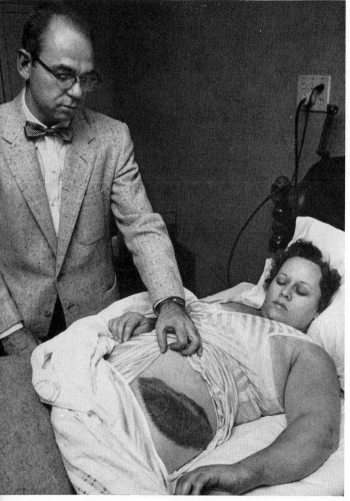

AN UNLUCKY TARGET of a meteorite, Mrs. Hewlett Hodges was bruised by a 10-pound fragment that pierced her roof (*top picture*) and struck her left side.

A FLATTENED FOREST in Siberia, long thought to have been hit by a meteor in 1908, is now believed to have been the work of a comet which exploded just before reaching the ground. A "ball of fire" crossed the sky, followed by a tremendous blast. Men and animals 100 miles away were bowled over, and pressure waves were recorded in London.

OUT WHEN AN IRON METEORITE OF 15,000 TONS OR MORE PLUNGED TO EARTH AND EXPLODED, SCATTERING MILLIONS OF FRAGMENTS

2

Cloudy Beginnings

WHILE knowledge of the earth's size and shape is as ancient as Greek geometry and as modern as Canaveral's rockets, man's understanding of the planet's origin—and its exact composition—is notoriously imprecise. "In the beginning . . . the earth was without form, and void," *Genesis* announces with unimprovable terseness—but when *was* the beginning? It is unlikely that even Archbishop James Ussher, if he had it to do over again, would date creation today as unequivocally (or as recently) as he did in 1650 when he pinpointed it at the stroke of 9 a.m. Sunday, October 23, 4004 B.C. Once it was dignified as a marginal note in the King James version of the Bible, his date stood for nearly three centuries as an all but ineradicable bench mark of fundamentalist chronology.

Yet the earth certainly has not existed forever. If it were eternally old, the various radioactive elements still decaying in its crust would have vanished to nothingness long ago. The elements leached from the rocks of the continents and exhaled by the volcanoes would have turned the oceans into a sticky broth more saline than the Dead Sea. The earth is old indeed—today most geologists accept a figure of 4.5 billion years—but once upon a time there was no earth, and the circumstances of its birth present one of the most fascinating riddles still before science.

There has been no lack of valiantly attempted solutions. Some ancient mythologies pictured the nascent earth as a warm body of liquid. The philosopher Descartes, in 1644, saw it as a sunlike, incandescent body. Immanuel Kant and the Marquis de Laplace, in the 18th Century, thought it condensed out of a gaseous nebula surrounding the sun. Various later hypotheses—now known to be untenable—have described the earth as a child of the sun, either blasted out of it by some internal explosion or torn away from it by the force of a collision, or near-collision, with some wayward passing star. The whole tantalizing question of the earth's evolution is, of course, inescapably linked to the larger questions of the origin of the solar system, of stars in general, of galaxies—and of the entire universe.

As to even the first of these questions, however—the creation of the solar system—a contemporary American astronomer, Gerard P. Kuiper, has pointed out that all possible theories involve assumptions that are simply beyond man's power to verify. "It is not a foregone conclusion," says Kuiper, ". . . that the problem has a scientific solution. For instance, an enclosure in which the air has been stirred gives, after some delay, no clue to the nature or the time of the stirring. All memory of the event within the system has been lost."

WITH this warning, what can be said about the earth's first, embryonic days? Many astronomers now agree on a probable chain of events occurring inside an interstellar cloud of gases and dust that was as far across as the entire solar system is today. For a long time this dust cloud may have been formless, but at some point the force of gravity working within the cloud caused it to collapse into a flattened, revolving disk. In the course of 80 million years or so this disk sorted itself into a dense contracting center and a series of surrounding concentric rings. The center, amounting to almost 90 per cent of the mass of the original dust cloud, was the protosun, huge, cool, and therefore not yet incandescent. The rings, containing the remaining 10 per cent of the original aggregate of gas and dust, were the cloudy stuff from which protoplanets would form. Each ring was destined for a distinctive character as a planet, depending on its distance from the central mass and the exact nature of its raw materials.

Protoearth was a special case in the array of spinning rings. As noted in the first chapter, the earth and its moon are unique in the solar system, for no other planet has a companion proportionately as large. So within the dust-cloud hypothesis, two possibilities exist to explain the formation of the moon: either protoearth developed two increasingly dense nuclei, which grew as a pair, or else two quite separate protoplanets developed from the

BODE'S LAW

One of the most productive and puzzling laws of science was published by the German astronomer Johann Bode in the 1770s. Bode noted that the distances of the various planets from the sun fell into a curious mathematical sequence. He published a paper which arbitrarily assigned numbers to the planets: 0, 3, 6, 12, 24, 48, 96, 192. Thus Mercury was numbered 0, Venus 3, Earth 6, Mars 12, and so on, each number being double the last one.

• *When 4 was added to each of these numbers and the result divided by 10, figures emerged which almost exactly equaled the planets' distances from the sun, measured in astronomical units. (An astronomical unit is the distance from the earth to the sun, 93 million miles.)*

• *The table on the opposite page shows how Bode's calculations work out, compared to the true distances as measured by modern scientific methods.*

• *The only trouble with the law was that there were no planets at positions 24 or 192. But astronomers, searching in position 24, located the asteroids. Uranus, which was discovered in 1781, occurs at position 192 and conforms almost exactly with Bode's calculations. Only the outermost planets, Neptune and Pluto (illustration below), fail to obey the law.*

• *Today, many astronomers dismiss Bode's law as a coincidence. Yet it remains one of the most mysterious statements of natural law formulated by man.*

MERCURY   VENUS   EARTH   MARS   ASTEROIDS   JUPITER   SATURN

same ring of raw material, and later captured each other in a near-collision.

Whichever the case, protoearth was probably 500 times heavier and 2,000 times its present diameter, just as all the protoplanets were far larger than the bodies they evolved into. Over the millions of years their heavier elements sank inward to form massive cores enveloped by lighter gases, mostly hydrogen and helium. Meanwhile their sun was contracting too. In due time it reached a critical density where nuclear reactions in its interior began to evolve heat.

Up to this point the whole process had taken place in darkness. But now the sun began to shine and to evaporate streams of ions from its surface. These hot streams swept the nearer planets free of the gases that still clung to them. The planets themselves grew warm, and the blowing-away of gas was enhanced by evaporation. After some hundreds of millions of years, with most of their mass boiled away by solar radiation, what remained was the sun-warmed, shrunken, virtually naked inner planets and the gas-enveloped outer planets of the present day.

The whole leisurely sequence is reasonably consistent with what is known about the existing solar system. All of the planetary orbits except that of Pluto lie within a few degrees of the sun's equatorial plane, and Pluto's is only 17° away from that plane. (Pluto may not even be a real planet, but an escaped moon of Neptune.) The planets all revolve about the sun, and rotate on their own axes, in the same direction as the sun rotates, which is counterclockwise as seen from over its north pole—though for some reason a few of the satellites turn clockwise. The planets' distances from the sun fall into a pattern of the most remarkable regularity. Further, their combined rotational momentum, which is 49 times that of the sun, squares with the theory. If they had been born in some solar catastrophe the sun's rotation, as well as its bulk, would dwarf theirs.

What is known of the earth's own structure also fits in plausibly. When the dense core of protoearth came into being, the shrinking process itself, as well as the heat-yielding radioactive elements present, began to raise the temperature of the whole mass. Eventually the earth became molten, but as the energy of contraction was exhausted and the initial radioactive content decayed, it began to cool down, a process that may or may not still be going on.

UNTIL the earth could be weighed, speculation about its anatomy could be no better informed than early philosophizing about its origin. Various natural philosophers had offered a variety of proposals: an earth filled with water (its cataclysmic outburst, in early times, causing the Flood); an earth whose crust was dust, floating on a supporting bath of oil; even a hollow earth, with cavities alternately full of fire or water. All these geogonies,

THE PLANETS' POSITIONS

PLANET	BODE'S PREDICTED DISTANCE	ACTUAL DISTANCE
Mercury	0.4	0.39
Venus	0.7	0.72
Earth	1.0	1.00
Mars	1.6	1.52
Asteroids	2.8	2.65
Jupiter	5.2	5.20
Saturn	10.0	9.50
Uranus	19.6	19.20
Neptune	38.8	30.10
Pluto	77.2	39.50

(Figures are in astronomical units. One unit equals 93 million miles.)

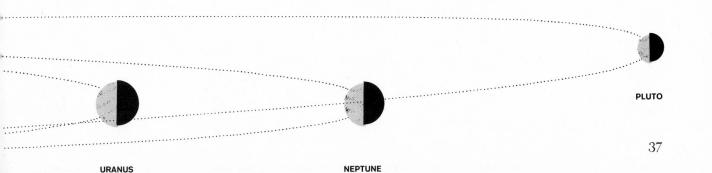

PLUTO

URANUS

NEPTUNE

37

as they were called, necessarily vanished in 1798 when the English physicist Henry Cavendish "weighed" the earth. His starting point was Newton's law of universal gravitation, which holds that every body in the universe attracts every other body with a force directly proportional to both their masses and inversely proportional to the square of the distance between them. Cavendish built a yard-long dumbbell, hung it from a thread, measured the attraction between its twin balls and two larger spheres, calculated the gravitational constant—and from this, along with such known quantities as the earth's diameter, derived a weight of 6.6 sextillion (6.6 followed by 20 zeros) tons. As estimates go in problems of such magnitude, it was and is a good one.

For its volume, which is about 260 billion cubic miles, the earth is the heaviest planet in the solar system. Its average density is five and a half times that of water. (Saturn, at the other extreme, is so light it would float in water.) But the average density of the rocks that make up the earth's crust—light granites and dense basalts together—is only a hair more than half the density of the earth as a whole. To the scientists who first pondered this, one fact immediately was clear: the density of whatever composes the earth's interior had to be far greater than that of the surface rocks. The earth neither had room for such lightweights as fire and water inside, nor was it like a giant Edam cheese, a great ball made of the same stuff all the way through.

Such an insight seems elementary today. But at the start of the 19th Century, when geology began to outgrow its prolonged infancy, facts of this kind were invaluable building blocks. Even today, every idea about the interior of the earth is conjecture—but it is conjecture based on a foundation of ingenious conclusions, largely drawn from observation of the natural disasters known as earthquakes.

ALTHOUGH only about a score of severe earthquakes wrench the earth in the course of an average year, there are approximately a million minor tremors during the same period, or about two per minute. They provide a continuous source of data for analysis of the earth's interior. As a result of a century of such study, seismologists know that nearly all of the major earthquakes originate in two long, relatively narrow zones. The principal zone is a belt in the lands that border the Pacific Ocean, running up the west coast of North and South America, and down the coast of Asia. The second major zone runs from west to east across Europe and Asia, from Spain and northern Africa through Italy, Greece, Turkey, India and Burma, to join the Pacific belt at Celebes. The first zone, known as the Pacific "ring of fire" because of the presence of most of the world's volcanoes along its path, is also the site of more than 80 per cent of all earthquakes, while the second zone is responsible for an additional 15 per cent or so. The remaining quakes occur at scattered locations elsewhere on the earth.

Nearly all earthquakes originate in fractures of the solid rock of the earth's crust along one zone or another. These fractures, called faults, occur when stresses that develop within the earth become too great for the brittle crust to bear. A spectacular example is the San Andreas fault in California. The land mass east of the San Andreas fault is steadily inching its way south, and every so often the motion goes beyond the stretching ability of the underlying rock. When this happens, the rock ruptures. On

April 18, 1906, the ground shifted as much as 15½ feet along 200-odd miles of the San Andreas fault, causing an earthquake that demolished much of San Francisco. It was the most extensive earth shift ever recorded for a single quake. The 1906 San Francisco earthquake was neither the first nor the last to occur as the result of movement along Pacific Coast faults: major quakes shook California in 1857, 1922 and 1940, and others can be expected from time to time before the rearrangement of the earth in that restless region is complete.

A MAJOR earthquake is one of nature's most awesome events. In violence it may exceed the detonation of a billion tons of TNT, and while the most severe disturbance is localized, the shock may convulse wide areas. The Lisbon earthquake of 1755, for example, not only wrecked the heart of that city and killed thousands of its people, but also made itself felt over a million and a half square miles of Europe. All over the Continent the waters of lakes and rivers were violently disturbed, and sea waves from the quake rushed all the way across the Atlantic to the West Indies in a few hours. The quake occured on November 1—All Saints' Day—when the faithful all over Europe were in church. In the great cathedrals, awed spectators watched the chandeliers shake and swing to the shock waves from Lisbon.

The Lisbon quake was not the first, by any means, to have alarmed Europeans. But it was the most destructive by far, and the scale of the disaster reminded scientists how little they knew about the nature of earth tremors. One of them, the English astronomer-mathematician John Michell, collected all the reports he could find and was able to calculate that the shock wave had traveled at a speed of more than 20 miles a minute. Michell prophetically guessed that the source of the shock was an earth movement deep in the crust: " . . . it could not be much less than a mile or a mile and a half [deep]," he wrote, "and . . . it is probable that it did not exceed three miles."

Less than 30 years after the Lisbon disaster, a series of severe earthquakes convulsed the Calabrian district of Italy, taking a toll of 35,000 lives. This second disaster, as well as Michell's inspiration concerning the great depths —far below the reaches of the deepest mine—at which the destructive shocks were born, served to bring more and more scientific effort to bear on the earthquake question. An urgent need was felt for some instrument that would measure the upheavals. Purely subjective reporting developed a rough scale of earthquake intensity, ranging in steps from slight to catastrophic. Later it became known that the shock waves at an earthquake's center produce an up-and-down motion and that, as they travel outward like ripples in a pond, these waves gradually become more horizontal. But there were no clues as to the direction from which distant shocks came, and the speed of travel, while realized to be rapid, was not known with any precision. It seemed possible that some new apparatus would not only supply this missing information but also, because of the depth at which earthquakes evidently begin, provide vital information about the earth's unknown interior.

Despite these incentives it was not until 1855—a century after the Lisbon tragedy—that the first seismograph was constructed. Today hundreds of these instruments, with a variety of refinements, are at work in seismological laboratories around the world. No single seismograph can disclose the point

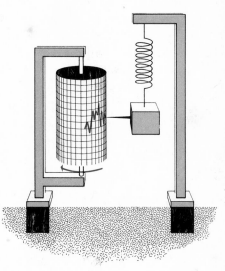

A seismograph, shown in this simplified drawing, records an earthquake in the following way: the two metal frames, anchored in rock, pick up earth vibrations. A heavy pendulum, suspended from one of the frames by a wire coil to keep it static, traces the movements of the other frame and its rotating drum on the unfurling graph paper—thus giving an accurate measure of the earthquake's force.

at which an earthquake's tremors start. All, however, can show how far away an earthquake is.

Basically, a seismological station has three seismographs, one mounted vertically, and two mounted horizontally at right angles so that one instrument will react to waves that pass to the north or the south, while the other responds to waves from east or west. In essence, each seismograph consists of a support, firmly anchored to the bedrock; a massive body that hangs freely suspended from the support; and a spring connecting the two. As an earth tremor shakes the support, the flexible spring keeps these bedrock motions from reaching the suspended mass, which tends to hold its original position. In the process, the spring stretches or contracts and these changes in the spring are recorded. Together, a set of three seismographs can narrow the possible sources of incoming waves to two spots on earth, only one of which is likely to be in an earthquake zone.

One of the first fruits of this new instrument was the realization that an earthquake's shock is transmitted in several different forms. The slowest is called a surface wave, which travels like an ocean wave along the curve of the earth's thin crust. Other waves, unsuspected before seismographs revealed them, drive, instead, straight into the body of the earth at a speed substantially greater than the surface waves'. They proved to be of two kinds, primary—or P—and secondary—or S—waves. Of this speedy pair, P waves are the faster and more penetrating, moving without hindrance through the dense matter of the earth's interior. The slower S waves have a transverse movement—most commonly seen when a taut cord is plucked, or when a whip is cracked. A fact of significance, as will be shown, is that transverse waves travel well enough through solids, but disappear when they encounter liquids or gases.

At any seismograph station, the first sign that an earthquake has occurred is the arrival of a train of P waves—the fastest ones. Later—the interval depending on the distance to the station from the earthquake's focus—the S waves arrive. Still later, the slower surface waves, journeying along the thin, curved medium of the earth's crust, make their distinctive squiggle on the seismograph's revolving drum. (In some cases, seismographs can also point to the source, and indicate the force, of a volcanic eruption—or of a nuclear explosion.)

So far as exploring the earth's interior is concerned, the most useful facts that seismographs provide are the travel times of earthquake waves from their centers to the seismological observatories that dot the earth. From a sufficiently complete set of travel times, it is possible to infer the speeds of P and S waves at various depths in the earth. It has been found, for example, that these speeds tend to increase gradually as the waves pass nearer the earth's center. There are also several precisely defined depths at which sudden shifts in the speed of travel occur. Such shifts must signify radical changes in the properties of the earth's interior matter, and the boundaries they mark between concentric layers of chemically or physically different kinds of material are therefore known as discontinuities.

The uppermost of the discontinuities is named after its discoverer, Andrija Mohorovičić. Above the Mohorovičić discontinuity there lies only the crust of the earth, a thin shell of rock about three miles thick under the sediments that coat the ocean floors, but with an average thickness of some 20

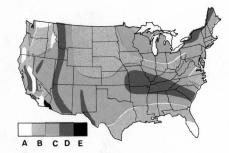

A B C D E

An earthquake map of the U.S. shows that no state is free from the threat of tremors. The darkest zones (E) indicate regions where quakes are most severe. Even in areas one shade lighter (D), a quake could knock a house off its foundations.

miles under the continents. This crust seems to have two chief components: a three-mile-thick layer of heavy basalt that surrounds the entire earth, and blocks of lighter granite rock, as much as 40 miles thick, superimposed on the basalt to form the continents.

At the Mohorovičić discontinuity, the P and S waves accelerate from 4.3 and 2.4 miles per second respectively to 5 and 2.9 miles per second. Their rate of travel then increases steadily for the next 1,800 miles downward, until it reaches speeds of 8.5 and 4.5 miles per second respectively. At this depth, the speed of P waves suddenly drops to 5 miles per second and their direction of travel changes sharply, while the S waves disappear. Evidently a dramatic change in the earth's interior takes place at this 1,800-mile-deep boundary between the earth's mantle and its core.

THE whole region between these two discontinuities, the mantle, contains over 80 per cent of the earth's volume, as compared with the crust's $1\frac{1}{2}$ per cent. At present it is only possible to guess at the nature of this region. Some geophysicists surmise that much—perhaps most—of the mantle is composed of various phases of dunite, a rock with properties that seem to fit in well with what little is understood about this vast region. Seen on the earth's surface, dunite is a green or rust-colored, coarse-grained rock. But the mantle may also contain peridotite, a greenish-brown rock in some regions and eclogite, a pale pink similar rock, in others.

Below the 1,800-mile-deep discontinuity lies the earth's core. Much indirect evidence supports the notion that at this depth the core is composed of molten iron, perhaps with some nickel and a trace of cobalt. First, the core must be very dense, in order to help account for the earth's great weight. This points to iron as the chief ingredient of the 42 billion cubic miles of the core, for iron is the only heavy element relatively abundant throughout the universe. Moreover, at the estimated pressures and temperatures of the earth's core, iron would have a density—at least 588 pounds per cubic foot—that fits the weight requirement, and it would also be a molten liquid. That the earth's core *is* liquid may be inferred from the inability of earthquake S waves to pass through it (their transverse vibrations can travel only through solids). Finally, the existence of the earth's magnetic field is most readily understood in terms of electric currents generated in a body of liquid metal.

All these lines of reasoning leave little doubt that the earth's core is principally composed of molten iron. But this is not the whole story. On the basis of further seismographic studies, some geophysicists think that still another major discontinuity exists—this one located about 800 miles from the center of the earth and indicating another, different region *within* the core. Thus, working from the earth's surface downward, there would be a crust (a few miles), mantle (1,800 miles), outer core (1,375 miles) and inner core (800 miles). The difference between the inner and outer cores could be a chemical one—perhaps a slightly altered alloy of iron with nickel —or simply physical: perhaps the inner core is solid rather than liquid. Refined measuring systems in the future may permit more informed guesses, but direct knowledge of the earth's core lies farther beyond man's reach than outer space.

The dramatic increase in density, from surface crust to inner core, is less surprising when the steady increase in pressure at increasing depths within the earth is calculated. The overburden of light, thin crust and denser, far thicker mantle, for example, weighs down on the sphere of the earth's outer core with a pressure of 10,000 tons per square inch, while the incredibly compressed cubic inch of matter at the earth's exact center is supporting 20,000 tons of pressure on each of its six faces.

With such increases in pressure, it is logical to expect increases in temperature, and even by the 17th Century, miners at work in deep, dry shafts in Germany had reported steady rises in temperature with increasing depth. For those shallow portions of the earth's crust that man has thus far probed, this increase in heat is at the rate of 1° F. for each 60 feet of depth. If this rate of increase held good all the way to the center of the earth, the core's heart would be a hell-fire of 350,000° F.—or 35 times hotter than the surface of the sun.

Hardly any geophysicist is prepared to believe this; estimates of the core's maximum temperature range between 4,000° F. and 8,000° F., compared to the sun's estimated surface temperature of 10,000° F. In any case, the present temperature distribution within the earth—whatever it may be— is not permanent. Both the mantle and the core surely hold a substantial residue of radioactive isotopes—uranium, thorium, potassium—that release heat as they decay. And many geophysicists believe that the earth's interior temperature is gradually rising. This is nothing to worry about: both the mantle and the crust are superlative insulators, and it will take millions of years for temperature changes within the body of the earth to be apparent on the surface. As it is, surface temperatures are entirely controlled by the sun; its effect is thousands of times greater than that of the heat flow from within the earth.

That man will ever penetrate the planet's core is inconceivable, except in science fiction; but that he will send his instruments down through the crust and into the mantle is now inevitable. One means to that exciting end is Project Mohole, a title derived from the name of the crust-and-mantle boundary. Taking advantage of the fact that the crust is thin under the ocean floor, American scientists in 1961 sank test drillings as deep as 1,035 feet below the floor, from a ship anchored off Southern California. The experiments moved the National Science Foundation to commit up to $50 million for the three- to seven-year drilling job that Mohole entails—or perhaps $16 million or so to get through each mile of crust.

What Dr. Alan T. Waterman, director of the foundation, calls "man's greatest single geological project," will be well worth it in scientific advances. En route down to the mantle, Mohole drills will bring up a continuous core sample of the sediments, the rocks and the fossils contained in the suboceanic crust. (Meanwhile, Soviet drillers will be probing the mantle on their own from sites on land.) From the pierced mantle itself will come whatever it contains—and from that point on, knowledge will replace guesswork as to its composition, density, radioactivity and other properties. And science will have stronger clues than ever to the origin and history of the earth, of the solar system, of life itself.

The earth's magnetic field has taught geophysicists a good deal about its interior. Mariners of the West have known about the magnetic compass for nearly a thousand years, but it was not until late in the 16th Century that the pioneers of science really understood how a compass works. Until then

Pinpointing of an earthquake's place of origin, or epicenter, is done by three or more seismic stations in different cities. Each determines the interval between the arrival of the fast primary waves and the slower secondary waves, and from this time span estimates the distance they traveled. Three circles with radii representing these distances are drawn on a map. At their intersection is the epicenter (E).

it had been assumed that the constellation of the Great Bear, or perhaps Polaris, the North Star—or even some unknown, massive mountain in the frozen North—was the source of the attractive force on a magnetized needle. William Gilbert, court physician to Queen Elizabeth I, was the first to show that the earth itself is a giant magnet. Earlier observations had shown that a compass needle, when hung free to move in any direction, not only pointed northward but also dipped—with the angle of dip becoming greater the farther north the experiment was performed. Gilbert attempted to duplicate this phenomenon in the laboratory, using as a substitute for the earth a sphere of naturally magnetic iron ore. Compass needles reacted to this magnetized sphere just as they did to the earth, dipping at an increasing angle as they were moved nearer to the sphere's poles. From these observations Gilbert was able to infer correctly that the earth was also a magnetized ball.

Gilbert's treatise, *De Magnete*, was published in 1600 as the climax of 17 years' work. He described how he had established that *magnus magnes ipse est globus terrestris* ("the earth itself is a great magnet") and, although he owed a debt to earlier investigators, the clarity of his study makes *De Magnete* a milestone in the history of modern science. By now, more refined methods of measurement and subtler theoretical analyses than Gilbert could command have firmly verified his central thesis.

ALTHOUGH the earth does behave like a magnet, however, it is far from behaving like a perfect one. For one thing, the earth's magnetic field is quite irregular in direction and fluctuates with time in an irregular way. For another, the terrestrial magnet is not constant in strength: in the past century alone, the earth's magnetic field has weakened by 5 per cent. Still odder are a number of known reversals in the earth's magnetic field, the evidences of which form a part of geologic history. From time to time the field has slowly vanished, to reappear with the field directions of the North and South Magnetic Poles interchanged. All these peculiarities in the earth's magnetism are welcome to the geophysicist, for they serve as important clues in reconstructing the earth's past.

After measuring the intensity and direction of the earth's magnetic field all over its surface, one can construct a chart of the field in which so-called isogonic lines play a role not unlike that of contour lines on a relief map. Such a chart is indispensable for navigation, since it shows the direction in which a compass needle will point from any geographical region (there are few places on earth where a compass needle points to true, geographic north). When all irregularities are smoothed out on an idealized chart of the earth's magnetic field, a pair of geomagnetic poles can be identified, corresponding to the poles of Gilbert's model. An idealized model of the earth's magnetic field, on this basis, would envision this field as resulting from the presence of a bar magnet of immense strength hidden deep in the earth's interior, about 200 miles from the center and tilted by 11.5° from the earth's axis of rotation.

The geomagnetic poles, moreover, are *not* the earth's Magnetic Poles, beloved grails of polar explorers, which are better known as the "dip" poles. There a freely suspended compass needle will point straight down. The earth's north and south dip poles are some distance from the geomagnetic poles, and to complicate the picture further, the dip poles wander. In 1948, the North Magnetic Pole was located 70 miles southeast of its present position. Forty-four years earlier, it had been another 200 miles distant to the southeast. Geophysicists are unable to predict the future positions of the earth's dip poles with certainty, although they know the rate of change is around three to four miles per year for the north, and that the south dip pole is drifting at a somewhat greater speed.

In all probability, the earth's magnetic field originates in electric currents generated in the planet's outer core of molten iron. Such a mechanism would invoke two physical principles no different from those that underlie the operation of an ordinary electric generator, or dynamo. The first principle involves the intimate connection between electric current and magnetic field: electric currents are always surrounded by magnetic fields, and all magnetic fields are caused by electric currents. The second principle is that of electromagnetic induction: when a conductor of electricity (such as a wire) is subjected to a changing magnetic field or is moved through a magnetic field, a current is induced in it.

In a dynamo, coils of wire mounted on a shaft are moved through a magnetic field by rotation. Ideally, if the wires offered no resistance to the current and if there were no friction in the moving parts, such a dynamo could be coupled together with an electric motor so that the two would run forever—motor turning dynamo shaft, and dynamo generating current to turn the motor. In the real world, however, both electrical and mechanical resistance are inevitable, and some energy must be provided from outside to make the system work.

The dynamo concept of the earth's geomagnetic field holds that such a motor-generator combination—comparable, but vastly different in detail—exists in the earth's molten core. Because the earth's imagined dynamo, like a real one, is not wholly efficient, energy must be provided to keep it going. In the case of the earth, according to the dynamo theory, the source of this mechanical energy is convective (circulating) movements that may arise in the earth's liquid outer core from the intense heat of the smaller, solid, inner core or from chemical differences between core and mantle. In the outer core, the molten iron does not simply heat, circulate, cool and return to reheat in orderly fashion, like the air from a hot-air furnace. Instead, because of the effect of the earth's rotation, the paths of the fluid are complex, swirling ones.

THE dynamo theory suitably accounts for both the orderliness and the irregularity that are observed in the earth's magnetic field. The symmetry imposed by the planet's rotation accounts for the nearly approximate alignment of the earth's magnetic and geographic axes, while the nonuniform character of the liquid core's convection swirls accounts for the absence of perfect agreement between the two.

Thus the earth's innermost parts form a dynamic system that extends its influences all the way to the surface. What was realized theoretically for years but only proved by modern rocket probes is that these magnetic forces generated in the core also reach into space for thousands of miles before they fade to insignificance. As will be seen, this enormous zone of the magnetosphere plays an important part as mediator between the earth and the many bursts of radiant energy and physical particles continually emitted by the sun.

THE PLANETS FORM AROUND THE SUN OUT OF GAS AND DUST SWIRLS. EARTH AND MOON ARE AT LOWER RIGHT IN THIS PAINTING

The Unquiet Planet

Ever since the earth first took tentative shape in the blackness of space, mighty forces have been at work on it, from the outside and from within. What goes on in its interior is no longer as unfathomable as it once was: from clues provided by earthquakes and eruptions, the greatest events on the earth's surface, man is beginning to understand the mysterious stirrings of his planet.

The Fires within the Globe

Our earth, once so cold, long ago warmed up, on the inside, to temperatures between 4,000 and 8,000°. Thanks to the insulation of the earth's mantle and crust, little of the interior heat ever manifests itself on the surface. But hot springs and geysers, in a minor way, and volcanoes, in a spectacular way, give evidence of the searing heat that prevails far below. Volcanoes are fired by the same nuclear and frictional forces that maintain this locked-in heat. Their outpourings of lava and gases originate near the mantle's upper boundary. Hot magma (molten rock) squeezes upward, usually following fissures left by quakes, and sometimes erupts at once, sometimes remains for long periods in vast chambers within the crust before pushing to the surface. But exactly what triggers an eruption, science has not yet learned.

THE MULTILAYERED EARTH has a hot inner core, probably composed of solid iron and nickel, a cooler outer core of molten metal, a warm rocky mantle and a thin cool crust.

THE STEAMING CRATER of Nyamlagira volcano in the Congo is a scene of broken rock and clouds of gas (*right*). From such vents in the crust have come most of the atmosphere and water on earth.

THE FIERY FOUNTAINS of Kilauea in Hawaii (*below*) spew forth a lava lake. In some places in the crater the flow reaches a depth of 350 feet. Lava from thousands of such eruptions built the islands.

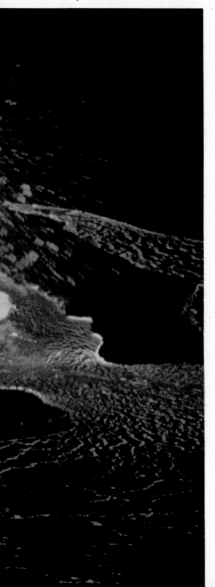

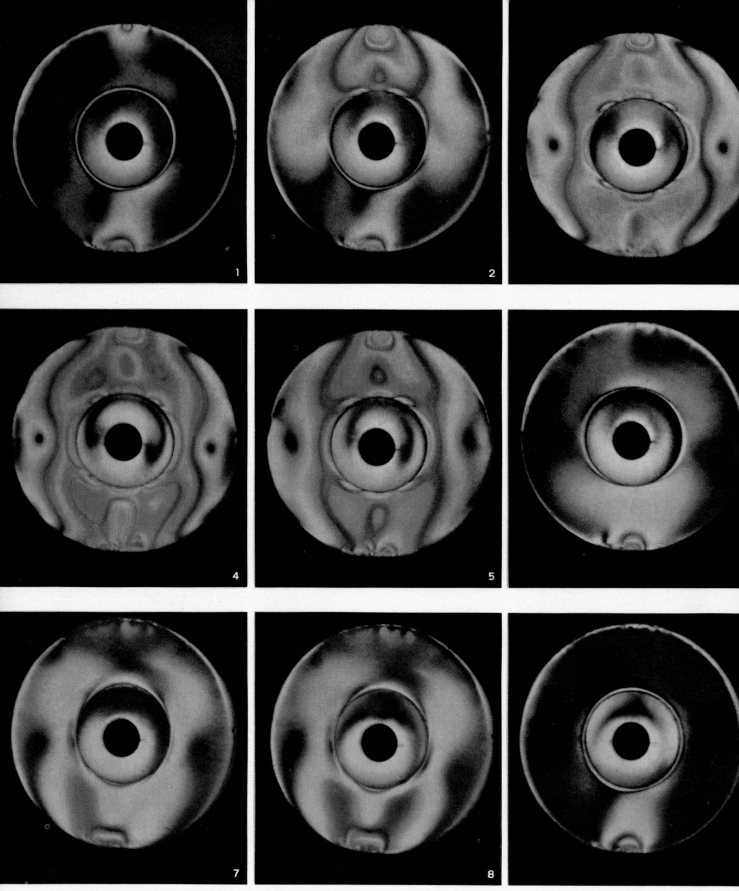

THE EARTH'S VIBRATIONS after an earthquake are simulated as waves of color sweeping through the interior of this two-inch disk. A sharp blow at the top of the model starts a shock wave (1), which spreads quickly through the entire disk (2 and 3), then gradually fades in a series of slow, rhythmic pulsations (4 to 8) until the stresses die out completely (9). In the model, photographed in polarized light in a New York University laboratory, the earth's rocky mantle is represented by a hard rubber ring, the molten outer core by gelatin and the solid inner core by an aluminum disk.

A STRAIN METER DEEP IN A MOUNTAIN TUNNEL USES A 75-FOOT QUARTZ ROD TO MEASURE CRUSTAL EXPANSION AND CONTRACTION

The Pulse Beats of the Earth

From laboratory experiments like the one shown on the opposite page and from instruments such as the earth strain meter developed by Dr. Hugo Benioff of the California Institute of Technology (*above*), science is learning more about earthquakes and something about the continual, less evident stretching and compression of the earth's crust. The moon, for example, creates tides on solid land just as it does in the oceans: twice a day, with each tide, any point on earth may rise and fall several inches. Also, for days after a severe earthquake the earth vibrates at certain frequencies like a struck gong. These frequencies are far too low to be audible—one "tone" is 20 octaves below middle C—but they are powerful. There is even speculation that they indirectly move the earth's inner core a fraction of an inch. Scientists are studying still other movements along fault lines, which they believe may help forecast when and where earthquakes will strike.

FATHER JOSEPH LYNCH, A FAMED EARTHQUAKE STUDENT, WATCHES SEISMOGRAPHS IN FORDHAM'S UNDERGROUND OBSERVATORY

A QUAKE'S SIGNATURE is written with a beam of light on a strip of photographic paper (*right*). This strip from one of Fordham's seismographs is marked off in minutes (Nos. 1-12), and was made on a drum that revolves every half hour. From top to bottom, this portion thus spans five and a half hours. In the sixth half-hour line, the shocks of an earthquake appear: first the primary waves (P), followed by the slower secondary waves (S), and finally the surface waves (L). From the interval between the first two waves (5 minutes, 18 seconds), seismologists calculated how far away this quake was—in Montana, 2,195 miles from New York, on August 18, 1959.

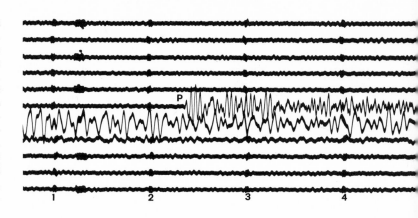

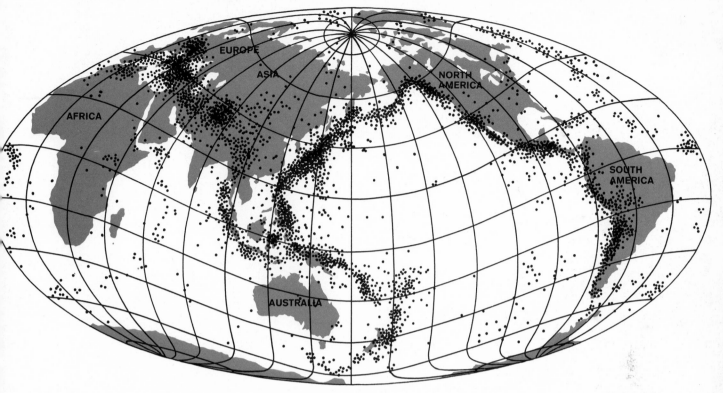

MAJOR EARTHQUAKE ZONES APPEAR AS THICK CLUSTERS OF BLACK DOTS ON THIS MAP, WHICH COVERS 20 YEARS OF ACTIVITY

The Trackdown of Earthquakes

When an earthquake occurs, its vibrations travel rapidly through the body of the earth. These vibrations are detected by seismographs which keep a ceaseless vigil all over the world, recording the earth's tremors as abrupt, zigzag lines on sensitized paper (*below*). By comparing data from several stations, seismologists can pinpoint the disturbance and measure its force.

With their world-wide network of observatories, seismologists have found that the globe's seemingly solid, stolid mass is in an eternal tremble. They also have mapped the globe's earthquake belts, as shown in the map above.

And recently seismologists have discovered that earthquakes can occur at considerable depths within the earth. Although most quakes—and the most disastrous of them—originate a few miles down in the earth's crust, a number occur at an intermediate level in the mantle—between 43 and 186 miles down—and some as deep as 446 miles. All these deep quakes occur in the two main earthquake belts. Seismologists hope that study of these deeper shifts and cracks will lead to knowledge of the underlying causes of all earthquakes and, finally, to an understanding of the relationship of the earth's crust to the mantle.

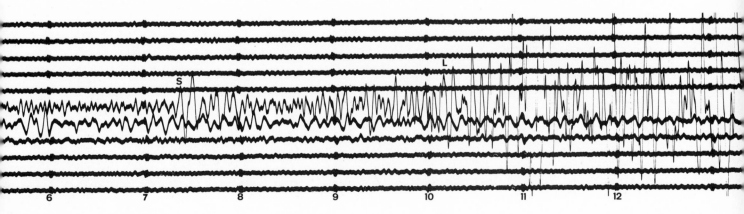

AN EXPOSED FAULT in western Nevada reveals where the earth's crust reared over 15 feet to relieve vast pressures from below. The sudden movement set off a localized earthquake in December 1954.

A TWISTED TRACK is crimped by the movement of a California fault in 1906. Faults in many areas, as well as the San Andreas one, shifted that year when the San Francisco earthquake occurred.

A DEPARTMENT STORE LURCHES OVER AND BIG FIRES BREAK OUT

Death from a Violent Earth

The forces distorting the earth's crust are like the winding of an alarm clock—accumulating energy that will ultimately be released in a sudden burst of violence. A major earthquake expends many times more energy than the most powerful man-made explosion. Its destructive effect may be magnified by landslides in the mountains, fires in the cities and huge waves at sea that can wreak death and damage thousands of miles from the original disturbance. Earthquakes rank

DURING A 1948 EARTHQUAKE THAT KILLED 3,895 IN FUKUI, JAPAN

A SUDDEN LANDSLIDE dumped this stretch of highway into Hebgen Lake, Montana, during the 1959 earthquake near Yellowstone Park, one of the most violent recorded in the U.S. It killed 28.

A STRANDED FLEET of small craft jams the streets of Shiogama, Japan, in the wake of tsunami waves. Formed by earthquakes in Chile in May 1960, the waves traveled 10,000 miles in 24 hours.

among the great disasters of history. The deadliest on record include: Shensi Province, China, 1556—830,000 dead; Calcutta, India, 1737—300,000 dead; Kansu Province, China, 1920—180,000 dead; Tokyo, Japan, 1923 —over 100,000 dead. The toll of the famous 1906 San Francisco earthquake was a relatively low 452. Two earthquake disasters occurred as recently as 1960: over 12,000 died in Agadir, Morocco, on March 1, and 5,700 died in Chilean quakes three months later.

AN INTENT PILOT, Ralph McCoy, keeps *Cuss I* positioned over the drill hole more than two miles below by watching sonar screens that show the location of underwater buoys.

A PRECIOUS CORE from hundreds of feet down in the bottom ooze is sliced into sections by a paleontologist so that fossils imbedded in its clay can be removed and studied.

"CUSS I" DRILLS IN THE DEEP PACIFIC DURING MOHOLE TRIALS

Drilling Down to the Mantle

At nightfall on March 26, 1961, a powerful ocean tug towing an ungainly barge churned through heavy Pacific swells about 260 miles south of Los Angeles. The odd barge was the *Cuss I* (*above*), fitted with a 98-foot derrick amidships and three miles of steel drill pipe in 60-foot sections on its deck. At about midnight the barge was maneuvered to the center of a ring of buoys and held there while its derrick began lowering a diamond-studded drill toward the ocean floor.

The operation was a crucial test for Project Mohole, a plan to drill through the earth's crust and obtain samples of the mantle, which man has never seen. Nobody had ever tried to drop a drill through two miles of sea water, and there were doubts that *Cuss I* could be held still enough to do it without bending or breaking the drill pipe. Why drill at sea? Because the crust is only three miles thick under the ocean, and up to 40 miles thick under the continents.

During two anxious weeks *Cuss I* drilled five test holes, and proved that the technique was feasible. Mohole scientists will try to go all the way to the mantle sometime in the late 1960s.

AN ANXIOUS MOMENT comes as the shaft goes down through the "guide shoe" at the ship's center well (*opposite*). There was constant danger that the shaft would snap when waves shifted the barge.

3

Anatomy
of the Skies

THE sea that covers nearly three fourths of the globe is only the second biggest thing on earth. Incomparably vaster is the ocean of the atmosphere,
which dominates the lives of men and most other creatures as surely as
water dominates the lives of fish. Without the atmosphere's oxygen, living
things die almost at once. Without rain erosion and the weathering of
rocks, there would be no soil for plants to grow in. Without carbon dioxide
the plants could not produce carbohydrates, the primary link in the food
chain that supports all animal life. Without the high-altitude umbrella of
ozone to absorb the lethal ultraviolet rays of the sun, human existence—if
any—would be quite different. Yet this is only a fractional list of the free
services performed by the atmosphere and taken for granted by the nearly
three billion human beings who at this moment are drawing breaths of it.

The atmosphere is an invisible and probably inexhaustible mixture of
air, water vapor, smoke and dust particles—including, in recent years,
quantities of radioactive fall-out particles dispatched skyward by nuclear
explosions. At sea level, the very bottom of the ocean of air, a cubic foot of
the mixture weighs about an ounce and a quarter. The entire atmosphere

weighs 5,700,000,000,000,000 tons, barely a millionth as much as the earth, and the force with which gravity holds it in place causes it to exert a pressure of 15 pounds to the square inch at sea level.

The human body copes with this burden by exerting an equal outward pressure to balance that of the atmosphere, just as fish do in order to live under far greater pressures deep in the ocean. The density of the air dwindles with increasing altitude, shading off into the virtual void of interplanetary space but remaining tangible enough to support airplanes and balloons for a dozen or so miles up.

UNTIL men and instruments could get off the ground to find out better, everything beyond the earth's thin shell of ordinary, breathable air was simply called the ether for want of a more accurate label. In recent years scientific views of the atmosphere have had to undergo repeated rapid revision, always in the direction of greater complexity. One contemporary way to classify the sky is to divide it into five regions, going out from the earth's surface: troposphere, stratosphere, mesosphere, ionosphere and exosphere. Three quarters of the bulk of the whole envelope is concentrated in the bottom layer of the troposphere, along with the haze and dust, the clouds and storms—and all of life. Its upper boundary is the tropopause, fixed by hot-and-cold air exchanges at altitudes as low as five miles above the poles, as high as 10 miles above the equator. Within the tropospheric zone, air temperature drops about 3° F. with every 1,000 feet of elevation. The tropopause being lower at the poles, its temperature there falls only to about -60° F., but over the equator it gets down to -100° F. Everywhere within the troposphere the air—hot or cold, dry or humid, thick or thin—is a constant mixture: nitrogen 78 per cent, oxygen 21 per cent, argon 0.9 per cent, carbon dioxide 0.03 per cent, with traces of half a dozen other gases, plus a variable load of water vapor.

Starting in the cold stratosphere, a layer extending 10 to 15 miles higher, and in the warmer (up to 50° F.) mesosphere, which goes up to the 50-mile level, there are crucial chemical changes in the air. In the first of these, ozone is added to the mixture. This is the same clean-smelling gas that is often noticeable around electrical generators and ultraviolet lights. It is "heavy oxygen," each of its molecules containing three atoms of oxygen, and it is formed when an electrical discharge or strong ultraviolet rays pass through ordinary oxygen. In the upper atmosphere, ozone soaks up much of the ultraviolet radiation streaming earthward from the sun.

A cold front, the leading edge of an air mass whose cold air is dense and therefore heavy, advances from left to right below, driving under a lighter mass of warm air. As the warm air is displaced upward, cooling reduces its capacity for moisture, and clouds and then precipitation are produced. Thus a cold front is often marked by a line of storm clouds.

COLD AIR MASS

WARM AIR MASS

Every second, a billion billion primary cosmic-ray particles, travelers from far outside the solar system, reach the neighborhood of the earth, with a total power input of more than a billion watts. When they collide with the atmosphere's component atoms and molecules, the collisions produce showers of secondary particles. It is these "secondaries" that continue down to the earth's surface. Eight of them strike every square inch of the ground every minute; thousands strike every human being every hour. These particles are very penetrating; there is no escaping the ceaseless bombardment. But thanks to the breakup in the atmosphere, the barrage is harmless and has no perceptible influence on life. If they were primary cosmic rays, the effect would be lethal.

Starting at 50 miles and ending at 350 to 600 miles is the ionosphere, where more radical changes occur in the atmosphere. X rays, as well as ultraviolet rays from the sun, ionize the rarefied air: they produce electrically charged (rather than neutral) atoms and molecules, together with unattached electrons. In this region, primarily a layer of oxygen, the temperature goes as high as 2,000° F. But the air is so thin—the entire ionosphere, despite its huge size, containing only 0.001 per cent by weight of the atmosphere—that "temperature" has little practical meaning. No object passing through this layer would meet enough friction to heat up.

THE ionosphere's reflection of radio waves, which makes possible long-distance broadcasts, was understood decades ago, as was the service rendered by the lower, denser layers in incinerating nearly all of the millions of meteors that daily rain down toward the earth. But it was not until man began his counterbarrage into space, with the rocket probes launched during and since the International Geophysical Year, that any real knowledge was gained of the exosphere, the outermost layer of all. Only in 1962 was one of its components, the magnetosphere, defined as a gigantic trap that imprisons subatomic particles from the sun. At about the same time, deep space probes disclosed something of the exosphere's composition: a 900-mile layer of thinly dispersed helium, surrounded by a layer of hydrogen that extends over 4,000 miles farther before tapering off into the emptiness of space. Atoms and molecules are so far apart in the exosphere that they seldom collide and, in fact, some escape from the earth for good.

From this quick tour, working from the inside out, it is apparent that the atmosphere is anything but inert. Its major action, among many, is to serve as an enormous engine, using the sun's radiation as a power source

Pushing along behind a cold air mass, a warm system of less dense—that is, lighter—air climbs up its trailing edge, forming a long slope and producing a broad band of rainfall as the warm air rises and cools. Clouds soaring high above the cold air may appear as far as 1,000 miles in front of, and several days before, the arrival of the warm front they herald.

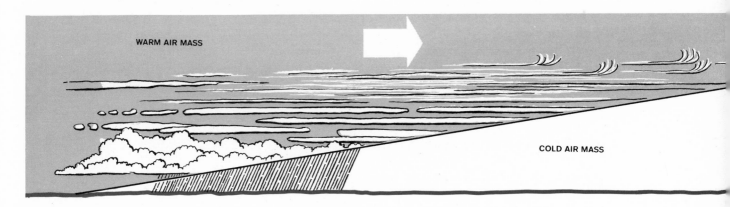

WARM AIR MASS

COLD AIR MASS

to drive the currents of air that stream and eddy around the earth. In other words, the atmosphere makes the winds, and thereby the weather. To understand how this atmospheric engine operates, one should keep in mind that all bodies, at all temperatures, radiate electromagnetic waves of one kind or another. In order of decreasing wave lengths, these include radio waves (long, short, on down to the microwaves used in radar); infrared waves; the waves of visible light; ultraviolet waves; X rays; and—shortest of all—gamma rays.

All these waves have the same physical nature, but their different lengths result in rather different behavior. The hotter an object is, the more electromagnetic energy it emits and the shorter the average wave length. The heat of the sun's surface is such that its predominant radiation is in the visible light range of wave lengths. However, the troposphere—in the confines of which most of what we call weather takes place—is not directly affected by these light rays. Instead, whatever solar radiation that may escape being reflected back into space by dust or clouds, or being absorbed by the ozone layer, passes right through the lower levels of the atmosphere until it strikes—and warms—the earth's land and water surface.

The earth accepts these solar rays and, in turn, gives off radiation largely of the longer, infrared wave lengths. Both the carbon dioxide and the water vapor in the atmosphere are excellent absorbers of infrared; as a result, they take up nearly all of such energy that radiates from the earth's surface. The entire troposphere becomes heated in this way. The ultimate source of this heat is the sun, since its rays warm the earth's surface and maintain its infrared radiation. Nonetheless, the actual heating of the atmosphere is from below, as with a pot on a stove, and not from above.

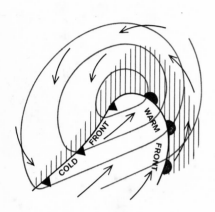

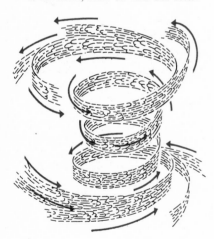

A low-pressure cell, shown above by isobaric lines that connect points of equal pressure, can form if a mass of cold air envelops a center of light, warm air. Given a counterclockwise twist by the earth's rotation, the air spirals inward (arrows, below) toward the center of low pressure, causing precipitation in the shaded areas as the warm, moist air rises and cools.

THE earth is not uniformly warmed everywhere by the sun's rays and thus its surface is not everywhere equally radiant. As we have seen, sunlight arrives at the earth nearly vertically in the equatorial zone, but at an oblique angle near the poles, so equatorial air is much warmer than polar air. It is this difference in temperature that turns the atmosphere into a heat engine, causing the winds to blow. If the earth did not rotate, these air currents would be quite orderly: warm air near the equator would rise and flow toward the poles, while cold air at the poles would sink and flow toward the equator in an endless, interchanging cycle. The earth's rotation modifies this simple pattern: in each hemisphere, working away from the pole and toward the equator, there is first a westward drift of air in the lower atmosphere, then an eastward one in mid-latitudes, and finally another westward drift near the equator. Each hemisphere's pattern of air flow is a mirror image of the other's: the easterly winds of the northern tropics—the trade winds—blow from the northeast, while the same easterly trades below the equator blow from the southeast. The name trade wind originated in the days of sail, when these steady winds were the mainstays of ocean commerce.

The westerly winds of middle latitudes do not share the trade winds' regular, stable pattern. Instead, they are roiled into immense high-altitude eddies, thousands of miles across. Below these large-scale eddies (three to six of which are over each hemisphere at any one time) are many smaller ones that swirl about for a few hours or days before they vanish and are replaced by others. The larger eddies are more persistent: one of them may move eastward for weeks before losing its identity in random turbulence. The birth and growth of these wind swirls account for the changeable weather of the earth's middle latitudes.

A smaller eddy that forms around a center of low-pressure air acquires a rotary motion and starts to spin—counterclockwise in the Northern Hemisphere and clockwise in the Southern. Such a spinning eddy is called a cyclone, but is not necessarily the storm wind that is sometimes given the same name. Here is a chance to watch the atmosphere's heat engine in action on a small scale. Why does a cyclone spin? The air at its center is lighter— lower in pressure—while the air surrounding the eddy is heavier—higher in pressure. Thus, the heavier air flows *inward*, toward the center, and it is this inward flow that is deflected by the earth's rotation. Consider the opposite case: here, the eddy forms around a deep, dense air mass at higher pressure than the air around it, and the air flow is therefore *outward* from its center. In consequence, the spin is in exactly the opposite direction and such an eddy is known as an anticyclone.

These great whorls of air make the major marks on weather maps. The United States is often swept in winter by highs from northern Canada that are very cold and dry. When such a cold air mass overlies a region, the weather will be correspondingly cold and clear, with the possibility of some cumulus clouds in the afternoon because of the heating of the earth by the sun. In summer, moist lows from the Gulf of Mexico often dominate weather in the eastern United States, producing hot, humid, windless days.

The line of contact between two air masses of different temperature is called a front. A cold front represents cold air replacing warmer air; a warm front moves in such a way that warm air replaces cold. The warm air along a front of either kind cools as it rises, producing cloudiness and precipitation. This effect is more pronounced along a cold front, which leads to more violent storms. The approach and passage of a front is one of the most fascinating of meteorological events. A warm front is signaled by cirrus clouds (mare's-tails) high up in the sky. These represent the condensed moisture at the leading edge of the oncoming warm air that has overrun the retreating cold air. Soon a milky film of cirrostratus covers the sky, and some hours later the ominous gray veils of altostratus clouds appear. Then low, thick, dark nimbostratus clouds darken the sky and rain begins to fall. Finally the warm air completely replaces the cold, from top to bottom, the temperature levels off and the rain stops. More or less steady weather then follows until the approach of the next front.

THE sequence of events when a cold front arrives is faster and more dramatic. The cold oncoming air is too heavy to override the warm air in its path, and instead burrows underneath. Forced upward by the intruding cold air mass, the warm, moisture-laden air condenses, forming a great vertical bank of dense cumulonimbus clouds. A well-defined cold front typically appears as a squall line of dark, ominous clouds, straight as a ruler from horizon to horizon, sweeping in from the west or northwest. When it strikes, the wind shifts abruptly from southwest to northwest, the temperature falls and a torrent of heavy rain begins, driven by strong, irregular gusts. A violent thunderstorm may occur, adding sight and sound to the tempestuous proceedings. After half an hour or so the squall line is almost out of sight to the east, and a band of clear sky appears in the west. Then the northwest wind blows more steadily and dry, cool, clear weather sets in. Of course,

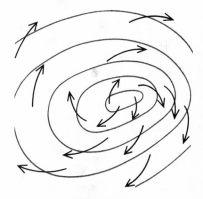

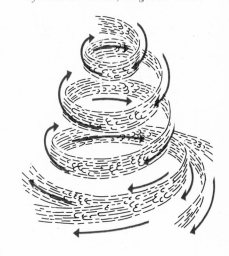

A high-pressure cell is formed by a process exactly the reverse of that which creates a low-pressure cell (opposite). A mass of cold, dense air tends to sink and spread out (above), replacing lighter surrounding air. As it spirals outward (arrows, below) from its center of high pressure, the cold air, given a clockwise twist by the earth's rotation, brings clear skies.

not all cold fronts bring with them such boisterous effects, but the pattern is familiar to dwellers in the middle latitudes.

The turbulent, unstable atmosphere near a squall line sometimes produces a vortex of rapidly spinning air. The vortex appears as a narrow, funnel-shaped cloud that extends to the ground, but its modest aspect conceals winds of hundreds of miles an hour. A vortex of this kind is called a tornado on land and a waterspout over the ocean; very little is known about conditions inside the whirlwinds because any instruments that have happened to be in their paths have invariably been destroyed.

Few people have looked such a whirlwind in the eye and lived to tell about it. One who did was Will Keller, a Kansas farmer who dared to peek out of his storm cellar as a tornado passed over in 1928. Above him was the hollow vortex, 50 to 100 feet across, its walls lighted by zigzag lightning flashes. Smaller vortexes were forming inside the main one and emitting hissing noises as they broke free of it. In 1955, a motorist encountered a thick dust cloud on the road near Scottsbluff, Nebraska. Realizing it was no ordinary dust cloud, he stopped his car. Then, according to a report in the U.S. Weather Bureau's *Monthly Weather Review,* "there was a roar and a crash of glass as the windshield and windows were broken . . . . He pulled his wife's head over in his lap and bent over to shield their faces. There was a moment of comparative calm and he raised his head to peer through the broken windshield. Large boards, tree limbs, and a boulder the size of a man's head were floating around the car . . . there was a crash and that is all he remembers until he regained consciousness in a hospital. Actually, both occupants were thrown from the car . . . . The wife was apparently killed instantly. The car was rolled into an unshapen mass of metal."

Usually a tornado is a few hundred yards across and travels at perhaps 25 miles per hour for a distance anywhere from a fraction of a mile to 100 miles or more before it vanishes. The central United States is probably the most tornado-prone part of the world, and they form so rapidly and unpredictably as to make protection against them chiefly a matter of descending into a strong storm cellar whenever a thunderstorm appears. Waterspouts are generally milder than tornados, though still capable of violent destruction. The lower portion of a spout contains some salt water drawn up from the sea beneath it, but mostly fresh water that has condensed out from its basic body of cloud. Some waterspouts range up to a mile in height.

Many localities have other peculiar winds of their own that are more or less unrelated to the global pattern. Simple examples are the sea and land breezes familiar along many coast lines. These winds owe their existence to the fact that the temperature of the ocean surface stays fairly constant while that of the land surface may fluctuate widely. On a hot day a beach becomes warm and the air above it rises, while cooler, denser air from over the water—the sea breeze—is drawn in to replace it. At night the beach cools rapidly and the air circulation is reversed: the air over the land is now denser, and a land breeze flows offshore.

The sea and land breezes' grown-up relatives are the monsoons of Asia, which are governed by the contrasts in land and sea temperatures in summer and winter instead of in daytime and nighttime. In winter the Asiatic plateau is bitterly cold, so that the overlying air is much denser than that above the China Sea and Indian Ocean to its east and south. A steady, cold, dry wind blows offshore from October to April, deflected by the earth's rotation into a northeast wind in the China Sea and northern part of the Indian Ocean. In the summer Asia swelters, and the air above it rises while cooler air moves in from the ocean. This summer monsoon brings air that has picked up considerable moisture in its sea passage, and its arrival deluges southeast Asia with prolonged, drenching rain. A monsoon climate of this kind has only two varieties of weather, wet in summer and dry in winter, in contrast to the fickleness of middle-latitude weather.

Other regional winds are conditioned by landscape as well as temperature. Cold, dry air may spill over a mountain range suddenly after having collected on the windward side of the range for some time, surging down into adjacent valleys with great force. The mistral consists of cold air from the Rhone Glacier that pours down the Rhone Valley to the sea for much of the year, while the bora of the Adriatic has a similar birth in the mountains of Yugoslavia. The geography of the Mediterranean, bordered by high mountains on the north and the hot Sahara on the south, is responsible for a number of notorious winds. At times a hot wind from the Sahara, the sirocco, blows north across the Mediterranean, accumulating enough water vapor to bring rain to Sicily and the Italian coast.

THOSE who live along the fringes of the world's oceans have good reason to fear the coming of fall, when tropical cyclones are most likely to be born at sea, to mature as they move in the grip of the trade winds, and to cause disaster if they sweep over the land. The western shores of the North Atlantic, North and South Pacific, and Indian Oceans are most often the targets of tropical cyclones, but they are unknown only in the South Atlantic and eastern part of the South Pacific. These violent tropical storms are quite infrequent (only 48 occur on the average each year in the entire world), but their high power sets them apart, along with earthquakes, as the most destructive of natural phenomena.

At birth, one of these typhoons, or hurricanes, forms as a zone of low atmospheric pressure over a tropical ocean. Warm air laden with moisture flows toward this zone and ascends within it. The water vapor in the rising column of warm air condenses into clouds and rain, liberating a great deal of heat in the process, which further speeds the upward flow of air. Perhaps a quarter of a million tons of water are extracted from the ocean and the converging air every *second* by a hurricane, and their condensation over one day releases energy equivalent to the explosion of a 13,000-megaton nuclear bomb. As the heated air rises faster and faster, new air converges on the storm center with ever increasing speed; winds of as much as 200 miles per hour may be generated in this way. The rotation of the earth deflects wind flowing toward the storm center to the right in the Northern Hemisphere and to the left in the Southern, leading respectively to the counterclockwise and clockwise circulation already noted in the cyclones of the middle latitudes. At the center of a hurricane is an area of calm, a few miles across, called the eye. A ring of dense clouds, from which a deluge of rain falls, surrounds the eye, and in this ring the winds are at their most furious; the wind speed may change by a hundred miles an hour or more in a distance of a mile within the ring.

The hurricane itself is a nightmare of shrieking wind made all the more apocalyptic by torrents of rain and darkness as dense clouds blot out the sky. If the eye passes overhead the turmoil comes to a crescendo and abruptly stops; the wind falls to a breeze, the rain ceases and bits of blue sky appear through thin, patchy clouds. But the lull is brief and soon the full fury of the storm strikes again, now with the wind from the opposite direction. The recession of the hurricane is marked by a sequence of weather exactly the reverse of the events heralding its approach.

Such a storm is fueled by the heat and water vapor it sucks from the sea surface, and it weakens and disappears in short order when deprived of this power supply. Thus hurricanes seldom penetrate far inland, and if they miss land entirely by swinging poleward, the colder water in their paths quenches their violence before long.

IN a single year the engine of the atmosphere, using such forceful instruments as typhoons and monsoons and such peaceful ones as sunlight, lifts 100,000 cubic miles of water into the air from the seas and the continents. Everything that goes up in this massive evaporation process must eventually come down, and most of it precipitates as rain. In order for rain, snow, sleet or hail to fall, clouds must form. Even air that is supersaturated with moisture cannot usually produce clouds unless myriads of minute "condensation nuclei" are present. The nuclei may be salt particles from sea spray, or fine dust, or smoke particles from forest fires and industrial plants, or the combustion products of volcanoes—or even the water-attracting oxides of nitrogen left behind by lightning. It has been figured that Krakatoa's 1883 eruption filled the atmosphere with enough condensation nuclei to provide 1,000 world-wide rainy days.

The water-vapor molecules that join a nucleus form cloud droplets (or ice crystals, if the air is well below freezing). These cannot fall as rain: they hold only a millionth as much water as an ordinary raindrop. In absolutely still air they would take eight hours to fall a quarter of a mile, and in moving air they are affected by gravity hardly at all. It is their growth to bigger size, called coalescence, that makes precipitation possible. In turbulent air bigger droplets collide with and "collect" smaller ones; in cold air, droplets evaporate and then condense on nearby ice crystals.

Only when a droplet grows to raindrop size, at least 1/125th of an inch in diameter, can it fall out of the cloud. It may never reach the ground; often a torrent may spill out of clouds high above a desert, only to evaporate entirely on the way down. Raindrops that reach the earth in a fine spray, called drizzle, have fallen from relatively low clouds, with little time to collide with other drops while falling. The raindrops that arrive in a vigorous downpour come from deep clouds where the colliding of droplets, and the "capturing" of little ones by bigger ones, is going on quite actively.

For snow to form, a cloud must be chilled to a few degrees above or below zero. The cloud droplets are supercooled and freeze together into crystals. Because the crystals carry a thin film of unfrozen water, they mat into snowflakes when they collide. In extreme cold the crystals are drier and fall as granular snow. Rain that starts in warm air and falls through a cold layer does not turn into snow but into the translucent ice pellets called sleet. Frozen raindrops from high clouds, moving through a thunderstorm and hurled about in violent updrafts, pick up concentric layers of snow and ice. Finally they plummet to earth as hailstones, pea-sized or golf-ball-sized, depending on their rough-and-tumble experiences aloft.

A RARE RED-GREEN AURORA FLAMES OVER CONNECTICUT. RADIATION FROM SPACE MAKES THE UPPER AIR GLOW LIKE A NEON TUBE

The Shield of the Air

Intangible and invisible, the atmosphere envelops the earth like a protective shell. It screens out the lethal rays of the sun and most of the bombarding cosmic rays from space. It incinerates most meteors before they reach the surface. It insulates the world from the cold of space and hoards the warmth bestowed by the sun. Even when unleashing storms, it is a zone of majestic beauty.

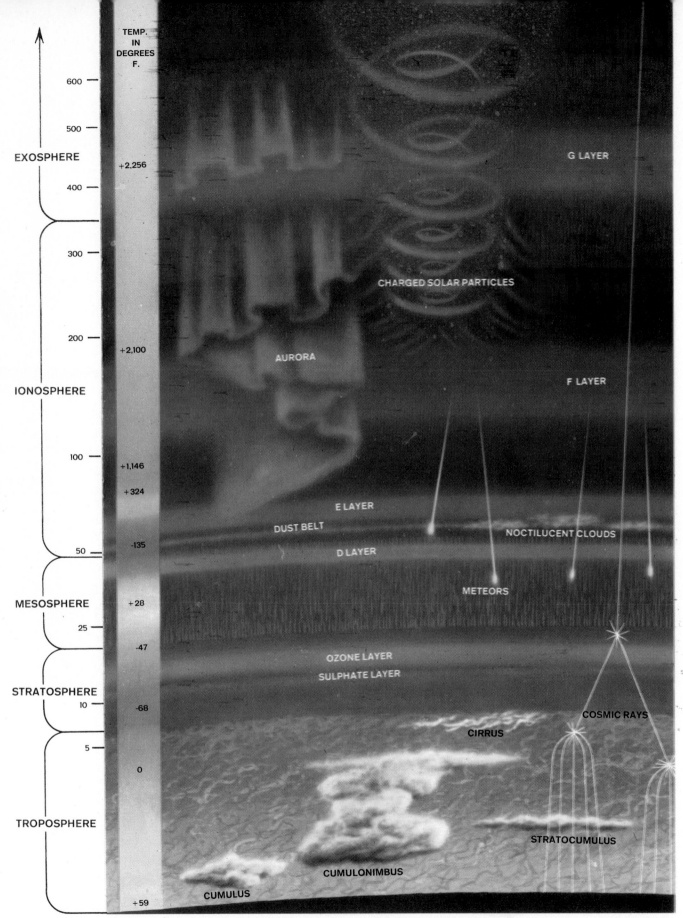

TEMP.
IN
DEGREES
F.

600

500

400 — +2,256

EXOSPHERE

300

200 — +2,100

IONOSPHERE

100 — +1,146
+324

50 — -135

MESOSPHERE — +28

25 — -47

STRATOSPHERE

10 — -68

5

0

TROPOSPHERE

+59

G LAYER

CHARGED SOLAR PARTICLES

AURORA

F LAYER

E LAYER

DUST BELT

D LAYER

NOCTILUCENT CLOUDS

METEORS

OZONE LAYER

SULPHATE LAYER

CIRRUS

COSMIC RAYS

STRATOCUMULUS

CUMULONIMBUS

CUMULUS

THE FIRST 600 MILES of the atmosphere, mapped in this cross section, are a complex stack of air layers. The gradations at the left show how temperatures fall and then rise with increasing altitude. At the upper levels, auroras appear like hanging curtains. The spiral swirl is a thrust of particles from the deep radiation zone of the magnetosphere.

A PACIFIC SUNSET SPREADS BANDS OF COLOR OVER THE HORIZON. THE LOWER ATMOSPHERE SPLITS THE SUN'S RAYS LIKE A PRISM

The Many-Layered Atmosphere

The atmosphere is neither as simple as it looks from below nor as shallow as scientists recently supposed. The troposphere, where man exists, is merely the lowest level of many. It ends at five to 10 miles up and contains the air currents which shape most of the earth's weather. The stratosphere occupies the next 10 to 15 miles. In it are two narrow layers containing concentrations of chemicals. The lower contains particles of sulphate which may play a role in rainfall. Above it is a layer of ozone, a form of oxygen, which blunts the force of deadly ultraviolet rays coming from the sun and thus makes life possible on the earth. Next is the mesosphere, a warm layer in which most of the meteors from outer space are incinerated. It is replaced, at 50 miles, by the ionosphere, whose top shades off somewhere between 350 and 600 miles up. Auroras flicker in the ionosphere, and near its bottom float noctilucent clouds which sometimes may be seen glimmering at dawn or dusk. The lettered layers D, E, F and G in the ionosphere are zones where air particles have been ionized by solar radiation. They are important to man because they reflect radio waves back to earth, and make wireless reception possible.

Last comes the exosphere, in which atmosphere slowly dwindles to nothing. It contains a huge radiation band known as the magnetosphere, and is believed to extend to 40,000 miles.

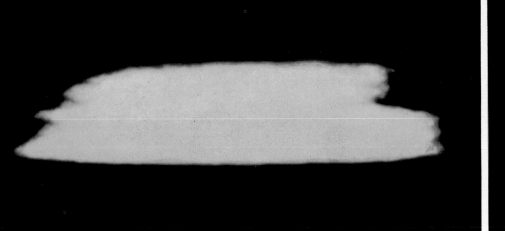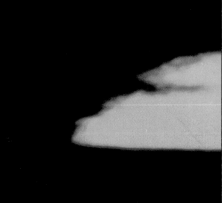

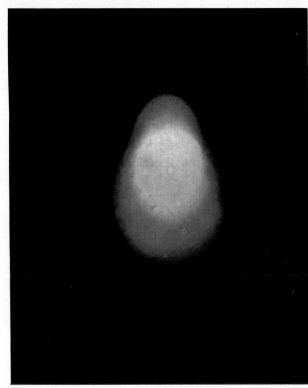

LOW-LYING VENUS, usually pearly-white, is seen through atmospheric distortion as a multicolored, pear-shaped body. As with the sun, green is dominant on top and red below.

The Flash Phenomena

Like the oceans of water, the ocean of air is in constant motion, and all light coming to the earth from space is blurred by its ripples. Astronomers have been able to see out through the atmosphere only dimly up to now. Until telescopes can be set beyond the atmosphere, in space or on the moon, what man sees in the sky must often be a mirage. Viewed at sunrise or sunset through the rippled air, the sun, for instance, may sometimes appear as fluffy as a cloud, flattened and perhaps seeming to split into thin horizontal strips. The sun's colors will vary from the blinding white of noon to soft red or violet hues tinting the horizon. Sometimes the setting sun may unleash a flash of red below or green on top, like the almost instantaneous lighting and blowing-out of millions of candles. These bursts of color are caused by special atmospheric conditions when the sun is close to the horizon.

The remarkable photographs here, taken from the Vatican Observatory at Castel Gandolfo in Italy, prove that the flash mirage lies not in the

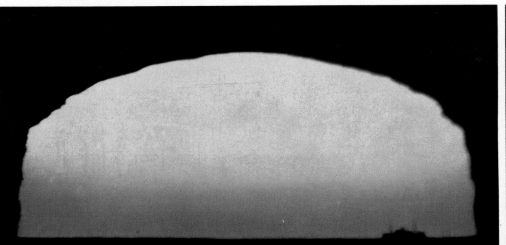

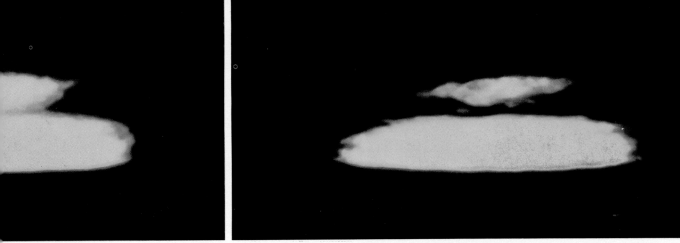

beholder's eye, as some scientists have suggested, but rather is a result of the way the atmosphere affects light. The golden white light of the sun is actually a mixture of all the colors of the rainbow. It happens that green light rays are more affected by travel through the air than the red ones, which are only slightly distorted. When the sun is low on the horizon at sunset, its light must pass a long distance through the earth's atmosphere. The red rays in it tend to disappear below the horizon first, while the green rays, which have been bent in their passage through the air, remain visible. Under certain conditions, the red and green actually appear to separate. When they do, the so-called green flash is created. Rarely, the flash may last for several minutes.

Similar atmospheric interference often affects the light coming from bright bodies much smaller than the sun, such as Venus. When it is near the horizon, this planet is sometimes distorted into ever-changing, overlapping images that are brilliantly splashed with the flash-pattern colors.

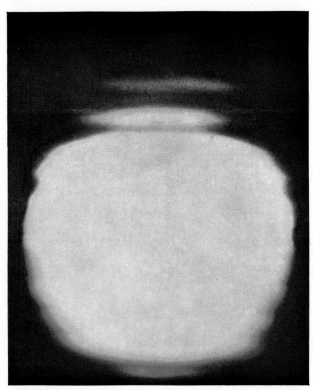

A BLUE-TOPPED SUN is created by a light bulb in a glass globe to simulate a sunset's distortions. A blue flash sometimes occurs with a green one, but is much less prominent.

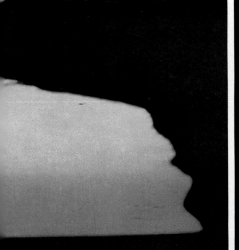

SOFT PLUMES of cirrus clouds float four to eight miles over the earth. They are fair-weather clouds unless they thicken into the hazy cirrostratus form that signals impending rain.

GRAY LAYERS of stratocumulus loom as a menacing front advancing on a clear sky. Composed of rolls or folds, and at times patchy, they threaten rain but do not always deliver.

The Benign and Furious Moods of the Clouds

Clouds have always been heralds of fair or foul weather. They are made of water vapor that has evaporated from the earth and formed droplets or ice crystals of microscopic size in the atmosphere. Too lightweight to descend as rain, the droplets may ride the air currents indefinitely before they condense around dust, salt or other

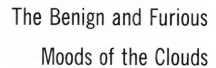

A TORRENTIAL RAIN BEATS DOWN UPON THE SOUTH PACIFIC OFF SAMOA. THE BALEFUL-LOOKING CLOUD MASS FROM WHICH IT IS FALLING

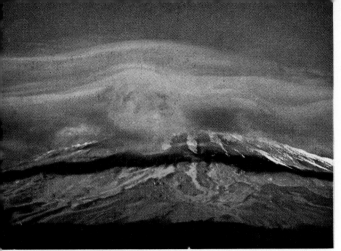

A THIN CLOUDCAP hovers in fixed position atop Mount Kilimanjaro, Tanganyika. It is formed into a lens shape by drafts of air sweeping up and down the mountain slopes.

A BOLD THUNDERHEAD of cumulonimbus warns of an approaching storm. Flung high by fast-rising air currents, the frozen top is hammered anvil-flat by a warm layer above.

particles. Clouds were first classified in 1803 according to the Latin names for their shapes: *cirrus* for ringlet, *cumulus* for heap and *stratus* for scattering. The term *nimbus*, for rainstorm, was applied later. In varying combinations, the terms describe the patterns of the clouds. The fragile cirrus clouds spray out as high as 40,000 feet.

Cirrocumulus crowd the sky like mackerel scales at 20,000 to 40,000 feet, while cirrostratus appear as a milky blur. Cumulonimbus are thunderheads that rise to great heights. Cumulus are fleecy white puffs 4,000 to 6,500 feet up. Nimbostratus are drizzle clouds, and stratocumulus are the low-flying messengers of rain or snow.

S THE BOTTOM OF A THUNDERSTORM CUMULONIMBUS FORMATION WHICH MAY EXTEND FROM SEA LEVEL TO AN ALTITUDE OF 40,000 FEET

A FLAMING FOUNTAIN arcs from the Arizona desert as a rainbow appears. It is caused by sunlight passing from behind the viewer through drops of moisture. The drops act as prisms, splitting the white light of the sun into its many component colors. Colors are brightest when the water droplets are the largest, often after a summer thundershower.

Mystic Mists in the Air

Two of the most striking phenomena that occur in the earth's lower atmosphere are dim, dun fogs and brilliant rainbows. Rainbows (*opposite*) are caused when the sun's rays strike a heavy but translucent cloud of raindrops left hanging in the air after a shower. This thin film of moisture acts as a prism, separating and reflecting the whole spectrum of visible color that is contained in sunlight.

Fogs are also the result of heavy concentrations of water vapor. They form most frequently when the air just above ground level cools suddenly and condenses its load of water vapor into tiny droplets about 0.1 millimeter across. The most persistent fogs occur when air temperatures are "inverted," that is, when the cool ground air is overlaid with warmer air and cannot move away. When this condition exists over a densely inhabited region that produces a good deal of smoke and other fumes, a noxious smog results.

A GROUND FOG obscures the earth like vapors of steam, turning an English landscape into a Japanese print. Such a morning mist along gentle slopes is a sign of fair weather ahead. Already, the sun's rays are piercing the fog to disperse it. Like dew and frost, ground fog develops in the after-midnight hours, often on windless autumnal nights.

Darting Fingers from the Sky

Before or during almost all of the 44,000 thunderstorms that beat down on the earth each day, darting fingers of light streak through the air, usually followed by claps of thunder. This is the anger of the skies—heard and seen—which made men fear the ancient thunderbolt-hurling gods. Lightning is still a violent, fearsome thing. It may come in great sheets, in balls or in zigzag or forked streaks. The accompanying rumbling of thunder is produced by the sudden expansion of air that has been heated by the bolt; thunder is heard after a flash because light travels faster than sound. The flashes result from atmospheric

A FREAKISH FLASH of lightning is attracted to a pillar of water flung up by the detonation of a Navy depth charge. A camera recording test blasts caught the bolt by accident.

A STREAKED SKY is seen from inside a ranger lookout tower in Clearwater National Forest, Idaho. The camera shutter was left open for two minutes, photographing a number of

A TRIPLE BOLT is made by three consecutive flashes of lightning. All three, discharged within thousandths of a second, follow parallel courses through the already ionized air.

bursts of electricity, which may leap between different clouds or between sky and earth wherever sufficient tension from opposite charges is built up. Erect structures on the earth's surface attract the ground-seeking bolts. To avoid fire, lightning rods are set atop high buildings to "coax" the bolts and conduct their electric charges, as high as 100 million volts, to metal plates in the ground. Death by lightning comes to more than 150 persons in the U.S. every year, but on the beneficent side, lightning brings nitrogen from the air to the earth by converting it to an oxide, which then falls with the rain to fertilize the soil.

separate lightning flashes. The thickest ones are closest to the tower; the thinner ones thread out in the distance. Lightning starts about 10,000 forest fires a year in the U.S.

A SPIRAL OF FLAME streaks earthward during a thunderstorm in Switzerland. This rare bolt has ignited chemicals in the atmosphere, giving it the appearance of twisted cloth.

75

A TWISTER'S TIP thunders along a Texas highway, flinging bits of destroyed houses into the air. Many tornadoes often whirl through the air at the same time. A dozen other funnels were counted in the area where this one struck.

The Ferocious Winds

The strongest winds that blow upon the earth's surface are those that whirl within the vortex of a tornado. Australia and North America know them best. About 150 tornadoes hit the U.S. each year, converging on the southern states in the spring and on midwest states in summer. A tornado's funnel starts (usually after a thunderstorm) as a gently whirling downward drift of clouds. When it gathers force and touches land, tons of dust and debris travel up the funnel, which may revolve at 200 to 500 miles an hour. The inverted whirlpool of air can lift an entire house and deposit it elsewhere, intact or in smithereens. Tornadoes also form at sea, where they are known as waterspouts. These are much less violent and do little damage.

A TORNADO'S WAKE in a suburb of Kansas City, Missouri (*below*), shows a broad, clean-cut lane of destruction. The width of such a path varies widely, from a few feet to 450 yards, extending as the vortex veers from side to side.

A DEMOLISHED BARN litters an Iowa farmyard after a tornado. Most of the damage from such storms is caused when buildings "explode" in the extreme low air pressure of the tornado's center. But objects in the buildings may remain untouched. In this case, five horses are still standing in their stalls moments after the debris stopped falling.

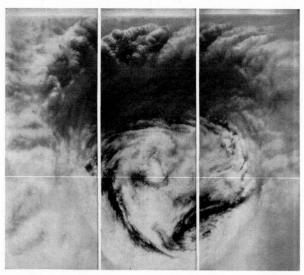

A HURRICANE EYE, five miles wide, is seen in the center of these strips filmed by a U-2 reconnaissance plane flying at 65,000 feet. The main force of the storm is below 50,000 feet.

The Violence of Wind and Wave

To man and his flimsy structures, wind-driven water is among the most dangerous of natural phenomena. Since 1900 more than 50,000 persons have been killed as the ocean has licked over the land. The friction of air passing over the surface of water, as gentle as this rubbing of gas and liquid may seem, is enough to heap it into waves. The height of waves is proportional to wind speed: an 80-mile wind blowing uninterruptedly over the ocean raises 40-foot rolling seas. The highest waves tower to 100 feet and result when two smaller swells merge at sea.

Sometimes, as at the right, a monstrous wave will glide across many miles of ocean and pile up on the coast with little or no trace of the wind that started it on its way. More often, the great whirling motions of the atmosphere stir up storms at sea which strike the shore with huge breakers and winds ranging from 75 to 200 miles an hour blowing around a central area of calm. There are several names for these whirlpool-like storms. In the Far East, they are called typhoons; in the Philippines, *baguios;* and in the Western Hemisphere, hurricanes—after the ancient thunder-god of the Carib Indians, Hurakan.

A VIOLENT WAVE, 60 feet high, caused by a northeaster, crashes against the sea wall at Winthrop, Massachusetts. Although the wind has died away, the sea is still agitated.

4

The Emergence of the Crust

THE solid earth underfoot is not as solid as it seems. Actually it is undergoing constant stirrings. Sometimes these take place before our eyes, as when volcanoes spurt out molten rock or earthquakes wrack the globe's thin crust. But usually the shifts are on a far slower and larger scale, as whole regions rise or subside, tilt or warp. In either case, no plain, no cliff is permanent. By studying the record of past change written on the face of the earth, we can not only trace the geologic past but also infer what the future holds in store.

The most striking fact about the earth's surface is that most of it—nearly three quarters—is drowned in ocean. Still more land would be submerged if the millions of cubic miles of ice that now smother polar and mountain areas were to melt and thus raise the sea level by an estimated 200 to 300 feet. An almost equally conspicuous fact is that the relative distribution of land and sea areas on the earth's surface shows a rough symmetry, with each great land mass being on the opposite side of the earth from an ocean. It is possible, for example, to divide the earth arbitrarily into halves in such a way that one contains 81 per cent of all the land area, and the other only

19 per cent. An earth so divided would have its "North Pole" in France, and its "Northern Hemisphere" would include Europe, Asia, Africa, North America and the bulk of South America. Opposite it would be a watery "Southern Hemisphere" with its pole in the neighborhood of New Zealand. Is this arrangement of land and sea the result of mere chance, or is there some explanation for it? As yet, no one can say for sure.

The continents of the earth are great plateaus of rock that project an average of about half a mile above the level of the sea. Ordinary maps, which divide land from sea at the tidal zone, do not give a true picture of continental outlines, for they fail to show the gently sloping undersea margins that form the natural continuations of most coast lines. These continental shelves extend out to sea in shallow water for as much as 100 miles. Their aggregate area is over 10 million square miles, a little larger than North America. It is the precipitous brinks of the continental shelves that are the true limits of the continents—a fact that our descendants would encounter at firsthand should the accumulation of glaciers in a new ice age lower the earth's sea level.

The unrevealing face of the oceans also conceals the fact that the huge oceanic basins themselves—which average two and a third miles in depth—possess as varied an assortment of irregular terrain as do the continents. The Mid-Atlantic Ridge, for example, is a broad submarine mountain range that runs from Iceland south almost to Antarctica. Unseen by seafarers thousands of feet above, its peaks project a mile or more above the ocean floor. Mariners are familiar only with the few great mountains that thrust high enough to be visible as islands—the Azores, Ascension and Tristan da Cunha among others. Isolated elevations, called sea mounts, abound in oceanic basins, and long, narrow trenches, some deeper than Everest is high, scar the basin floors here and there. But for all this resemblance to the land, there is no proof that the geologic character of the sea bottom is anything like that of the land. On the contrary, all evidence indicates that the materials of the ocean floor are not only quite different from those of the continents but also have a rather different history.

An additional basic fact about the earth's crust, whether above or below water, is that it is virtually all solid rock. This is not immediately apparent, for sediments cover the ocean floor, and above water soil, vegetation, and rock fragments such as sand and gravel are littered everywhere. But this cloak of crustal debris occurs in superficial layers measurable in feet or yards, while the thickness of the underlying bedrock is measured in miles. Furthermore, the rocks at the surface of the earth's crust are much the same as those deeper down, right to the level of the mantle. Mine and well shafts, the deepest of which descend as far as five miles, go through the same stuff all the way down. Similarly, volcanic rock shows no great differences, whether it has risen in molten form from chambers just below ground or from depths as great as 40 miles.

Rocks have been classified and subclassified almost endlessly by zealous petrographers, but all belong to three great groups: the igneous, the sedimentary and the metamorphic. All igneous rocks were once molten and are believed to have come from deep in the earth, cooling at various rates and assuming various forms ranging from smooth basalt to grainy granite. Sedimentary rocks, as their name implies, are formed of layers of such materials as sand and clay washed down into lake beds and ocean floors. Those sediments may be laid down by water, by ice or by wind. Cemented under pressure and often raised up again by later earth movements, they include the familiar sandstones and shales, limestones and dolomites. It is in these rocks, particularly in shales and limestones, that fossil deposits are found. The metamorphic rocks are also aptly named: they are changed in form, reborn by heat and pressure during periods of deep burial. Thus slate was once clay, quartzite is a changed form of sandstone, and marble is reconstituted limestone or dolomite. Geologists are not unanimously agreed on these groupings. For example, some of them believe most granite is metamorphic rather than igneous in origin.

However formed, rocks are complex mixtures of various elements in the form of mineral compounds. Of the 92 natural elements known on the earth, only eight are commonly involved in rock formation; they constitute 98 per cent of the earth's crust by weight. The most abundant element in the crust—47 per cent of it—is oxygen. Silicon is next, at 28 per cent. From there, the percentages drop sharply: aluminum totals 8 per cent, iron 5 per cent; and sodium, magnesium, potassium and calcium less than 4 per cent each. These eight common elements, together with several not so common ones, combine chemically in simple or complicated ways to form nearly 2,000 known minerals. But it is hardly surprising that in terms of volume, oxygen-silicon compounds predominate and that only a dozen or so mineral compounds account for the bulk of the earth's crust.

Man's only direct experience with rock formation comes from what he has seen of active volcanoes—orifices in the earth's crust from which molten rock, hot enough to flow like incandescent taffy, pours forth. This is the prototype of all igneous rocks. Such molten stuff is called magma when underground and lava when it emerges, and the nature of a volcanic eruption depends upon the rock's composition and content of gas and water. A viscous magma, laden with gas, tends to escape explosively, spewing fragments of solidified lava and billowing clouds of steam and hot gases. A thinner magma, with a smaller gas content, pushes out in quieter fashion, forming tongues of white-hot lava that creep downhill until they harden.

The giant volcanoes that have formed the Hawaiian Islands rear as high as 30,000 feet above the ocean floor, 14,000 feet or so of this eminence being above sea level. Lava from the active volcanoes of Hawaii often emerges as an incandescent, highly fluid stream, sometimes spurting up in transient fountains when a pocket of gas comes to the surface. Such flows may travel for long distances before solidifying; characteristically, they produce wide-based mountains. At the other extreme are volcanoes with thick lavas, which build up steep, narrow cones.

Magma does not always reach the surface by the volcanic route. In fact it sometimes does not reach the surface at all. If it can find no outlet, or if there is not sufficient pressure behind it to force one, it may merely thrust its way up into cracks or between layers of rock near the surface. Sometimes it forms underground lakes, pushing up the surface above like a blister but not breaking through. Often it runs along natural fissures, occasionally engulfing and melting what lies in its path. Magma which has worked its way into a vertical crack and hardened there like a wall is called a dike. Dikes vary in width from a few inches to several yards and may be many miles in length. They

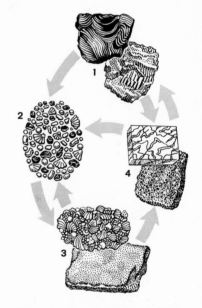

The cycles through which rock disintegrates into sediment and the sediment is compressed into new rock are illustrated in the diagram above. Sediment (2) is formed of particles from all kinds of rock, plus the shells or other remains of animals. It is compressed, primarily, into sandstone and limestone (3), shale and conglomerate.

These sedimentary rocks may erode or they may be changed by heat, chemical action or pressure into metamorphic rock like marble or gneiss (4). These, remelting, can contribute material to igneous rocks (1) which are formed of molten matter. These igneous rocks, in turn, may be changed into metamorphic rock or may be eroded into new supplies of sediment.

may be revealed millions of years after their formation when the softer rock around them has been eroded away, leaving the dikes, exposed to the elements, running like long fences across the surface of the land. A few dikes are immense. One in Rhodesia is 300 miles long and up to five miles wide.

A horizontal sheet of solidified underground magma is known as a sill. The magnificent Palisades that line the bank of the Hudson River opposite New York City are, in reality, a tremendous sill. Their appearance is deceptive; they look like a series of immense crumbling stone columns. But these columns are only one edge of the sill, and their vertical appearance derives from the shrinkage of the original magma as it solidified.

Sills are dwarfed by the most gigantic of all molten rock formations. These are batholiths, enormous bodies of granitic rock that may be tens of thousands of square miles in area, extending downward to unknown depths. What causes batholiths is a subject of controversy. Some geologists think that the magma has simply forced its way into older rock formations on a huge scale, pushing them upward and aside as it rose toward the surface. Others think that the intense heat generated by a large amount of magma enables it to swallow up and melt the rocks above it, thereby growing in volume at the expense of existing rocks rather than forcing them aside. A third school holds that batholiths were never magma—that they are not of igneous origin at all, but are metamorphic. This point of view contends that no lava field, above or below the surface, could be as big as some batholiths, and that only the exertion of subterranean heat and pressure on a grand scale can yield such masses of homogeneous material.

The texture and appearance of magma varies enormously according to whether it has been cooled rapidly on the surface of the earth in the form of lava, or whether it has remained underground in batholiths and cooled very slowly. The rapid cooling of lava gives it a fine-grained character ranging all the way from obsidian, which is the most quickly cooled of all lava and looks like blackish glass, to basalt, a smooth, dark, dense material that is the most common of all volcanic rocks. By contrast, subsurface magma cools so very slowly that its structure is much coarser. A typical dike or batholith is made of granite, which is a grainy rock, speckled in color and full of relatively large particles of different minerals.

TAKEN over-all, the earth's crust appears to consist of a spherical shell of basaltic rock, in which the vast blocks of granitic rock that make up the continents are embedded, or—perhaps more accurately—"float." But this picture of the crust may be a little oversimplified since granite and basalt are both igneous rock, and there is a good deal of the other two basic types —sedimentary and metamorphic—on the earth's surface. However, in terms

This cutaway profile of the earth's crust shows how it is shaped by recurring movements of sedimentary rock layers subjected to pressure from below. Where the layers are forced to bend, geologists describe the resulting folds as anticlines, synclines or monoclines. A fault is a line where the layers of rock are actually broken and shifted. A raised section created where the rocks are squeezed up is known as a horst; a rift valley where they subside is called a graben. An overthrust fault, usually accompanied by severe folding, slides the rock horizontally. The structure called an unconformity results when rock tilted up by a previous disturbance is covered with new rocks and sediment.

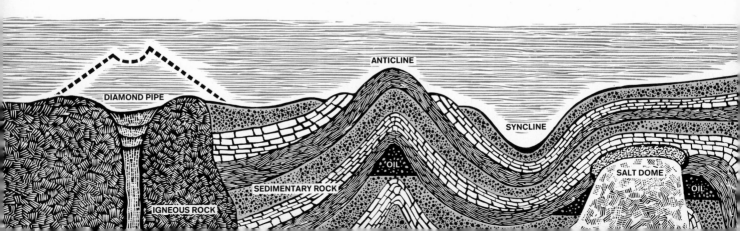

of total quantity, both are so much less abundant than igneous rock that the general picture of a basalt shell with granite continents will do.

At the beginning of the 19th Century, the threefold division of rock classes was only a hazy concept. Geology at that time was a highly practical, applied science concerned chiefly with the mining of commercially important deposits of metals and other minerals. Nevertheless, there were those who went beyond the pick-and-shovel stage and speculated on how the rocks got there in the first place and why there were so many different kinds. The theorists quickly found themselves in two rival camps. One group held that the earth had originally been covered with a thick primordial sea and that everything now found in the crust—hard stones, soft stones, large and small stones, even fossils—had been precipitated slowly out of this broth. For their allegiance to this view of the oceanic origin of the earth's crust, these men were known as Neptunists. Their opponents held that the principal factor in crust formation was the outpouring of volcanoes past and present. For their support of fire, they were known as Plutonists.

THE Neptunists had some persuasive evidence to support their view; the layers of sandstone, clay and shale, in fact all the sedimentary rock in the world, had obviously been laid down in water, possibly out of a primordial broth, just as they claimed. But how about granite, shouted the Plutonists; how do you get around the fact that you have only to dig down through your sedimentary layers to find granite practically everywhere? How do you account for all that granite? The Neptunists answered that granite was simply the first thing to precipitate out. In a primordial sea full of grains in suspension of different materials, something had to precipitate out first, and why couldn't it be granite? Granite was dense and very hard, and was obviously the first to settle. The later settling of other things could account very neatly for the sedimentary layers on top of the granite, layers which were slowly compressed into rock by the sheer weight of still other sediments on top of them.

To the Plutonists, faced with the immense forces on display in a hundred volcanic landscapes, such an explanation was arrant nonsense. The granite bedrock was hard, they insisted, because it had been fused and tempered by the earth's interior fire. The softer rocks above it had been subjected to lower temperatures, and hence were not quite so hard.

As one and another Plutonist traveled around the world, noting the brutal evidence of volcanism in many places, the domination of the Neptunist view began to wane. Charles Darwin, as a student, was exposed to one Neptunist die-hard—and very nearly lost his taste for earth science in the process. The scene is preserved in his memoirs:

The continued reshaping of the crust is responsible for the distribution of minerals and fuel deposits. The diamond pipe is formed by an eruption which forces a narrow passage to the surface. Erosion has worn away the volcanic cone, exposing the pipe filled with diamond-bearing rock. Oil, formed by heat and pressure from decayed organic substances, rises through porous sandstone. It collects where folding or an unconformity has created nonporous shale traps. Salt domes, pushed through the rock from deeper formations, also form oil traps. Coal seams, originally laid down in horizontal layers, are often bent and brought up to the surface by crustal disturbances.

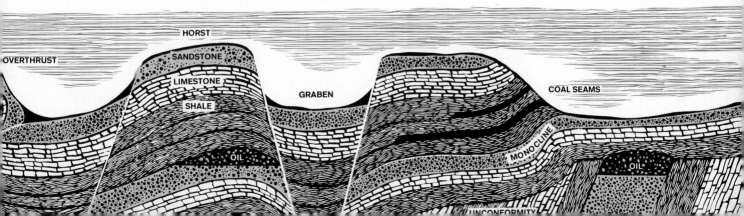

"I heard the Professor at Salisbury Craigs discoursing on a trap dyke with volcanic rocks all around us, say it was a fissure filled with sediments from above, adding with a sneer that there were men who maintained that it had been injected from beneath in a molten condition. When I think of this lecture, I do not wonder that I determined never to attend to Geology."

Yet these learned schools were disputing over nothing more than the portion of the earth's crust available for inspection at the surface. The even more staggering modern concept of continents as buoyant blocks of granite was yet to be formulated, since it had apparently occurred to nobody to wonder why the continents project upward the way they do.

ON a world average, the continents protrude almost three miles above the ocean floors today. Moreover, what evidence there is strongly suggests that this elevation, or a comparable one, has persisted since the continents' origin. What, then, keeps these weighty continental blocks from sinking downward until they are level with the rest of the earth's crust? Even the most rigid shell of basalt could not withstand the constant pressure of such enormous masses of granite. The answer to this appears to be the same as the answer to why a cork floats: in both cases, the bodies are buoyant because they are less dense than the material in which they are immersed. In the case of the continents, it is the earth's mantle that plays water to these colossal corks. Granite is about 20 per cent lighter than the material of which the earth's upper mantle is composed. Basalt, on the other hand, is only 10 per cent lighter. The continents thus *must* ride higher above the mantle than does the crust's basaltic, basement layer.

Another problem presents itself here. A cork does not float *on* water but *in* it. A block of wood, being heavier than cork, will float deeper. How deep is determined by a simple law discovered 2,200 years ago by Archimedes: if the block of wood weighs a pound, it will float just deep enough to displace a pound of water. Looked at in this way, it is not hard to see that a cork or a block of wood, being less dense than water, is actually held up by the water. In the same way, do the great blocks of granite that compose the continents have roots substantial enough for them actually to be floating like corks?

There are two ways of investigating this point. The first utilizes the same principles that enabled scientists to work out the sequence of the layers of the earth by measuring earthquake waves. By making very accurate measurements of the movements of quakes in the crust, it is possible to perceive vague outlines of the structure of the crust. The second method makes use of gravity measurements. Extremely sensitive instruments will detect differences in the force of gravity at different points on the earth's surface, and from these differences it begins to be possible to estimate the varying amounts of granite and basalt that lie unreachably below. Both approaches yield the same conclusion: the continents indeed have massive roots that reach deep down to support the three miles or so that these blocks extend above the ocean floor.

A simplified model of the crust used by many geophysicists in their calculations supposes a more or less uniform, three-mile-thick layer of basalt atop the mantle. Upon this are superimposed continental blocks, an average of 20 miles thick. The blocks are so heavy that they press the underlying basalt layer down about 14 miles into the mantle, thus making the mantle's surface slightly dimpled rather than being perfectly spherical. So, although the continents cover only a trifle over a quarter of the earth's surface area, in terms of total volume they actually comprise about two thirds of the crust, and the basaltic, basement rock about one third.

The idea that a continent—or indeed any major land mass, such as a large island—floats on the mantle is known as the theory of isostasy. A direct verification of the theory is found in the fact that the entire Scandinavian Peninsula is rising in the air. Pressed down by the weight of glaciers during the ice age, it has been rising ever since the glaciers departed 9,000 years ago. Scandinavia is now believed to stand nearly a thousand feet higher than it did under the burden of the icecap, and parts of it are currently going up at the rate of three feet a century. Some estimates indicate it still has about 650 feet to go before it reaches equilibrium.

Just as the roots of continental blocks thrust deep enough to dimple the underlying mantle, so the roots of major mountain systems push down even deeper in order to support their weight, and to justify their greater height. The first suspicion that mountains, as well as thrusting up, also extend down into the earth came from experiments performed in the 18th Century with no more complex an instrument than a plumb bob. On a level plain, a plumb bob points directly toward the center of the earth. This being so, one would expect that near a mountain the plumb line would be deflected by the gravitational pull of the mountain's mass. In 1738, the French mathematician Pierre Bouguer went to an Andean peak—Mount Chimborazo, in what is now Ecuador—on an expedition sent by the French Academy to help settle scientific arguments over the length of a meridian arc. While making gravitational measurements on Mount Chimborazo, he noticed that the gravitational attraction of the mountain caused a much smaller deflection of his plumb bob than would be expected from such a great mass. Bouguer suspected that the granites in the mountain and under it were for some reason comparatively lightweight. He noted in his journal that it was as if the mountain were made of eggshells. Before long, there was speculation in the French press that he had discovered "hollow mountains" which might be inhabited.

In a sense, Bouguer was right. What he did not realize was the reason for the mountain's "lightness": what underlay Chimborazo was a great block of light, granitic rock instead of the heavier basaltic rock normally found at depth.

Another gravity study, in the Pyrenees a century later, actually gave a negative result: the plumb bob, instead of swinging toward the mountain, was deflected away from it. In efforts to account for such anomalies, an English astronomer, George B. Airy, reasoned that mountains must have "roots" extending far down into the basaltic layer, and that a mountain of light density floats in the heavier rock as an iceberg floats in water. Out of such speculation the theory of isostasy was born, and it is not hard to extend the theory from mountains to the continents themselves.

Isostasy, however, says nothing about how continents came into being. This is one of the most difficult questions that one can ask about the earth, and is the subject of intense study and controversy at this moment. There are many more hypotheses than there are continents—nearly as many as there are geologists. No single theory is free from serious objections.

The simplest is known as the convection-current theory. It suggests that differences in heat deep in the earth cause the plastic rock in the mantle to flow in a regular pattern and that new material reaches the surface on a massive enough scale to create continents. It is a good theory, as will be shown, but it does not entirely satisfy geophysicists because there is hardly any observational evidence to support it. At the other extreme the theory of continental drift, which holds that the present continents are fragments that broke off from a single initial continent, is almost impossible for a serious geophysicist to believe—yet there are facts which no other theory explains as well.

Some idea of the extraordinary complexity of this subject may be gained by taking a brief look at the history of the continental-drift theory. Its chief exponent was a German meteorologist, Alfred Wegener, who felt the need to explain the parallel development of living things throughout the world. Similar plants and animals have existed in widely separated regions throughout geologic history, a fact that troubled biologists early in this century. A common explanation was the supposed existence of land bridges linking the various continents, but this notion is hard to accept, if for no other reason than that there is no trace today of most of the supposed bridges, which must have been substantial affairs if they were to persist for hundreds of millions of years. Wegener suggested instead that once there was a single, giant continental mass called Pangaea, and that the rest of the globe was covered by a single ocean called Panthalassa. In time Pangaea cracked apart, and the pieces wandered away from one another to produce the continents of today.

This simple idea permitted Wegener to account for a number of odd facts besides the simultaneity of evolution. For one thing it suggested an explanation for why South Africa, India, Australia and part of South America bear the unmistakable scars of prehistoric glaciers and ice sheets. This phenomenon is understandable if it is assumed that these lands once surrounded the South Pole which Wegener believed had been near the west coast of Africa. Similarly the coal deposits of Europe, North America and Antarctica point to a probable equatorial location for those continents in the past. Merely glancing at a globe seems to verify continental drift: the coast line of the Americas closely matches that of western Europe and Africa, as if the two had actually been torn apart at some time in the past. There are even matching geologic formations in Norway and Canada in the north, and in South Africa and Patagonia in the south.

Unfortunately for Wegener's daring and imaginative hypothesis, there are no known forces strong enough to shove the continents around the earth, let alone split one into fragments. Exceedingly precise measurements reveal no lateral motions whatsoever of the continents today, although the theory predicts that they should still be drifting. The oceans were just where they are now, according to geologic and biological studies of the sediments on their floors, throughout the period when the continents were supposed to have been wandering across the face of the earth. What is more, the very observations that seem at first sight to support continental drift are not so convincing on closer inspection. Winds, floating objects and the few verified land bridges—such as the one across the Bering Strait—account well enough for the appearance of similar plant and animal species around the

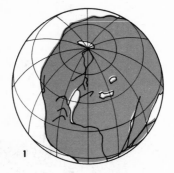

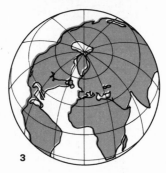

The theory of continental drift, as propounded by Alfred Wegener, held that all the continents originated as one huge land mass called Pangaea. Black lines show the outlines of present continents (1). Wegener theorized that various forces pulled Pangaea apart (2), gradually dispersing the continents toward their present positions (3). He cited the continents' jigsaw-puzzle effect as well as fossil and glacial evidence to support his hypothesis.

world. As far as the climate argument is concerned, later research has indicated that glaciers were present both before and after coal beds were formed in many places, which Wegener and his followers could only account for by supposing that the continents had come together again after having been originally dispersed. And the jigsaw-puzzle matching of the continents does not really work very well either.

For all these reasons the theory of continental drift was abandoned by nearly all geologists, just as the collision theory of the origin of the solar system was abandoned by nearly all astronomers when the weight of empirical data went against it. Theories in science live or die by the sword of experiment, and no matter how attractive they may seem to the layman, unless they agree with observation they cannot be taken seriously. The idea that the solar system is the fruit of an encounter between our sun and another star is dead today but, peculiarly enough, recent findings indicate that the continents may very well have shifted their positions slightly in the remote past. These findings were made by a most ingenious method and are based on the fact that many rocks contain compounds of iron. By whatever process these rocks are formed, during the time that they are hardening the mineral grains in them will become magnetized in the direction of the earth's magnetic field, just as iron filings line up in the magnetic field of a magnet. Theoretically, if there were never any continental movement or shifting of the poles, those grains, once hardened into position, would always point toward the poles. The fact that many such polarized rocks have their magnetic fields pointing in different directions suggests either that the poles have moved, or that the rocks themselves have.

There are good theoretical reasons for believing that the magnetic and geographic poles, while they are known to move slightly relative to each other, do not ever vary more than about 10 or 12 degrees. Therefore any polarized rocks which point farther than that from magnetic north can be assumed to have moved—or the continents in which they lie may have moved. This suggests *some* continental drift, but nothing on the grand scale that Wegener proposed.

More appealing is the suggestion from the rock magnetism studies that the *entire* crust of the earth has shifted relative to the earth's axis of rotation. Curiously, such a crustal shift is easier to account for than the relative motion of the individual continents, because the ocean floors are rigid enough to hold the continents in place while the crust itself is apparently not too firmly attached to the underlying mantle.

Two other theories of continental formation command more serious attention today. The older is the contraction theory, first proposed late in the 19th Century and later modified and extended into a consistent and logical—but not necessarily correct—picture. In this view the primitive earth, at some time prior to three billion years ago, had a thin, uniform cover of basaltic rock. As the underlying mantle cooled, the surface shrank and began to crack, since the inner part of the earth maintained a constant temperature and volume. Through the cracks steam, gases and magma escaped—forming respectively the oceans, the atmosphere and the nuclei of the continents. Then erosion went to work. It washed rock fragments into thick beds of sediment along the margins of the original small continents, and the pressure of these beds promoted further cracking just offshore.

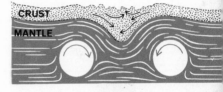

A theory that convection currents work to build mountains is illustrated in a working model sketched here. Drums turning slowly in viscous glycerine set up currents which simulate those in the earth's mantle. A layer of sawdust and oil represents the crust. Friction of the currents drags the crust into a downfold. If the currents are interrupted, the crustal layer floats up again (lower), lifting the thickened section to build up new mountains.

These new fractures permitted more steam, gases and magma to emerge from the earth's interior, adding to the oceans and the atmosphere and causing the growth of mountain ranges along the edges of the continents. As time went on, the continents grew larger and larger because of the new material added to their edges by the fracture system; the fractures in turn were largely induced by the deposit of sediments made by continental erosion.

The essential assumption of this theory is the contraction of the crust, which turns out to be rather hard to account for on the basis of pure surface cooling. It may be speculated that contraction was brought about by the escape of steam, gas and magma through chance fissures, and that the loss of this material led to the shrinking of what was the initial surface of the earth. Thus the original terrestrial skin could have been at what is now the Mohorovičić discontinuity, and everything above it today exuded from below during the past several billion years.

Attention must still be paid to the convection-current theory, which argues that there are immense flows of material within the mantle, much like those that occur in a pot of porridge bubbling on a hot stove. It is believed that the action of such currents would be to concentrate the lighter granitic crustal material into large continental masses on the surface, almost like froth. This theory must assume that both granite and basalt were part of the primeval precontinental crust, but there is nothing to indicate that this was not so. It also must deal with the fact that the flow of material in the mantle is not a flow at all in the sense that we understand it, but is incredibly slow, perhaps on the order of an inch a year. However, we are dealing with immense periods of time, and the important thing is to establish some movement, however small. An inch a year, over several million years, amounts to several hundred miles.

Both of these recent hypotheses have their strong points, and neither is physically impossible or even implausible. Many geologists today lean toward a combination of the two, with contraction playing the larger role and convection currents in a subsidiary position.

WHILE these two theories are currently receiving the most concentrated attention from geophysicists, new ones are constantly being suggested. It has been proposed by the marine geologist Bruce Heezen that the earth is *expanding*. Only in this way can he account for much that still remains obscure in the history of the earth. Expansion would crack the crust along fracture lines through which new material would well up, and as the sections of the crust moved apart, immense pressures would be exerted upon the contents to squeeze mountains upward. A novel and, at first glance, startling notion—but at the present stage of its development it is an idea to be further explored rather than a finished hypothesis.

But all these theories deal with the earth's crust in the broadest of views. Most of the shapes visible to the earth's inhabitants—great lakes and gentle hills, glittering icecaps and verdant plains, swampy deltas and parched deserts—are the products of other forces. Systems of almost unimaginable scope and power have formed—and still modify—the earth's continents, dividing land from sea. But it is thereafter that what we think of as landscape comes into existence. In the contemplation of landscape, too, we must envy the geologist, for his pleasure is enhanced by an understanding of how the multitude of shapes arrayed before him came into being.

NEARLY TWO MILES UNDERGROUND, AFRICAN GOLD MINERS TRUDGE ALONG A TUNNEL IN JOHANNESBURG'S ROBINSON DEEP MINE

The Great Treasure Hunt

Alone among all the earth's creatures, man learned to dig its treasures to make tools. Stone Age men scratched for flint, and their more knowing descendants mined their way through the Bronze and Iron Ages. The earth's coal fired the industrial revolution; now its uranium fuels the nuclear age. And its most dazzling prizes are the same today as they have always been: diamonds and gold.

A MONSTER DIGGER, reaching 420 feet from shovel to chute, excavates rock covering an Illinois coal strip. After it clears this overburden, other machines scoop coal from the exposed surface.

GRINDING AWAY at the face of a rich coal seam, this mechanical miner cuts out a ton every 30 seconds. Machinery in its wake gathers the broken coal, conveys it back to a shaft and hoists it to the surface. In the past two decades machines have tripled the rate of coal production; most miners now operate machines instead of swinging picks.

Coal: Ammunition for a Revolution

Ever since it started to turn the wheels and forge the steel of the new industrial order 200 years ago, coal has been man's prime source of power. Long before, the Roman armies had used it for their campfires, "mining" it simply by digging shallow holes into visible outcroppings. Today machines have taken over much of the hard digging, both on the surface and far underground. There is a lot of coal there. For example, a tenth of the area of the U.S. is underlain by coal, and most of the original reserve of nearly 2,000 billion tons is still untapped.

The creation of this storehouse of potential energy goes back about 345 million years to the time when vast swampy areas of the earth were covered by dense, sun-drenched plant forests. As the plants died in the marshes, crustal disturbances occurred. Shallow seas and layers of sediments inundated the forests, and later new swamps grew in their place. In some areas this alternation of swamp and sea occurred hundreds of times. Slowly, great pressures and ample time worked chemical changes, hardening and fossilizing the layers of decayed vegetation. The result was seams of coal, still rich in the solar energy absorbed by the plants so long ago.

CLEARING AWAY coal which they have blasted from the face of a narrow vein, these Kentucky miners, their backs bent to the low ceiling, still strain to the shovel as their grandfathers did. In the United States, such laborious pick-and-shovel mining is now confined mostly to abandoned mines and outcroppings being reworked by individuals.

SOUTH AFRICAN MINERS DIG FOR DIAMONDS AMONG THE EROSION-ROUNDED ROCKS OF AN ALLUVIAL DEPOSIT NORTH OF KIMBERLEY

Diamonds, Born in the Depths

Few substances look less alike than coal and diamond, yet both are fashioned from the same elemental carbon. No one knows exactly what goes on deep in the earth where the startling change from soft carbon to hard crystal is made. But to form diamonds, experiments show that carbonaceous material must be subjected to temperatures of at least 5000° F. and to pressures of over a million pounds per square inch. It is reckoned that these conditions must prevail at some points 240 miles down in the earth's interior. Once formed, diamonds are carried to the surface by molten magma during volcanic eruptions. When it cools, there remains a plug in the crust, called a diamond pipe. Within the pipe is a mass of

THE "BIG HOLE," an abandoned mine in Kimberley, shows the shaftlike shape of a diamond pipe. It produced $188 million worth of diamonds in 26 years.

GEM STONES VALUED AT THREE QUARTERS OF A MILLION DOLLARS SPARKLE IN A FRYING PAN AFTER BEING WASHED IN AN ACID BATH

bluish rock known as kimberlite, which is seeded with diamonds.

Long before the discovery of such pipes near Kimberley, South Africa, in the 1870s, miners in India and Brazil had been digging up diamonds scattered in dried-up river bottoms. These deposits were left by running water which picked up diamonds from volcanic pipes and dropped them miles away. Africa is rich in such alluvial beds as well as in pipe mines, and now produces 97 per cent of the world's annual diamond output of about 22 million carats, or four and a half tons. About 80 per cent are used industrially, since diamond, the earth's hardest material, is a useful tool as well as an ornament to beauty.

INDUSTRIAL DIAMONDS are mined in great quantity in the Congo. These stones will be used in abrasives and for drilling everything from teeth to oil wells.

The Bright Lure of Gold

Because it is rare, very beautiful, easily worked and never tarnishes, gold has always been the earth's most prized element. The Egyptians, first to mine it, considered it the "royal metal." Medieval alchemists strove to turn base metals into gold, a frustrated dream that nevertheless made for many of the early advances in chemistry. Europe's lust for it helped launch the voyages of exploration that opened the New World. Modern economists regard gold as "global money," the only totally acceptable medium of international exchange.

So thorough has been the search for gold that the days are gone when it could be panned commercially from the beds of streams, and a nugget weighing 208 (troy weight) pounds could turn up in a wagon rut, as happened in Australia. Now men must burrow deep for gold, and South African miners, like the sweating man at the left, have already blasted through rock to a depth of over two miles. For all the time, energy and lives spent in pursuit of gold, the amount taken from the earth seems pitifully small. It has been estimated that if world gold production from 1493 to 1955—a period encompassing the greatest strikes in Latin America, California, Australia, South Africa and Alaska—were melted down, it would bulk only as large as a 50-foot cube. Its value, however, at today's official rate of $35 an ounce, would be more than $60 billion.

A PROUD MINER, a migrant from Portuguese East Africa, labors in Johannesburg's Robinson Deep gold mine. Nearly depleted, the mine has produced more than 13 million ounces of gold in 68 years.

AN ARRAY OF GOLD shows the basic types mined (*opposite*). The rough is lode gold, found with quartz at a depth; the smooth nuggets come from surface mines. The $20 coin dates from 1855.

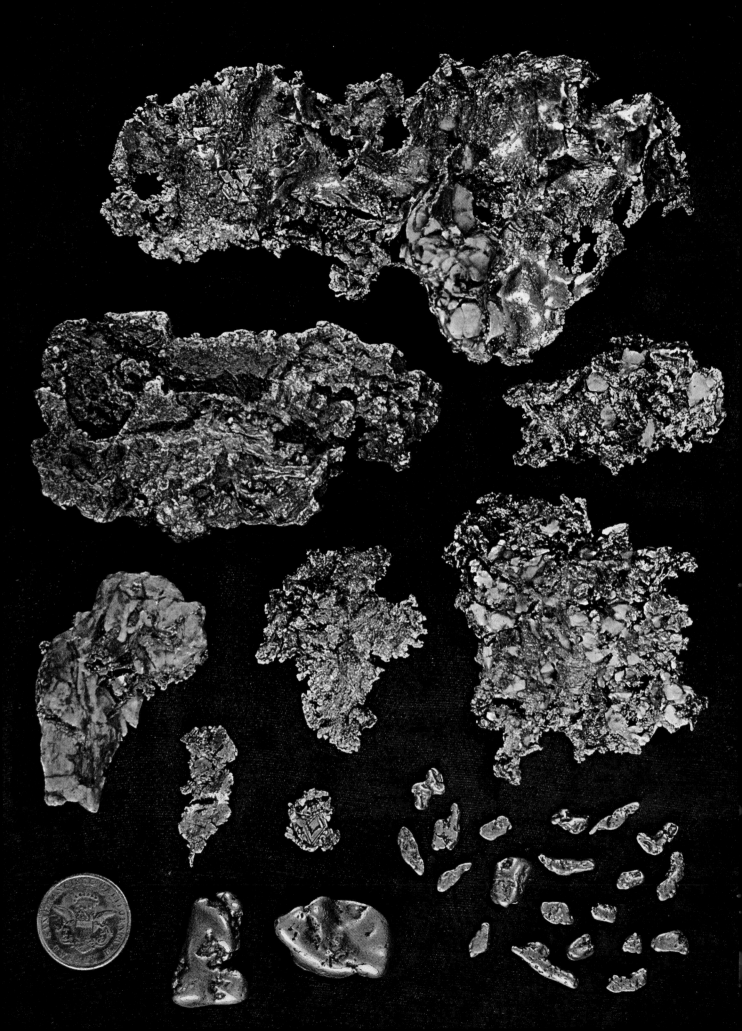

URANIUM-RICH VEIN of the yellowish mineral carnotite is tested by a prospector with a Geiger counter. Found mostly in the Colorado Plateau, carnotite is one of the main sources of uranium in the U.S. Before the nuclear age made uranium an element of prime importance, carnotite had only a modest value as a source of radium and vanadium.

URANIUM CONCENTRATE, CALLED "YELLOW CAKE," IS RAKED AND DRIED AT A MILL. ITS YELLOW COLOR IS LOST DURING REFINING

Precious Metal of a New Age

With the explosion of the first atomic bomb over the New Mexico desert in 1945, uranium—the basic ingredient of nuclear power and weapons—suddenly became the most sought-after metal of the nuclear age. As metals go, it is neither very rare nor particularly glamorous. Because it never occurs in a pure state, and seldom in heavy concentration, vast amounts of ore must be found, mined and refined in a long, costly process to produce small quantities of the final product (*right*). But the world's nuclear powers have created an urgent demand for it. Deposits of rich ore, such as those in the Congo, Romania, Canada and the U.S., are being intensively mined, while a world-wide search for more continues.

ELEMENTAL URANIUM, a heavy gray metal, is the basic source of fuel for nuclear reactors. Because of its strategic importance, all uranium is under governmental control.

PYRITE, QUARTZ

YELLOW WULFENITE

PEACOCK COAL

MICROCLINE, SMOKY QUARTZ

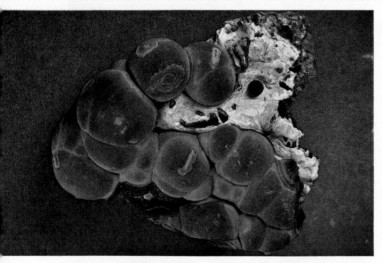

BOTRYOIDAL AZURITE, MALACHITE, LIMONITE

CHRYSOTILE (ASBESTOS)

The Glittering Faces
of Earth's Rocks and Minerals

Aside from providing the raw stuff of civilization's tools, the rocks which make up the crust of the earth have endlessly fascinated man simply by their natural beauty and extraordinary variety. Today in the United States there are over two million enthusiastic hobbyists who are captivated

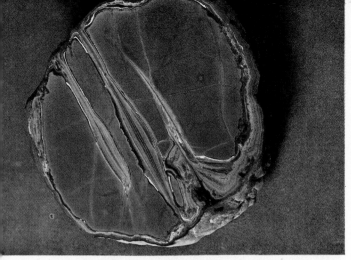

VARISCITE

PELE'S HAIR

GARNET

AMETHYST

RUBY SPHALERITE

CHALCANTHITE

by the lure of collecting strange and arresting specimens of the earth's remarkable alchemy. Altogether there are just under 2,000 different minerals in the crust and they present a bewildering and dazzling assortment of colors, shapes and textures. On these pages is a collection of rocks and minerals with striking contrasts. They range from the fragile, spun-glass effect of Pele's hair to the iridescent sheen of an ordinary lump of peacock coal, and from the rough fibers of natural asbestos to the brilliance of ruby sphalerite, which looks just like—but is not—a priceless gem.

ORDINARY LIGHT shows a nondescript collection of mineral-bearing rocks as they naturally appear. Only the trained eye can detect the characteristics that distinguish them.

ULTRAVIOLET LIGHT produces an array of distinctive luminescence in the same pile of rocks. Fluorite gives off a blue glow, calcite a red, willemite green and scapolite yellow.

A Weird Ultraviolet World

In the light of day not all minerals have the vivid beauty of those on the preceding pages. Many look drably alike, and to differentiate among them there are tests for such physical properties as texture, hardness and specific gravity. But a more spectacular test, involving the use of ultraviolet light, can turn even the dullest minerals into rainbows of ghostly color. The short wave lengths of ultraviolet light make it invisible to the human eye, but they produce in the atoms of some minerals an excitation which gives off energy in the form of longer-waved, visible light. This property, known as luminescence, is inherent in certain minerals and absent in others. Thus, though impurities and differences in crystal structure can complicate the tests, exposure to ultraviolet light is a valuable guide to a mineral's identification. This test has been used extensively both in the laboratory and in the field in prospecting for uranium, zinc and tungsten.

ODD DIAMONDS, otherwise normal, respond to ultraviolet light with a display of color. Only one gem diamond in 100 shows such color variation, instead of a blue-white light.

PURE SCHEELITE, a prime ore of tungsten, identifies itself with a display of blue hues. An all-white or a yellow tint would show that molybdenum was also present in the ore.

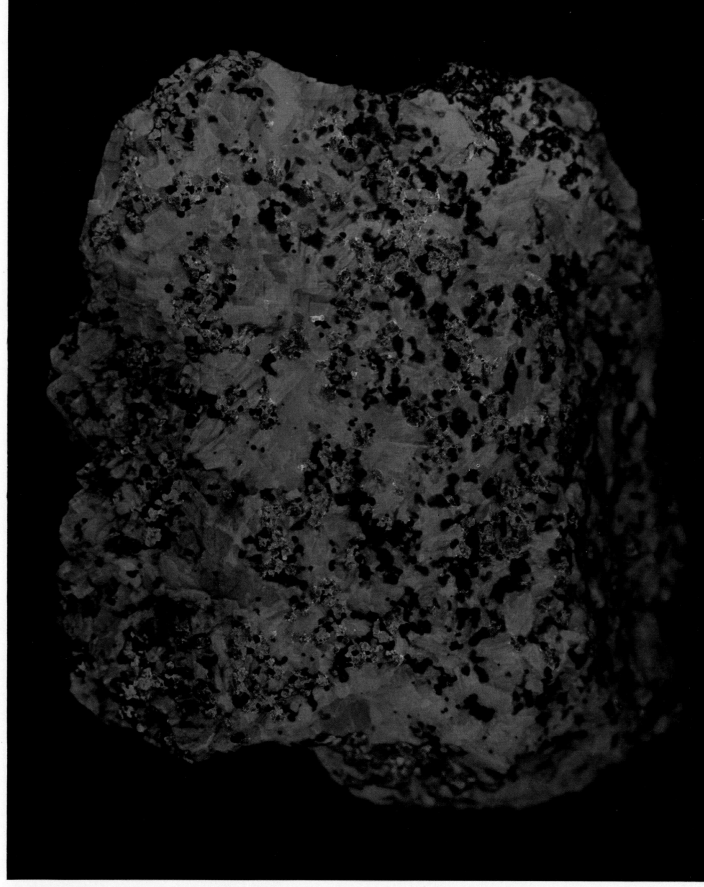

A GREEN GLOW is emitted under ultraviolet light by willemite, a zinc mineral. The red glow comes from calcite. The commercial value of luminescence was first realized accidentally in 1905 by mine workers in Franklin, New Jersey, who found that willemite dust glowed distinctively when exposed to electric sparks from milling machinery.

5

Shaping the Landscape

IT is not every day that a newborn volcano shoots lava out of a cornfield, or an island sinks beneath the waves, or an earthquake crumbles a city. While the earth is forever rearranging its features, most of its changes of face are leisurely rather than catastrophic. A human lifetime simply does not offer a long enough look to make the changes apparent. So until a few generations ago it was reasonable to assume, and most people did, that landscape was here to stay, pending the Last Judgment. That the hills were eternal or at least, as William Cullen Bryant put it, "ancient as the sun," was generally unquestioned.

But 19th Century geologists already were taking closer looks at the earth around them and beginning to find clues that had been available all along. Shore lines were everywhere advancing or in retreat; Niagara's brink was receding a few feet every year; some "eternal" hills were decaying while others appeared to be on the rise. In time it was realized that even the splash of a single raindrop on the soil, imperceptible to man although overwhelming to a mite or wood louse, counted for something in the remolding of the earth. In the course of this reappraisal of landscape, the ruins of the

Greek temple of Serapis at Pozzuoli, near Naples, became a sort of geologic Exhibit A. When this building was excavated and studied by scientists, it was found that several of its columns were still standing upright, and that three of them were riddled with holes drilled by a species of borer clam that is still common in the nearby Mediterranean. What was puzzling was that some of these holes were bored near the tops of the columns, there being no known way that clams could have climbed up there. The mystery was not settled until men could bring themselves to believe what the evidence so clearly showed: the temple, some time after its construction, had been engulfed by the sea when the land under it sank; later on it rose again, its columns still upright.

Nothing else on the face of the globe, it turns out, is immutable either. For two major sets of forces are engaged in a titanic contest, of which the pioneer Scottish geologist, James Hutton, said: "We find no sign of a beginning—no prospect of an end." These are the tearing-down forces of weathering and erosion, and the uplifting forces of diastrophism. The pawns in this conflict are the continents, and all that they are made of.

WEATHERING and erosion encompass all of the processes by which rock is worn away and its debris removed for deposit somewhere else. Diastrophism, from the Greek for "thorough turning over," refers to the processes by which the earth's outer shell is uplifted, tilted, fractured and folded, and dragged down from below. If either contending force ever gained full sway, this would become an unrecognizable world. Erosion by itself would wash most of North America into the oceans within 25 million years, leaving only a wide low plain, which ultimately might be entirely covered by the sea. Diastrophism, unchecked, would contort the earth's surface into contours as jagged as the uneroded mountains of the moon. Such things do not happen because a global balance of power seems to exist between erosion and diastrophism, though their coexistence is anything but peaceful.

Once the nature of the struggle between these two sets of forces was understood, scientists were able to clear up most of the immemorial mystery of the earth's topography, and to assign causes and effects. The jumbled rocks were no longer indecipherable. The Rosetta stone of geology was deciphered—the study could begin.

The sources of the great diastrophic heavings that lift up the mountains are deeply hidden from view, but most of the agents of erosion work openly for all to see. The greatest of these is running water. We have noted that the atmosphere sucks up about 100,000 cubic miles of moisture a year. Most of this falls back into the oceans, but about 35,000 cubic miles of it reaches the land as rain, snow, sleet, hail and dew. A great deal of the precipitation goes underground, and a great deal more evaporates again before flowing very far, but an estimated ten million billion gallons runs off to replenish the seas. This is the flood that year after year is the paramount instrument in shaping the land.

It is not so much the water itself that acts as the sculptor but rather the particles and chemicals that it carries along. The change in color from clear, swift mountain stream to the brown, placid currents of a major river shows how each tributary adds its portion of particles to the main stream's load. The Mississippi River system, for example, drains an area of about a million and a quarter square miles. In a year, something over 600 million tons of mud, clay, mineral fragments and pinpoint-sized lumps of raw rock, all torn from the drainage area of tributary streams, are carried down to be added to the Gulf of Mexico's burden of accumulating sediments. From the first bright flake of mica swirling in a mountain brook to the last quartz sand grain stripped from a downstream bar, each particle serves as one of the Mississippi system's erosive teeth, nibbling at riverbanks and bottoms along the way.

The speed of water's flow is a vital factor in the erosive power of streams. A youthful, steep mountain torrent, flowing about 10 feet a second, not only carries fine particles in suspension and mineral salts in solution, but also rolls, pushes and tumbles masses of pebbles, gravel and even boulders downhill along its bed. As the grade levels off and the water loses velocity, the larger stones are left behind, then the smaller ones. A stream is a kind of sorting machine, grading its suspended load with fair precision. Coarse materials fall out first, gravels and sands reaching the bottom and the banks long before the finer fragments of mud can sink. It is this mechanism that provided the deposits of gold, tin and platinum that were exploited by placer mining; these heavy metals, tumbling down from waterworn ore deposits in the mountains, were often concentrated by the sorting action of running water. Similarly, when a rapid-running stream leaves the confines of a canyon, it changes its rate of flow as it runs out onto the flat and deposits an alluvial fan of well-sorted material, the coarser fragments lying nearest the canyon and the finer ones on the outer fringes of the fan.

CLASSICALLY a great river valley begins as tiny channels in the soft surfaces of hillsides. With each rainfall such a gully is deepened by runoff water. The stream always follows the shortest and easiest path downhill, and if it were the sole eroding agent, the cut it makes would, in cross section, be a deep slot with vertical sides. However it actually is V-shaped, the reason being that the sides are worn back by rain, frost and other agents at the same time that the stream is cutting away at the bottom. As the stream gets bigger, it can carry more and more grinding materials, and its cutting force will increase proportionately. Gradually undermined by the deepening gorge, any hard sedimentary layer on the banks will break off and tumble into the valley, thereby exposing new soft material to attack.

In time the rapids and waterfalls of the young river eat away the irregularities in its bed, and the resulting gentler slope reduces the current's vigor. As they age, streams which were once swift and straight broaden out their narrow, steep-sided valleys. They turn into old rivers like the Yellow and the Mississippi, meandering sluggishly across broad valleys. These valleys are characteristically smooth and flat because of the burden of mud and silt distributed by the river, and are known as flood plains. During seasons of high water a river may overflow its banks, unless confined by levees, and inundate the plain, adding a fine layer of silt to the entire area. Some rivers build their own levees by depositing silt along their banks during floods, and in time are unable to inundate the valleys except in times of extreme high water.

If the various beds through which a young river is cutting are of different hardness, the valley profile will look less like a V and more like a pair of facing staircases. In its Grand Canyon, the youthful Colorado has been eroding this kind of staircase valley for 10 million years, producing the most striking landmark in the United States. In spots, the canyon is cut 6,000 feet into the Colorado Plateau. Since Lake Mead, downstream, is 2,000 feet lower than the upper canyon bed, it is clear that the Grand Canyon is destined to be dug a lot deeper in the next few million years.

When those last feet have been removed, the Colorado will no longer be young. Down-cutting will be at an end and the river will undertake a new erosive project, side-cutting. Its side-to-side meanderings will mean eventual doom for every pinnacle, butte and mesa that now stands so spectacularly in the 12-mile gap of dissected plateau between the North and South Rims. Even the rims will be forced into retreat. Given enough time, and barring new uplifts and subsidences such as the region has repeatedly experienced before, the Grand Canyon of the distant future will be two lines of slanted bluffs athwart a 50-mile-wide flood plain through which, riding atop a thick blanket of its own sediments, will flow a gentle, elderly Colorado River.

STREAMS run; glaciers merely crawl; yet flowing ice is a spectacular agent of erosion. A glacier is an accumulation of snow gradually compressed into ice. Eventually its weight gets so immense that it begins to slide downhill, gouging the bedrock in its path with stones and boulders embedded in its bottom and bulldozing soil and whatever else may be in the way. But a river goes as far in a few seconds as an average glacier does in a year. Many glaciers in the Alps creep downhill only a foot a day; some in Alaska advance as much as 40 feet.

The lack of speed is no indication of a glacier's effectiveness in sculpting topography. A glacier 1,000 feet thick exerts a force of nearly 30 tons on each square foot on the valley floor underneath it, and the pressure enables the stones dragged along by the glacier to scour and polish the bedrock below. Valleys are not actually begun by glaciers, but glacial erosion re-models the contours left by running water. The result is a U-shaped valley with a broad, flat floor and steep sides, strewn with rock debris deposited as the glacier recedes.

The world's only icecaps today, covering Greenland and Antarctica, and the ice sheets that repeatedly spread over other continents in the past, have abraded landscapes much as mountain glaciers do, but on a vaster scale. Icecaps spread radially, scraping up all loose or protuberant material below them. The Laurentide ice sheet that once ground its way down over North America stripped much of Canada to bedrock, leaving innumerable shallow depressions now filled by lakes, and a denuded land that even today can barely support vegetation. Just as Scandinavia is thought to be still rebounding from the depressing weight of its most recent burial in the ice, parts of North America are still recovering from their Laurentide entombment. The ice sheet reached as far as St. Louis in the Midwest and New York City in the East, forcing the earth's crust downward as much as 1,000 feet and transferring southward the northlands' ancient beds of fertile soil.

The great ice sheets did more than transport the soil. Through centuries of ice advance and retreat, their forward edges bulged with outwash, partly a flour-fine mud made up of so-called "unweathered" materials. It contained fragments of quartz, feldspar, mica and calcite, planed from the bedrock. This gritty mud soon dried. Then the wild winds of the ice age took command, and swept the dry powder away in dust storms such as the world has never seen since. Today, from the Caspian through the plains of Central Asia to the basin of the Yellow River in China, and from the Rockies to western Pennsylvania in the United States, there are deposits up to hundreds of feet deep of the rich loam known as loess. It is composed of particles of the very rock dust that the ice sheets released to the winds. It is remarkable stuff: it may be carved with a knife, and caves dozens of feet high can be excavated from it. Roads that run through loess deposits grow more deeply rutted each season. In China, after years of use, they lie as much as 40 feet below the surface of the tilled land on either side.

The far-flung loess deposits show what wind can do to pile up eroded materials, but this should not permit an overemphasis of the wind itself as an erosional force. Not too long ago, as geological theories go, the weirdly balanced rocks, arches, natural bridges, spires and pinnacles of desert areas were all ascribed to wind—or aeolian—erosion. Now geologists know that water was the principal destructive agent, for wind must carry sand before it can cut, and even a strong wind cannot lift sand over tombstone height. Fine dust can be lofted much higher, but it is powerless to erode.

Natural arches and pinnacles often owe their bizarre shapes to mechanical weathering, a process which is noticeable in desert areas and which is accentuated by dry climate and wide swings in temperature. Sunlight plays a part in it: the dark-colored mineral grains in a granite block heat up faster than the lighter ones, and their different expansion rates bring on stresses that crumble the surface into a mass of loose crystals. Water, freezing in rock cracks and crevices, does more. It expands 10 per cent when it freezes, acting like a crowbar in forcing the cracks apart. Similarly, in forest areas plant and tree roots do the same thing, penetrating the soil-filled fissures and splitting the rock simply by growing.

Much weathering goes on underground. The raindrops that the earth soaks up fill the interstices between soil and sand particles, penetrate the pores of the porous rocks, and generally invade the crust to a depth of some hundreds of thousands of feet. They contribute to the water table, which is the upper surface of a more or less saturated zone that roughly follows the landscape contours. The water table appears above ground as lakes and ponds, trickles out in hillside springs or seeps in the hollows, and fills the lower portions of wells or gushes up from artesian bores.

There is probably more water underground at any one time than in all the lakes and rivers combined. This underground water leaches chemical compounds out of one formation, to deposit them in another. When the water carries enough carbonic acid—from dissolved atmospheric carbon dioxide and decayed organic material—and when it percolates through limestone formations, chemical weathering occurs. The acid eats away the rock, and the water becomes filled with dissolved limestone in the form of a calcium carbonate solution. In limestone flats the ground may collapse, producing the pits called karsts in Europe, cenotes in Yucatán, sinkholes in Florida, Virginia, Tennessee and Kentucky, and blamed nuisances in Indiana, where there may be hundreds of them in one square mile.

The same percolation has hollowed out such earth cavities as Luray Cave in Virginia, Mammoth Cave in Kentucky, and the all but endless Carlsbad Caverns of New Mexico, with their surrealistic arrays of down-growing stalactites and up-growing stalagmites, columns and solid rock veils, all made

The sketch above illustrates how caves are cut in layers of limestone. Water containing carbonic acid seeps down through fissures in the ground (A and B) and, stopped by a layer of more resistant rock, eats its way laterally through the limestone until it reaches the river (C).

In this sketch chemical weathering of the cave has continued until fissure B has become a sinkhole and the acidic water has managed to penetrate an underlying layer of shale. Meanwhile erosion has deepened the river and lowered its water level, leaving the original cave dry except for seepage.

of calcium carbonate precipitated, drop by drop, as dripstone. There are many minerals, for that matter, such as those in the ferromagnesian group, which originate deep in the earth and are unstable under surface conditions. The red and brown stains on rocks containing them are signs of their chemical decay under attack by carbonic acid and atmospheric oxygen.

Weathering can be considered to be the basic process on which all erosion rests, for it produces the first crumbled bits of rock, which are later used by water and wind to do their abrading work. Its importance to man is obvious, for it provides the chief ingredient for soil—without which the continents would be lifeless. Soil, although it also contains decayed organic matter, consists mostly of mineral grains—those transient fragments of rock dust which constitute the dirt of the continents, and whose destiny, in the distant future, is to be compressed into rock once again. The grit that makes up soil is an ideal medium for the goings-on of plant growth. Plants must have access to nitrogen in soluble form, being unable to absorb it directly from the air. They get it in two ways: lightning discharges convert it into oxides that rain washes into the soil, and certain bacteria in the soil convert it from gas into compounds the plants can assimilate. The humus, the earthworm castings and other animal excretions present in soil also act as reservoirs of soluble nitrogen. The nitrogen cycle is vital to life, and the weathered rock in the soil is vital to the perpetuation of the cycle.

At the outset of this chapter we saw that the sea plays at least a by-standing role in the diastrophic rising and sinking of shores. It is also an agent of erosion. Each year, every coast line on earth pays tribute to the tides and the wind-propelled waves in the form of coarse and fine debris that is pulled down to the sediment beds of the continental shelves. Yet the ocean can add to the landscape as well as take it away. The great sandspit called Cape Cod is being steadily devoured along the front that its Great Beach presents to the Atlantic, but is being steadily rebuilt with sand formations that hook around into sheltered Cape Cod Bay. The great offshore sandbars that culminate in Cape Hatteras and that provided the Wright brothers with good gliding terrain at Kitty Hawk, were all built up by the sea from materials borrowed from the North Carolina lands that lie inland of Albemarle and Pamlico Sounds.

But the sea's prime function in the erosion cycle is to serve as a repository, a dumping-ground for all the wastes of the land. It is the grave where all the pulverized continents would be interred if nothing ever balked erosion. Its mineral salts, including sodium chloride, are a great, well-stirred accumulation of material dissolved out of rocks. Its floor is an even greater accumulation of the sediments of earth. These are deposited in various ways. Undertow sucks sand, gravel and clay out from the shore. In some areas the shells of living organisms are abundant enough, as in the case of coral, to become important deposits. When sea water becomes locally supersaturated with certain salts, like calcium carbonate, they are precipitated out and form deposits on the bottom.

The buildup of deposits may cover the floors of such shallow extensions of the ocean as Hudson Bay and the Baltic, but elsewhere it is concentrated on the continental shelves, spilling down the slope to depths of two or three thousand feet. Not much sediment from the land actually gets to the deepest ocean bottoms. But at river deltas, most of which are underneath the water, tremendous burdens of sediments are borne by the sea floor and the underlying crust. The Piedmont district of Italy is a great alluvial plain composed of such stream deposits, and a similar plain stretches out from the western edge of the Sierra Nevada range in the United States. Nearly every river has a delta, except where the sea is deep or turbulent. The Mississippi's mud delta by now is perhaps 30,000 feet thick and nobody knows exactly how heavy. Some geologists think that parts of the gulf floor keep sinking as more sediment piles up. Others say that the floor is sinking by itself, and that the silt and debris from the Mississippi do not affect it.

As younger sediment deposits bury older ones, the latter gradually are compressed into solid rock. Gravel beds become conglomerate, sand becomes sandstone, clayey mud becomes shale, and calcite oozes turn into limestone. Even though most sediments end up in the ocean, the periodic upheavals of the crust, and the changes of sea level during ice ages and thaws, have succeeded in leaving sedimentary rocks almost everywhere. About 80 per cent of the earth's surface is sheathed in them, though by far the greater part of the crust still consists of igneous rock. The major sedimentary rocks have their own rates of deposition, which vary according to local conditions, but which can be estimated from one rock type or another, according to how long it takes for a layer a foot thick to build up. For shale, the most abundant sedimentary rock on the continents, the average estimated period is 100 years. For sandstone it is 450 years, and for limestone 6,000 years. Limestone takes longer because it originates with materials that come from the shells and skeletons of aquatic life, which are not so plentiful a source of sediment as rivers and streams.

By a well-informed reading of the events embodied in the sheath of sedimentary deposits, the geologist can unravel much of the history of erosion versus diastrophism. A limestone layer, whatever its present elevation above sea level, suggests that the region once formed the bed of a sea in which the ancestors of clams and snails lived. A seam of coal betrays an ancient swamp whose rich vegetation was partly decomposed when it was inundated by water and buried under later rock. A layer of salt or gypsum points to a body of salt water that later ebbed or dried up.

Sometimes the layers are all mixed up and the history takes some deciphering. One series of sedimentary layers may lie at an angle below the surface, and another series may lie horizontally above it. This is called an unconformity, and is good evidence that three geologic processes occurred there in a definite sequence. First, existing beds of sediment were uplifted, tilted, and left above sea level by crustal movements. Second, erosion worked away at the uplifted strata until they were worn flat, and third, the region finally sank again below sea level to permit more sediments to be deposited on top of them.

Studying the time-consuming sequences of mountain-building, erosion, sediment deposit and later uplift has been the main concern of geologists for the past century. Collaborating in the detective work have been another group of earth scientists, the paleontologists, or fossil hunters. Probing in the same sedimentary beds, they have found all sorts of traces, faint and plain, of the early forms of life on earth, sorting them out in sequence according to the rocks' relative ages and thereby giving the students of evolution their most useful evidence. The grand tableau that has been recon-

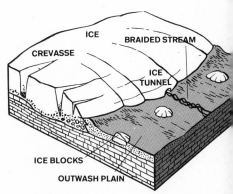

In this drawing of a glacial front, the glacier, riven by crevasses, has reached the point where it melts faster than its ice advances. In front of it is the outwash plain, composed of silt washed down by the melting of the ice. Through the plain flows a braided stream of melt-water issuing from a tunnel within the glacial ice. Buried in the plain are massive ice blocks left behind as the glacier receded.

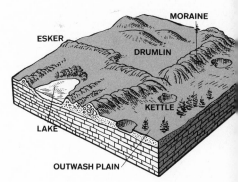

This sketch shows the same area after the glacier's retreat. The most striking feature is the moraine, a ridge made of dirt and rock the glacier carried downhill and deposited. Drumlins may also be made in this way. The esker is made of gravel left behind by the glacial stream. A depression made by the glacier's weight has become a lake, while the holes in the plain, called kettles, formed as the ice blocks melted.

structed with its stages of geologic change and increasingly complex life is far more impressive than any single, transitory landscape.

Up to now this chapter has talked in terms of natural forces, sometimes in harmony and sometimes in conflict with one another; and up to now, in terms of geologic time, they have been the only forces at work. But just recently a new factor, man, has come on the scene. It is far too early to tell how high he may rank permanently among the agents of erosion, but his record over the short span of recorded history is impressive. Paleolithic man, who was not very numerous anyway, left only the faintest of blemishes—he probably accidentally set a few forest fires—on the face of the earth. Early Neolithic farmers and herdsmen, around 10,000 years ago, took to burning patches of the forest cover in the Middle East, cultivating the clearings until the soil was exhausted, then moving on to burn more trees. But the first settlers in the Negev of southern Israel learned to check erosion in their hills by throwing a series of terraced dams across the slopes, each dam watering a tiny plot of farmland. After their land was conquered it turned into desert, never to be reclaimed until the present day. Ever since, the spread of civilization—in China, around the Mediterranean, northward through Europe and across to the New World—has brought denudation of the forest cover, overgrazing by livestock, and consequent gullying and destruction of land by the unchecked runoff of rain water and the lowering of the water table. The great central European forest, through which Caesar's legionaries could walk for two months without coming to the end of the trees, almost disappeared in the ensuing 19 centuries.

IN recent decades there has been some reversal of man-made erosion in the United States. In 1960, new forest growth exceeded forest cutting for the first time since the 17th Century. In Italy and the Netherlands, hundreds of miles of new, dry seacoast land has been reclaimed from the oceans since World War II. But at the same time, the expanding technology of an expanding world population has accelerated man's consumption of all mineral resources. Short of a catastrophe that would decimate the population, nothing is likely to stop this. New energy sources can delay the exhaustion of fossil fuels, but the world appetite for the earth's other raw materials can only increase.

Yet some scientists find hope in the rocks themselves. In every 100 tons of igneous rock, for example, there are eight tons of aluminum, five tons of iron, half a ton of titanium, about a tenth of a ton of manganese, lesser amounts of chromium, nickel, vanadium, copper, tungsten and lead. And in a ton of granite there are a dozen grams of thorium and a third that much uranium. If the power could be applied to extract all this, then industrial society might keep going indefinitely.

Harrison Brown, geochemist at the California Institute of Technology, has suggested that world population may eventually level off at about 30 billion people, who would "consume rock at a rate of about 1,500 billion tons per year. If we were to assume that all the land areas of the world were available for such processing, then, on the average, man would 'eat' his way downward at a rate of 3.3 millimeters per year, or over 3 meters per millennium. This figure gives us some idea of the denudation rates which might be approached in the centuries ahead. And it gives us an idea of the powers for denudation which lie in mankind's hands."

CAPPED BY HARD ROCK, THESE JAGGED STONE SPIRES RESIST THE RAINS THAT CARVE THE CLIFFS OF ARIZONA'S MONUMENT VALLEY

The Sculptured Earth

In the relentless rhythm of change, the earth sporadically raises up on the continents new mountain masses and high plateaus, while the unceasing motions of water and air sluice the dry land into the sea. In the course of their blind task of diminishing the continents, these forces of erosion often carve a landscape into shapes that men sometimes find beautiful—and always find strange.

BEADED COLUMNS guard the cliffs of Bryce Canyon in southern Utah. They are formed by rain water running down tiny vertical cracks in the rock, wearing them deeper with each rain. Layers of harder rock wear more slowly, forming bulges in the columns. The pink color comes from traces of iron oxide (rust) exposed in some of the rocks.

A Plateau's Eventful Past

From the high, arid plateau that covers 130,000 square miles where Arizona, New Mexico, Colorado and Utah meet, the Colorado River each day carries away some 500,000 tons of earth, rock and sand, leaving spectacular formations which include the Grand Canyon (*next page*) and the scenes shown here. In the exposed rocks, geologists have traced a long sequence of dramatic changes. During the first 600 million years a warm, shallow sea covered the area, retreated and returned again and again until it had left layer upon compressed layer of sand and mud in a bed of rock 12,000 feet thick. Then, about 10 million years ago, some mighty, unknown force raised the entire region thousands of feet above sea level, and rains and rivers soon began to chisel the otherworldly landscapes visible today.

TILTED LAYERS of rock in Checkerboard Mesa in Zion National Park are the compressed sand dunes of a prehistoric desert, piled up by the wind and later covered with water.

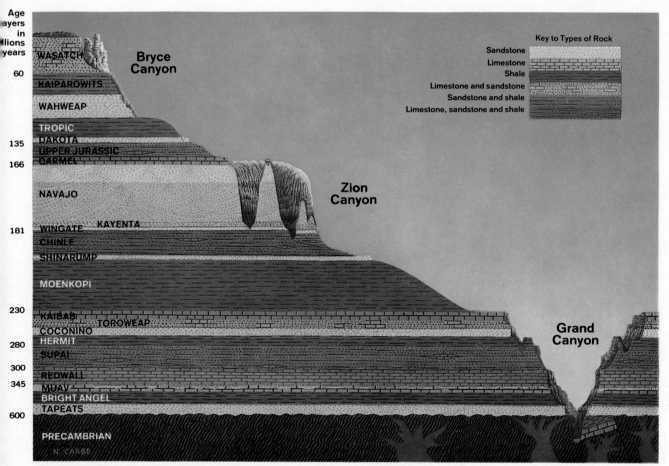

ERODED STEPS, cut into the Colorado Plateau like part of a giant stairway, expose progressively older layers of sediments, from the youngest rocks, at Bryce Canyon (*upper left*), to the oldest, near the bottom of the Grand Canyon. The tilted fragment of limestone and shale at lower right is the remnant of an earlier cycle of uplift and erosion.

A MILE-DEEP CHASM of glowing colors and shifting shadows, the Grand Canyon is the Colorado Plateau's classic example of erosion. The swift Colorado River gouged the canyon down to its present depth in about 10 million years, and the stream is now wearing away the tough Precambrian rock at the canyon's bottom at a rate of one foot each 2,150 years.

117

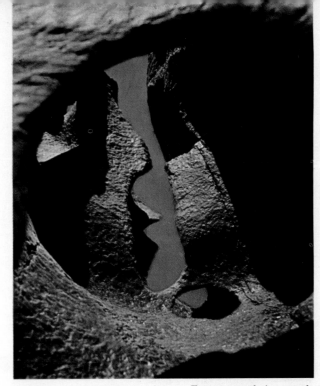

WATER-CUT "CAVES" near Aswan, Egypt, owe their smooth contours to the churning violence of the Nile River, which pours through these deep potholes during the annual floods.

The Caprices of Erosion

Unhurried but irresistible, the shifting currents of air and water gradually wear away the surface of the land, producing the familiar forms of hills and valleys, and eventually leaving a landscape flat. But some materials in their path resist this erosion more stubbornly than others do, and where hard rock is interspersed with weaker rock, some grotesque landforms are carved out, like capricious designs executed in a sculptor's dream.

RAIN AND WIND HAVE SCOOPED OUT A LAYER OF SOFT CLAY FROM

SNUB-NOSED COLUMNS, huddled together in the Devil's Garden in Utah, were formed when erosion opened up a maze of deep, vertical cracks in a once-solid layer of rock.

SAND-SMOOTHED ARCH in southeastern Utah was shaped by abrasive desert winds widening a tunnel which a stream of rain water had bored through a massive block of stone.

BENEATH THE WEATHERED EDGES OF A BED OF SANDSTONE TO FORM A DEEP, SHADOWED ARCADE AT TOADSTOOL PARK IN NEBRASKA

WIND-CARVED FIGURES of hard sandstone stand on slender pedestals of less resistant rock in Utah's Goblin Valley, their elongated shapes aligned with the prevailing winds.

THICKHEADED BOULDERS shelter the weak stems of rock beneath them from the rain, which has eroded about a foot from the rest of this slope on a ridge near Moab, Utah.

The Labors of Moving Water

Among the forces that leave their mark on the continents, streams and rivers do more to change the shape of the land than all others combined. Steep, turbulent streams batter and scrape the exposed rocks of newly lifted mountain areas with loose bits of stone, quickly digging out steep-walled valleys. A young, vigorous river such as the Colorado can break apart a six-foot boulder and reduce it to mud in four years.

As the jagged contours of the highlands are worn away, rivers enter a less urgent maturity. Their once-steep valleys become broad and flat, and the rivers flow at leisure along winding paths. But even an aging river can be a formidable agent of erosion: during the spring floods, the Mississippi daily sweeps some 10 million tons of earth from North America down to the Gulf of Mexico.

A YOUNG RIVER, the swift, turbulent Colorado (*left*), joins its sediment-laden waters with the clear blue flow of the slower-moving Little Colorado (*right*) in the Grand Canyon.

A MISTY PLUME of water, Bridalveil Falls (*opposite*) drops 620 feet into California's Yosemite Valley. The creek feeding the falls has worn a broad U in the valley's sheer rim.

A SEDATE RIVER, the Yellowstone, winds quietly through Yellowstone Park. Its loops steadily widen as the currents cut into the outer banks and pile sand along the inner edges.

121

DRIPSTONE FORMATIONS IN ELS HAMS CAVE, ONE OF THE MANACOR CAVERNS ON THE MEDITERRANEAN ISLAND OF MAJORCA, GLISTEN

The Weird Underground World
of Lost Rivers and Stone Icicles

All rocks contain some minerals which dissolve in water, a fact which hastens erosion and is responsible for the salty flavor of the oceans, where these dissolved minerals have been collecting since the continents first formed. The most soluble of all rocks is limestone, composed of easily dissolved

IN A FLOOD OF COLORED LIGHTS. STALACTITES GROW DOWNWARD FROM THE CEILING; STALAGMITES GROW UPWARD FROM THE FLOOR

minerals from the shells of sea animals. A stream encountering a bed of limestone may eat out a channel in the rock which meanders for miles underground, leaving a string of interconnected caves along its course. The water which seeps into these caves and drips from the limestone ceilings is often saturated with dissolved minerals; as it evaporates, minerals are deposited in iciclelike formations called dripstone. Water dripping from a stalactite on the roof of the cave will slowly build a stalagmite on the floor below. In time, the two may join to form a single column.

STRIPS OF THIS RICH GREAT PLAINS SOIL IN MONTANA, DEPOSITED 15 MILLION YEARS AGO, ARE LEFT FALLOW TO RETARD EROSION

Erosion's Fertile Debris

In obedience to the law of gravity, erosion carries the land bit by bit down into the sea. If the forces of mountain-building ever stopped operating, all of North America would be worn down to gentle plains only a few feet above sea level within 20 million years. For mankind, erosion is a mixed blessing. Much of the fine rock debris carried down from the highlands is dropped in lower areas as a blanket of life-giving soil. Depending upon the nature of the original sediments, the rainfall, the mineral content and the organic matter that builds up, these earth deposits may range from barren dusts to the rich black chernozem soils which can support crops in almost limitless abundance. Both the American wheat belt and the Russian Ukraine are overlaid with chernozem. Unhappily, erosion also destroys what it builds. The soils of the plains and valleys are slowly carried seaward, to pile up in deltas or be sluiced away by the flowing tides (*opposite*).

TENTACLES OF THE SEA curl inland, eroding the Dutch coast along the Waddenzee. In this view from 14,000 feet a very low tide has revealed pale plains of mud and sand, giving the tidelands the look of a river delta. The darker veins are channels cut deep by the land-stealing sea; when the tide is high they serve fishermen as navigation lanes.

STACKS OF ROCK AT DUNCANSBY HEAD ON THE SCOTTISH COAST ARE REMNANTS OF A PREVIOUS LINE OF CLIFFS. THEY WERE ISOLATE

A NEW SEASHORE on Florida's east coast is built of sand washed up by the sea. The old beach and shore line are visible in the distance beyond the newly enclosed lagoon.

The Sea's Irresistible Power

The ocean cannot match the total erosive power of all the earth's swift streams, but at some vulnerable points its waves shatter the shore like a battering-ram. In its rage the sea can hit a coast with a force of three tons to the square foot, in time reducing rock bastions to stark headlands and sheer cliffs. Often as the sea breaks down the land, it leaves behind such dramatic monuments as the castlelike stacks in the picture at the left. These formations occur when waves attack two sides of a headland and hammer their way through. The first results are sea arches. Then the arches break and their ends, the stacks, stand isolated from the shore.

But the sea can build as well as destroy. Where the shore slopes gently and the bottom is shallow, waves pick up sand and carry it landward, forming beaches and sand bars. Once a sand bar has formed, it may grow to enclose a lagoon (*above*). As waves and wind throw more sand over the bar, dunes build up and fill the lagoon. Thus the land encroaches on the sea.

WHEN THE ROCK BEHIND THEM WAS ERODED BY STORMY SEAS

127

The Ice-Carved Lands

Erosion by moving ice, in the world of today, is limited to a few glaciers, most of them on high mountains. But during the latest ice age, less than a million years ago, huge sheets of mile-thick ice ground heavily across parts of North America and Europe, leaving the marks of their passing prominently engraved in the land. As the ice advanced over Canada, it bulldozed the soil ahead of it; as a result, much of central Canada is barren, rocky ground while the rich cornfields of the Midwest thrive in a double thickness of fertile soil. The topsoil of New England was scraped away and deposited off the coast of Connecticut to build up Long Island. As the ice retreated, some of its melted waters collected in the ice-dug hollows where the Great Lakes stand.

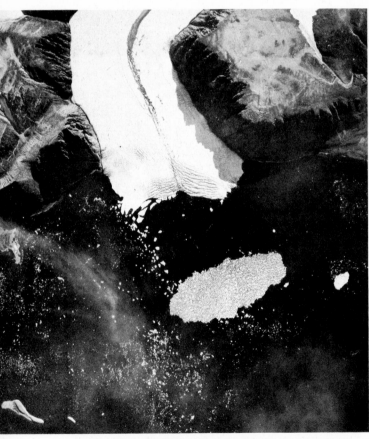

A NEWBORN ICEBERG falls from the tip of a Devon Island glacier in the Canadian Arctic. The glacier flows down a steep, gouged valley towering 1,300 feet above the ice.

A PARALLEL PATTERN of rock grooves and ridges, some a mile long and 200 feet high (*opposite*), is the work of an ice sheet that scraped across northern Canada's Victoria Island.

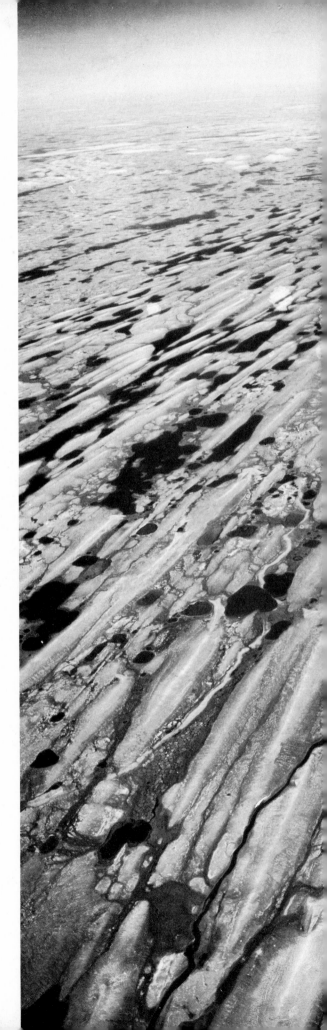

SPLIT IN TWO, this roll-like rock found in Illinois yields its secret— the perfect fossil impressions of a seed-fern frond. The tree-like species lived in the late Carboniferous period, 300 million years ago.

6

The Record of the Rocks

How old is the earth? In recent years the most practical way in which scientists could come to grips with this question has seemed to be in measuring the age of the rocks which form the earth's crust. And this study of ancient strata has certainly provided an enormous number of clues as to our planet's age, the evolution of its life, and the climatic conditions which have existed on its surface during many varied periods in the immensely distant past. However, there is a limit to how far back one can go in this manner, for there was an earlier period during which the earth did not have its present crust—or perhaps any crust. The dating of rocks is useful only back to the time when the rocks themselves came into being.

The measuring stick that is used is radioactive dating, a method which has become available to man in this century, or since he has learned enough about nuclear physics to understand how radioactive materials work. What is useful about a radioactive element is that it has a very precise decay rate, which means that it slowly but steadily, atom by atom, turns into a more stable element. Radioactive carbon, for example, which is created in the atmosphere by cosmic rays, loses exactly half of its store of radioactivity in 5,568

0 Years—death of animal or plant

5,568 years—1/2 left

11,136 years—1/4 left

16,704 years—1/8 left

22,272 years—1/16 left

60,000 years—about 1/1,000 left

The age of once-living matter often can be determined by measuring its content of radioactive carbon 14. All living things absorb some carbon 14 from the air. When an organism dies, this absorption stops and the carbon 14 it contains begins to decay into nitrogen. Since the rate of this decay is known—carbon 14's half-life is 5,568 years—the age of an organic substance can be established by a count of its radiocarbon. The diagrams above show the rate of carbon 14's decay; opposite are some of the things that have been dated.

years by conversion into nitrogen. A specialist with delicate measuring instruments can compare the amount of radioactive carbon remaining in a fossil with the amount of ordinary carbon, and in that way calculate how old the fossil is. For, in the next 5,568 years, the proportion of radioactive carbon will drop by one half, and in the next 5,568 years, by another half and so on, until ultimately none remains.

Radioactive carbon is a superb tool for the prehistorian, but next to worthless for the geologist, who must deal in periods of time far too great to give radioactive carbon's rather short half-life any meaning. He must find radioactive materials with a half-life of millions or billions of years. Luckily they exist. An isotope of potassium decays into argon, with a half-life of 1.3 billion years; thorium decays into lead, and an isotope of rubidium into strontium, with half-lives of 14 billion years and 60 billion years respectively.

A particularly useful radioactive tool for geologists is uranium, traces of which are found in many rocks and in widely scattered areas on the earth's surface. All uranium on earth will eventually become lead, with the release of helium in the process. However, this takes place with fantastic slowness. At the end of 2.25 billion years, three fourths of an original chunk of an isotope of uranium will still be uranium, and only one fourth will have turned to lead.

Today, the oldest known rocks are represented by some granite gneiss near Dodoma, Tanganyika, with an approximate age of 3.6 billion years. Older rocks may be discovered in the future; how old, nobody can say for sure. And even the 3.6-billion-year figure leaves open the question of how much older the earth is than its oldest rocks. However, the principle of radioactive dating can be applied to this apparently insoluble problem in a most ingenious way. Recently, radio-dating studies have been made of meteorite fragments, giving age estimates as great as 4.5 billion years for these bits of solar-system debris. Since it is generally assumed that all of the solar system came into being at the same time, most geologists are prepared to accept this as a figure for the earth's age.

WE toss millions and billions about very glibly. And yet they are such staggeringly large units of time that it is worth pausing to try and emphasize just how long 4.5 billion years really is. Hendrik Van Loon did it with this fanciful opening paragraph to his famous book, *The Story of Mankind:*

"High up in the North in the land called Svithjod, there stands a rock. It is a hundred miles high and a hundred miles wide. Once every thousand years a little bird comes to this rock to sharpen its beak.

"When the rock has thus been worn away, then a single day of eternity will have gone by."

A less dramatic but perhaps more useful way of emphasizing the age of the earth is to compare it with the evolution of man. It is generally believed that human beings as we know them today evolved from apelike, nonhuman ancestors during the last two million years. This slow process of evolution from primitive ancestor to modern man would have to repeat itself more than 2,000 times before the time thus consumed would equal the current estimate of the earth's age.

What is known about the slow process that first brought life into existence on the earth? So far, almost nothing. Biochemists and physicists, arduously calculating backward to guess at the raw materials which they believe were available in the earth's early atmosphere and in the oceans, have satisfied themselves that the building blocks were there for the formation of protein molecules—assuming that there was a way for protein molecules to have formed. Some recent studies have demonstrated that the lifeless but potentially rich chemical broth in the ancient oceans could have been organized into amino acids through the action of lightning. Amino acids have been turned into protein molecules in the laboratory; from this all else could follow. The major requirement is an abundance of time. It is estimated that the change from simple organic compounds to the earliest one-celled organism may well have taken far longer than the later development from one-celled animal to man. The fossil record shows not only that time was available, but that life did get under way very slowly.

GEOLOGISTS divide the whole span of earth history into two unequal periods, called eons. The first, and by far the longest of these, is known as the Cryptozoic eon, from the Greek for "hidden life." It covers the time from the earliest known rocks up to some 600 million years ago, a span of about three billion years. The second, or Phanerozoic eon—from the Greek for "visible life"—extends to today.

As might be expected, rocks from the Cryptozoic eon are by no means the commonest things on the earth's surface. They occur only where the cores of ancient mountain systems have been laid bare by erosion, or where deep gorges have been cut into high plateaus, or, most important, in the form of huge exposed "shields" in a few spots on the earth's surface. In North America the Canadian shield sweeps around Hudson Bay and covers Labrador. In South America the Guiana and Amazonian shields both exhibit vast outcrops. The Ethiopian shield stretches from South Africa to Arabia, the Australian from Perth to Darwin. There is a smaller shield covering most of Scandinavia and, finally, one in Siberia.

These ancient outcrops, rare as they may be in terms of the total volume of the earth's crust, constitute, nevertheless, an enormous amount of material. And yet in all their square miles of gneiss, schist and bedded limestone, the only fossils so far discovered in recognizable form are a few kinds of algae of the blue-green variety, and some colonies of fungus—plus the enigmatic burrows of an unknown wormlike animal. No trace of the worm itself remains.

This seems a pitifully small harvest from a three-billion-year segment of earth history. However, it may not be the entire story. Cryptozoan animals were all water dwellers, and probably developed few, if any, hard parts such as shell, cartilage or bone. There may have been many more of them, and a greater variety, than the Cryptozoan rocks show. This possibility is further borne out by the fact that some Cryptozoan rocks are rich in organic carbon, and this could represent the last transient traces of former living things. Nonetheless, the contrast between life on earth even at the end of the Cryptozoic eon and life in the earliest portions of the Phanerozoic is startling. Whereas we may never devise methods of reading the fossil story of Cryptozoan life. the story that follows it in the Phanerozoic is an elaborate and almost unbelievable chronicle of unfolding evolution. It has taken man a remarkably short time to gather a relatively immense amount of fossil evidence—once he stumbled on the concept that all living things are related and that they trace their descent back to the same origins.

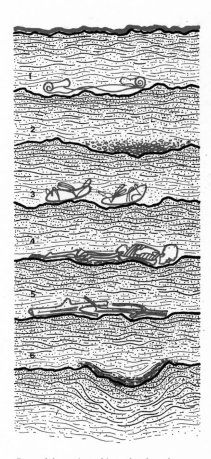

Some of the ancient objects that have been dated by the carbon 14 method appear in the drawing above. A tiny pulse of radioactivity proved the famous Dead Sea Scrolls (1) to be at least 1,900 years old, and some Japanese lotus seeds (2) were found to be 3,000 years old. Sandals (3) in an Oregon cave were carbon-dated at 9,000 years and objects around a skeleton in Illinois (4) at about 10,000. A Wisconsin tree (5) turned out to have died 11,000 years ago, and charcoal (6) found in Iraq kept men warm in 30,000 B.C.

133

The speed at which evolution progresses is a very complex matter and depends on numerous factors, among them geological and climatic change. If such changes are marked, there will be a corresponding tendency toward greater evolutionary change, which is not surprising, since a new set of living conditions may demand differences in animals to ensure survival.

The first step in organizing scientific knowledge is necessarily the classification of material into a useful pattern. In biology, for example, a distinction must first be made between what is a plant and what an animal. The peculiar organisms like slime molds which are both, or which in some instances spend half their life unmistakably as animals and the other half unmistakably as plants, must be set aside in a special file. But everything else must be organized in such a way that it falls into neat categories which not only identify the organism but also show its relationship to others like it. The method that the biologist usually uses in classifying animals is to divide them up first into large groups known as phyla. There are 22 such phyla, which are then subdivided into classes, orders, families, genera and, finally, individual species. Thus, a rose-breasted grosbeak is a particular kind of creature. That is its *species*, since it cannot be further subdivided into different kinds of rose-breasted grosbeaks. However, going the other way, it is a member of a larger group—a *genus*—of grosbeaks, of which there are several kinds in North America, and to all of which it is closely related. Grosbeaks, in turn, belong to a large *family* of finches, and to a still larger *order* of perching birds, which also includes thrushes, crows and orioles, since they have characteristics in common which they do not share with ostriches, say, or ducks. All of these are grouped in a *class* known simply as birds. Birds, finally, belong to a *subphylum*, vertebrates, which includes animals with an internal backbone, and finally to the *phylum*, chordates, which includes not only animals with backbones but also those with comparable internal supporting structures.

A startling example of evolution is a small fish called the Blind Cave Characin, which has no eyes. Long ago these fish were trapped in a black subterranean lake in some caves in Mexico. Eyes were of no use in the lightless water, and the fish eventually stopped growing them.

THERE are many kinds of vertebrates which are not birds, and they in turn must be divided into their own subdivisions. At the moment there are found living on the earth eight different classes of vertebrates. There are three distinct classes of fish; a single class of lampreys; a class of amphibians, which includes frogs and salamanders; another of reptiles, which includes snakes, lizards, turtles and crocodiles; another of birds; and finally one of mammals. In short, there is no backboned animal known which does not fall into one or another of those eight classes.

But the backboned animals are neither the oldest nor the most numerous phylum. Two other very important ones are mollusks and arthropods. The mollusks include clams, oysters and scallops; snails and conches; two other smaller groups of shellfish; and finally squids, octopuses and nautiloids, five orders in all. It may seem that the relationship between a clam and a conch is too close to permit their being placed in separate classes, but when their evolutionary lines are traced back, and the subtle differences which exist between the two are revealed, it will be seen that they are as different from each other as a man is from a fish, or a fish from a bird.

Arthropods constitute by far the largest phylum. This group contains four major classes: lobsters and crabs; centipedes and millepedes; spiders and scorpions; and insects. Again, this may seem like a highly arbitrary division, until it is realized all four have characteristics in common. More important, they share these characteristics with no other living creatures outside their phylum. One characteristic is an external skeleton. It is light and flexible, unlike the shell of a clam and equally unlike the internal bones of a man. "Arthropod" means "jointed legs," and each member of the phylum possesses them. Taken together, there are more than 750,000 different species of arthropods. By contrast there are 40,000 species of mollusks, and about 35,000 chordates. These are the three largest phyla. Without complicating matters by introducing others, it is possible to draw a fairly clear picture of the evolution of life with examples from only these three.

Having classified the animals, the next step is to classify the conditions under which the animals have evolved. When this is done, the story of evolution may be told. The classification of earth conditions is done by geologists. They know so little about the "hidden" ancient Cryptozoic eon that they make little attempt to break it down. But the Phanerozoic, extending over the last 600 million years, has been divided and subdivided with increasing precision the closer one gets to the present day.

There are three great subdivisions of the Phanerozoic eon, known as eras. First comes the Paleozoic era (ancient life), then the Mesozoic era (in-between life), and finally the Cenozoic era (recent life). Just as the ancient eon was far longer than the later one, so the three eras show an acceleration in time. The Paleozoic (subdivided into six periods) drew to a close 230 million years ago, for a total duration of 370 million years. In contrast, the Mesozoic (with three periods) lasted for only 167 million years. The end of the Cenozoic—which began only 63 million years ago—is, of course, not yet in sight. When it will end is impossible to determine, partly because evolution is continuing at an accelerating rate, partly because there is beginning to be a suspicion that man may soon acquire the power (if he does not already have it) of directing not only his own evolution but that of other living things as well, and partly because we have no assurance that our classification of eons and eras is the best that can be made. Our descendants, human or superhuman as they may be, will certainly be different from ourselves, and they may be so sophisticated or so well informed that they will perceive relationships in past time which are invisible to us, and will be able to make better divisions of eras and phyla than we now make. Be that as it may, the eras are, in turn, divided into periods, as shown in the marginal tables on pages 136 and 137.

The aspect of the earth at the start of the Paleozoic's first period, the Cambrian, was vastly different from what it is today. The sea occupied a much larger area than it does now, but it was very shallow. The continental land masses were low-lying and relatively small. Their rocks were bare of plant life except for lichens and a handful of other very primitive plants whose spores have since been detected in Cambrian fossil beds. There was no animal life on land at all. The general atmosphere was one of mildness and calm—and apparent agelessness, for the Cambrian period went on and on in this benign manner for 100 million years before sliding imperceptibly into the next period.

Beneath the surface of the sea, however, things were much livelier. The remorseless earlier progression from simple organic compounds to single-celled organisms, and from there to multicelled forms, had now reached the point where the sea was swarming with a variety of creatures, some of

Fossils of this sturdy, tongue-leafed ancient fern, the Glossopteris, have been found in such widely separated places as South Africa and South America. This suggests either that its seeds crossed the ocean, or that these land masses of the Southern Hemisphere were once connected.

GEOLOGIC TIME SCALE OF NORTH AMERICA

(Numerals indicate millions of years ago)

PALEOZOIC

PRECAMBRIAN (?-600)
The earth's crust forms, and the seas and the continental land masses appear.

CAMBRIAN (600-500)
Two great troughs in the East and the West fill with sediments which will later build the Appalachians, the Rockies and other mountain ranges.

ORDOVICIAN (500-425)
About 70 per cent of America is covered by shallow seas. There is some volcanic activity and the eastern land mass, including mountains in New England, begins to rise.

SILURIAN (425-405)
Much of the East is inundated by a salty, inland sea. Volcanoes are active in New Brunswick and Maine.

DEVONIAN (405-345)
Eastern America, from Canada to North Carolina, rises from the sea.

CARBONIFEROUS (345-280)
Large areas of the East become a great swamp which is repeatedly submerged by shallow seas. Forests grow, die and are buried—to become coal.

PERMIAN (280-230)
A period of violent geologic and climatic disturbances. Great wind-blown deserts cover much of the continent.

MESOZOIC

TRIASSIC (230-181)
The Appalachian Mountains, built in the Permian period and once as high as the modern Alps, begin to erode.

JURASSIC (181-135)
The Nevadian disturbance thrusts up a string of mountains, including the Sierra Nevada, stretching from southern California to Alaska.

CRETACEOUS (135-63)
The Rocky Mountains, from Alaska to Central America, rise out of a sediment-filled trough. The sea for the last time inundates much of the continent.

CENOZOIC

TERTIARY (63-1)
The Columbia Plateau and the Cascade Range rise, and the Rockies reach their present height. There is also extensive volcanic activity in the American Northwest.

PLEISTOCENE (1-0)
Four ice ages send glaciers across a continent much like the present.

them weighing as much as 10 pounds—millions or billions of times larger than the single-celled creatures of the earlier days.

The outstanding living form of the Cambrian period was the trilobite, whose name reflects the three lobes into which its body was characteristically divided. If any creature may be called the symbol of a period, then the trilobite was symbolic of those ancient seas. It was the great evolutionary triumph of its time, the most efficient thing the world had ever seen. It was not unlike a cross between a lobster and a sea slug, with an external lobster-like shell and numerous spindly legs which enabled it to creep over the bottom ooze. Its segmented body also allowed it to roll up into a tight ball like a pill bug—presumably for defense. Trilobites developed a wide variety of shapes and sizes, and were so much more advanced than anything else of their day that at their peak they are believed to have represented 60 per cent of all living creatures. And their day was a long one; it lasted more than 300 million years.

The trilobite was an early arthropod, and it shared the Cambrian seas with the pioneers of the mollusk phylum. Of the phylum to which man belongs—the chordates—no member had yet appeared. The ancestor of all the chordates was still scuttling or slithering anonymously around, still in another more primitive form, and it is doubtful if scientists will ever succeed in reconstructing relationships well enough to decide whether their Cambrian progenitor looked more like a worm or a starfish.

AFTER a hundred million years the Cambrian period ended. It was followed by the Ordovician, the change marked by considerable geologic disturbance in the Western Hemisphere. The oceans crept in for a time and divided North America into a group of islands. A huge mountain chain reared on the east coast from Newfoundland to Alabama, spawning many volcanoes which scattered their ash as far west as Minnesota. In the seas trilobites continued in enormous throngs, but their pre-eminence was threatened by the emergence of a number of mollusks, among them some spectacular cephalopods. These were cousins of the modern squid and certain of them grew tapering shells that were 15 feet long. The Ordovician period also saw the appearance of the first chordate. In retrospect, this pioneer among animals with backbones was anything but impressive. A fish, it belonged to the primitive jawless variety that is represented in modern times only by the hagfish and the lamprey. Yet this obscure fish *was* a vertebrate, the oldest one that the rocks so far have yielded up.

The following period, the Silurian, was much shorter than the two preceding ones, lasting a mere 20 million years. Throughout most of its time it was characterized by the same placidity, the low continents and shallow, warm seas of the Cambrian. But the eastern United States was slowly transformed by coastal uplift into a landlocked inland sea, which gradually evaporated toward the end of the Silurian, leaving an immense salt desert. These salt deposits have been extensively mined in New York, Pennsylvania and Michigan. Altogether, the dry salt lake may have extended over 100,000 square miles.

Elsewhere, life in these warm oceans continued to proliferate. The durable trilobite lingered on, but in a strangely modified form. Many types now were covered with bizarre spines, presumably as a protection against the superior mobility and rapacity of the evolving fish. Corals were very common, and were found as far north as Greenland. A gigantic water scorpion appeared, its nine-foot length an all-time record for arthropods. This huge scorpion completely overshadowed an obscure relative, only about two inches long, but which was to be infinitely more important to the overall course of evolution. For this small creature shares with an equally inconspicuous millepede the honor of being the first animal to venture on dry land. Tantalizingly, the fossil evidence does not reveal whether the respiratory systems of these pioneers were designed for water or for air breathing. Hence, we do not know whether they were true land dwellers or whether they merely nipped in and out of the water.

But the trail blazed by early scorpion and millepede was to become wider and wider. In the next age, the Devonian, 18 spiders are now known to have lived on land, together with a primitive wingless insect whose remains have been found in Devonian rocks in Scotland. However, the most significant advances during Devonian times were made by the vertebrates. Fish had evolved to the point where it was possible to distinguish two major groups: cartilaginous fish such as sharks, and bony fish, ancestral to most modern fish species. Among the latter a particular group went on to develop other novel characteristics which were to prove of immense importance. This group had true jaws. It bore the jawbreaking name of Crossopterygii and boasted two other principal innovations: internal air bladders which could be used as lungs, and stout muscular lobes on the fins. When one considers the conditions which prevailed during the Devonian period—shallow seas which came and went in response to the slow movements of the earth's crust—it seems almost certain that these developments were critical in helping their owners over the hurdle to a land existence. The capacity to gulp air, plus the ability to "walk" on sturdy stumps on exposed tidal flats, is believed by paleontologists to have been what made the Crossopterygii the ancestors of all the present-day frogs and salamanders.

Of equal importance to the development of vertebrates during the Devonian was the development of land plants. By this time the appearance of the continents was transformed. The once-bare, lichen-dotted, rocky landscapes were now misted with a rich green of giant tree ferns and many kinds of early evergreens. For the first time the countryside looked like a countryside. True, the plants were exotic and spindly, but they were plants, and recognizable ones. There were forests, and quiet pools with fish swimming in them, and insects crawling in the mossy shade.

The great development of plants was continued during the next period, the Carboniferous, which began 345 million years ago and lasted about 65 million years. It was a time of localized crustal activity. Many mountain ranges rose and volcanoes were extremely active. On land, there were vast forest swamps choked with plants and trees. These were buried in water over and over again across huge expanses of the earth's surface. Bedded down in mud, crushed by pressures from the sediments piling up above them, these forgotten forests were compressed into some of the world's great coal deposits, which give the Carboniferous its name.

Many insects developed during the Carboniferous, including one that resembled a dragonfly but had a two-and-a-half-foot wingspread. With them came the first traces of a new vertebrate group, the reptiles. These were the first backboned animals to free themselves completely from the

EVOLUTIONARY TIME SCALE

(Numerals indicate millions of years ago)

PALEOZOIC

PRECAMBRIAN (?-600)
The first life—algae, fungi, soft-bodied marine animals—develops on earth.

CAMBRIAN (600-500)
Trilobites and other primitive arthropods, with a few early mollusks, sponges and worms, dominate the primeval sea.

ORDOVICIAN (500-425)
Marine invertebrates—including clams, starfish, corals, seaweed—share the sea with several kinds of arthropods. Primitive fish, the first vertebrates, appear.

SILURIAN (425-405)
A few primitive animals, including scorpions and millepedes, and some rudimentary plants begin to live on land.

DEVONIAN (405-345)
The vertebrates of the sea grow in variety and size. Several species of fish develop lungs and strong fins and become amphibious. The land for the first time supports large, treelike plants.

CARBONIFEROUS (345-280)
The first reptiles appear, but giant insects dominate the forests. Fish flourish, including over 200 species of sharks.

PERMIAN (280-230)
Vertebrates—amphibians and reptiles—make rapid progress. Modern insects appear. The trilobite is at last extinct.

MESOZOIC

TRIASSIC (230-181)
Vertebrates, notably reptiles, begin to replace invertebrates as the dominant form of life. The first dinosaurs appear. Lobsters and complex arthropods appear in the sea.

JURASSIC (181-135)
Warm-blooded animals—mammals—make their first appearance, but the reptiles still dominate. Dinosaurs reach their peak and the first birds appear.

CRETACEOUS (135-63)
Dinosaurs, after 100 million years, finally become extinct. Small, primitive mammals increase markedly. Many modern trees develop, among them the birch, elm, oak and maple.

CENOZOIC

TERTIARY (63-1)
Bony fish abound, and some sharks 60 to 80 feet long appear. Mammals begin to dominate the earth, among them saber-toothed tigers and early horses.

PLEISTOCENE (1-0)
The age of mammals continues with an important addition—man.

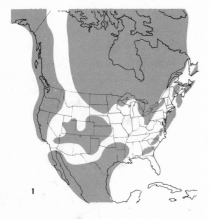

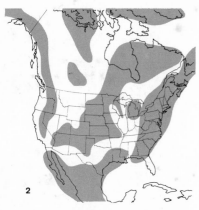

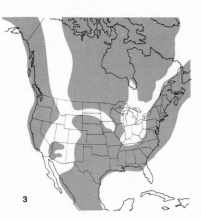

The maps above and on the opposite page show how much of what is now North America was covered by the sea at various times in the distant past. In the Cambrian period (top) the sea covered large areas of the United States although much of Canada was dry land (shown in color). In the Ordovician period (middle) the sea was even more extensive, although most of the Atlantic coast had risen above the waves. By the late Devonian period (bottom) the land had won considerable gains, but water still covered much of the Middle West and the Rocky Mountain region.

water. Amphibians must return to water to mate and lay their fragile eggs; their young, just as the tadpoles of frogs still do today, must pass through a free-swimming aquatic stage before they can return to land in mature form. The great innovation supplied by the reptiles was that their eggs had tough cases and could be deposited anywhere without danger of dehydration, and their young could take up a land existence the moment they were hatched. This final liberation from the bondage of the sea ranks as a major event in the history of life.

The last of the Paleozoic periods, the Permian, was one of the most violent in earth history. Mountain-building increased in intensity, and for the first time in hundreds of millions of years, there was a drastic change in the climate. For the Permian experienced severe ice ages which covered parts of Africa, Australia and South America with glaciers. Other parts of the world turned to deserts. Drying seas produced the three largest salt deposits in the world, one in Russia, one in Germany and one stretching from Kansas to New Mexico in the United States. Altogether, this was one of the most inhospitable periods for life ever known, and the strain on many organisms was severe. The denizens of the fetid Carboniferous swamps, both plant and animal, were ill fitted to withstand the rigors of cold and extreme dryness. Many failed to survive. The great stands of scale trees and seed ferns faded away, replaced by the hardier conifers. Reptiles adapted well, but in the sea the durable trilobite finally reached the end of the line. At last it became extinct.

THUS ended the Paleozoic, 370 million years of slow but steadily accelerating evolution. An uncounted number of types had come and gone, but in the process all the major life groups had become well established. The Mesozoic period which followed, and which lasted 167 million years, was notable primarily for the replacement of invertebrates by the reptiles as the dominant type of animal. Once they had firmly anchored themselves on land, these animals experienced a veritable evolution explosion. They were stronger and more agile than the amphibians, which, in the words of Julian Huxley, "pottered with much belly and little leg, like Falstaff in his old age." Throughout the early Mesozoic reptiles flowered in a great variety of shapes and sizes, gradually getting bigger and bigger as time went on. Some of them returned to the sea in the form of rapacious, dolphinlike animals, but with long, toothed snouts. Others wallowed in the swamps munching enormous quantities of marsh and river plants. By the middle of the era they had evolved into the largest land animals the world has ever known. This was the age of dinosaurs, and although many reptiles were not dinosaurs, the most conspicuous ones were. There was the diplodocus, a "typical" dinosaur with a long neck, a tiny head containing an even tinier brain, a fat body, huge legs and a long tail. End to end, the diplodocus was 85 feet long, larger but not quite as heavy as the similarly shaped but squatter brontosaurus. Tanklike animals called stegosaurs lumbered through the woods, their backs protected by huge, bony plates set on edge, and their tails armed with three-foot spikes. They were slow-moving and even slower-witted creatures, their brains averaging a mere two and a half ounces in weight, housed in a 10-ton body. Another group of dinosaurs were meat eaters. Agile and voracious, they ran along on their hind legs, dangling small forelegs as they went. Some were no larger than chickens. Others, like the allosaurus and the tyrannosaurus, were undoubtedly the most fearsome animals ever known and preyed on the huge, inoffensive plant eaters. Still others took to the air, gliding over the sea on leathery wings with a spread of 25 feet. These were not birds, nor were they bats. They were flying reptiles with small bodies and thin, hollow bones. Their wings were so enormous in contrast to the size of their other parts that there is a great deal of puzzled speculation as to how they functioned; their legs, for example, were mere fragile appendages, too frail for walking, and are believed to have been used for clinging to cliffs. It is thought that the pteranadon spent all its waking hours gliding over the sea, riding like a kite on the winds rising over the wave crests.

Although the Mesozoic was dominated by reptiles, the first birds appeared then, as did the first mammals. Both were obscure and unimportant for a long time. But both had adaptations which were clear improvements over what had gone before, and their emergence into a dominance of their own was only a matter of time. Birds and mammals are both warm-blooded, which gives them an immense advantage over insects, amphibians and reptiles. All of the latter, if it gets too hot, suffer heat prostration. A small lizard, living in burning desert sands, must scamper quickly from one patch of shade to another, or it will expire in a few minutes. It is only the bird or mammal, gasping or sweating as it may, which can stay out in the hot sun for long periods of time. Similarly, when the temperature falls, cold-blooded animals become totally inert. Mammals, with fur and a layer of subcutaneous fat to help retain body heat, and a high rate of metabolism for the continued production of heat, can stand extremes of cold almost indefinitely. They give up a certain elasticity in the process. They require a steady supply of food in order to keep their internal furnaces stoked, the extreme example being the shrew, which must eat heartily every hour or two, or it will starve to death. By contrast, a python needs a good meal only about once a year.

Mammals also suffer if their body temperatures are not kept within a narrow range. An insect may not function well—or it may not function at all—when its internal temperature falls to 35°, but it will not necessarily die. A man will die, however, if his temperature falls below about 65°. Warm-bloodedness requires constant temperature and a constant supply of energy, but these things are made possible by a far greater mental alertness and physical adaptability. With the need goes the capacity to fill it, and in the last 63 million years, during the Cenozoic era, warm-blooded animals have become dominant.

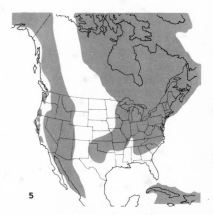

In the great stretches of prehistoric time that succeeded the periods shown in the maps on the opposite page, the seas continued their general retreat from North America. In the Carboniferous period, however, a great ocean almost 2,000 miles wide engulfed western America (above, top), and by the Cretaceous period (middle) the sea had once again overwhelmed much of western Canada and all but a small portion of Mexico. Not until the Miocene period (bottom)—about 25 million years ago—did the present continent emerge almost entirely above sea level.

T HIS has been a painfully short and perhaps dangerously sketchy account of the history of life. Even so, it reveals the vague outlines of some general rules in evolution. Evolution guarantees nothing. It is an accidental, wholly random process. The fact that an amoeba is developed does not guarantee the eventual development of a man. Under the changing conditions on earth, conditions which were themselves shaped by the evolutionary process, man did happen to emerge. If the conditions had been slightly different, something else might have emerged instead. And yet there are guidelines, basic tendencies. There is a trend away from simplicity and toward increasingly complex forms. There is also a tendency for evolving life to flow into a greater number of niches in the environment, thus increasing the total amount of life that the planet can support. These two tendencies go together, since greater complexity permits new life niches to be explored.

Single cells which accidentally mingle together in groups may, again accidentally, exhibit certain differences between them which make further going-around-together advantageous to the group as a whole. A few may have longer hairs than the average, and the sculling motion of those hairs may enable others in the group to be moved faster than they could move by themselves. Those others, in turn, may ingest food a trifle more efficiently. If such peculiarities were to give a group of cells even the slightest advantage over single cells moving freely in the water, then the chances of survival for the group would be better than for any single cell. Those groups whose useful differences became more pronounced over many generations of further accidental change would have the best chance for survival among groups, and hence the greatest opportunity for further change. In time the differences between individual cells would become so great that they could no longer exist separately. Each would have become specialized for performing a particular function such as sculling, feeding or reproducing. From then on the cells would have to hang together or die, and a true multicellular organism would have evolved. In this process the opportunities for further evolution would become greatly enlarged. And evolution itself would show a corresponding tendency to speed up.

All these things have happened. Primitive forms were followed by more complex ones, flowing with increasing abundance and increasing rapidity from the sea onto the land, and into all the cracks in the land. Each period of time had its most efficient and successful type. The trilobites and other arthropods of the Paleozoic had their long day of dominance. They were superseded by the reptiles of the Mesozoic, which were in turn superseded by the far more efficient and adaptable warm-blooded animals of the modern era. Evolution is still going on; the basic tendencies toward increased specialization still exist—and if nothing should occur to interrupt the process, we might be able to assume that in due course another dominant, and better, type would supplant the mammals.

But it must be emphasized again that nothing is certain in evolution. There is no guarantee that this will happen. On the contrary, there begins to be some suspicion that it may not. For the first time in the history of life, there has appeared a creature who is aware of life, and from that time on life can never be the same; for if we become aware of something, we then have the ability to tinker with it.

MAN has evolved to the point where he can reason, remember, read and write, devise scientific instruments and laboratories. Out of this comes the momentous discovery that there is such a thing as evolution. And out of that comes the science of genetics—and with it the key to shaping the further course of evolution. In short, man's future destiny may be guided by him and not by chance. Along with it he will guide the destinies of all other living things. It is unthinkable that he will permit the development of an improved type which might replace him as the dominant organism on earth. Instead, he will choose that type himself and turn himself into it. At least he will have the opportunity to do so. He may not grasp it, but it will be there.

A 50-MILLION-YEAR-OLD RELATIVE OF THE MODERN POMPANO, THIS FOSSIL FISH, MENE RHOMBEUS, ONCE SWAM IN ITALIAN SEAS

The Rich Fossil Legacy

Not all of earth's creatures return to anonymous dust. In the ancient rocks that encrust the world are preserved the imprints, and often the bones, of billions of organisms great and small. For 200 years scholars have studied this fossil record to reconstruct the development of life. Now, in search of the ultimate building blocks of life, science is penetrating the nucleus of the living cell.

IN A DINOSAUR GRAVEYARD, a skeleton is freed from the rock in which it was preserved. Workmen at the Dinosaur National Monument in Utah use a drill to break the bulk of the rock, and later use more delicate tools. At Dinosaur Monument the remains of many animals are only partly excavated so that visitors can see how fossilization occurred.

FRAIL BLUE BONES are the mineral-impregnated remains of a cat-sized, tree-climbing carnivore called Uintacyon, which roamed the forests of Wyoming some 55 million years ago.

FILMY LEAF IMPRINT, from a platanus tree of the Miocene period, closely resembles the leaf of a modern sycamore. The colors come from minerals that infiltrated the leaf's cells.

The Imprints of Vanished Life

Until about 1750, fossils were widely regarded as the remains of familiar plants and animals drowned in the Biblical flood. With the development of the theories of evolution, scientists looked more closely and recognized the traces of fantastic vanished life forms, ancestral to modern living things—but quite unlike them in many ways.

It is astonishing that fossils exist at all. Living tissue, even bone, is extremely perishable and, unless quickly buried in some soft material that later becomes rock-hard, will decay and disappear. Often when a scientist excavates a skeleton or a piece of wood, he finds that minerals have seeped into the cells, petrifying them to solid rock. More rarely, only an imprint of a mold of the living thing is found. The "fly" below is such a mold, a hollow space in a piece of amber exactly duplicating the form of an ancient insect.

THE FOSSIL FORM OF A FLY IS PERFECTLY PRESERVED IN AMBER, STICKY PINE RESIN THAT HARDENED 30 MILLION YEARS AGO

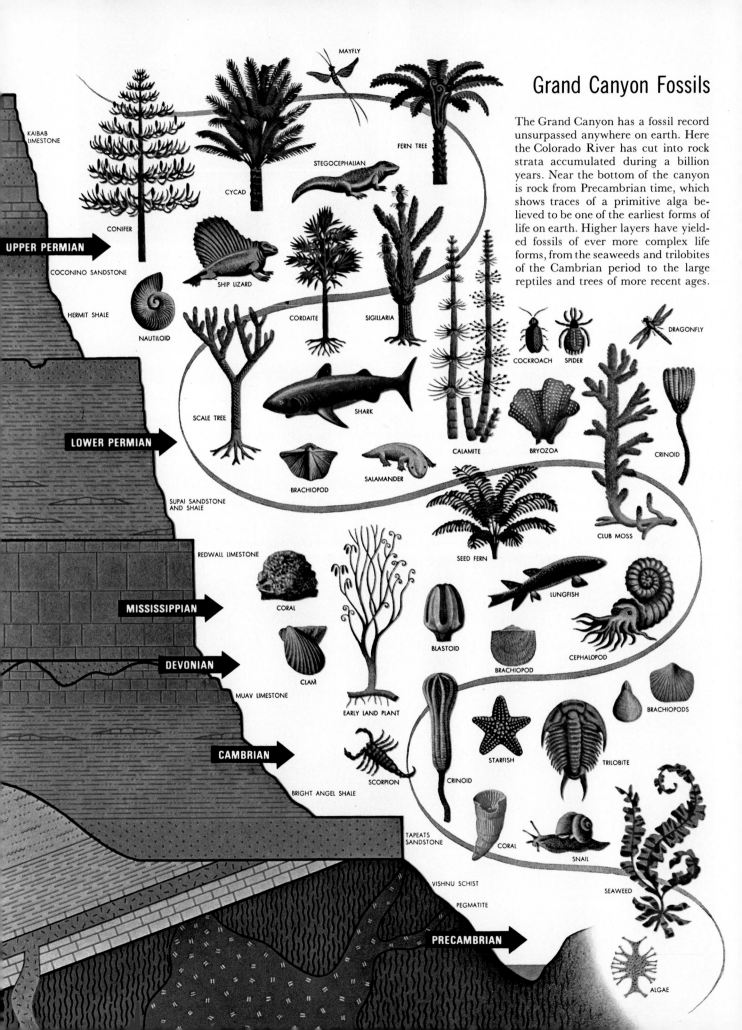

Grand Canyon Fossils

The Grand Canyon has a fossil record unsurpassed anywhere on earth. Here the Colorado River has cut into rock strata accumulated during a billion years. Near the bottom of the canyon is rock from Precambrian time, which shows traces of a primitive alga believed to be one of the earliest forms of life on earth. Higher layers have yielded fossils of ever more complex life forms, from the seaweeds and trilobites of the Cambrian period to the large reptiles and trees of more recent ages.

KAIBAB LIMESTONE

UPPER PERMIAN

COCONINO SANDSTONE

HERMIT SHALE

LOWER PERMIAN

SUPAI SANDSTONE AND SHALE

REDWALL LIMESTONE

MISSISSIPPIAN

DEVONIAN

MUAV LIMESTONE

CAMBRIAN

BRIGHT ANGEL SHALE

TAPEATS SANDSTONE

VISHNU SCHIST

PEGMATITE

PRECAMBRIAN

CONIFER

CYCAD

MAYFLY

FERN TREE

STEGOCEPHALIAN

SHIP LIZARD

NAUTILOID

CORDAITE

SIGILLARIA

SCALE TREE

SHARK

BRACHIOPOD

SALAMANDER

CALAMITE

BRYOZOA

CRINOID

COCKROACH   SPIDER

DRAGONFLY

CLUB MOSS

SEED FERN

CORAL

CLAM

EARLY LAND PLANT

BLASTOID

LUNGFISH

BRACHIOPOD

CEPHALOPOD

BRACHIOPODS

SCORPION

CRINOID

STARFISH

TRILOBITE

CORAL

SNAIL

SEAWEED

ALGAE

and the Life of Today

The Grand Canyon today supports a wide variety of animal and plant life. Willow trees thrive in the wet warmth of the riverbank, which at places is 6,000 feet below the canyon rim. Blue spruce and Douglas fir inhabit the upper, Canadian, zone. With the plant life go the animals that normally live in these various climatic zones. In all their variety, they are a dramatic illustration of the wealth of species that have evolved from the few, primitive forms with which life on earth began.

CLARK'S NUTCRACKER

MOUNTAIN LION

QUAKING ASPEN

BLUE SPRUCE

LYNX

DOUGLAS FIR

CHIPMUNK

MULE DEER

WHITE-TAILED SQUIRREL

CANADIAN ZONE

GOPHER

BROWN BAT

BLUE PENSTEMON

SCARLET BUGLER

WESTERN TANAGER

TRANSITION ZONE

SERVICEBERRY

YELLOW PINE

LOCO WEED

PORCUPINE

RUFUS DEER MOUSE

LIVE OAK

UTAH JUNIPER

CACTUS

BULL SNAKE

SPOTTED SKUNK

BLUE FLAX

ANTELOPE

CACTUS

CHIPMUNK

CACTUS

GOLDENROD

GRAY FOX

COLLARED LIZARD

WILD GERANIUM

UPPER SONORAN ZONE

HORNED TOAD

CACTUS

BAT

LARKSPUR

MESQUITE

SNOWBERRY

MOUNTAIN SHEEP

KING SNAKE

LOWER SONORAN ZONE

JIMSON WEED

WILLOW

GOPHER

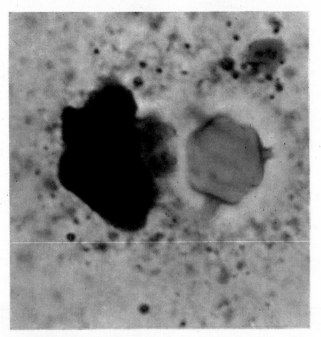

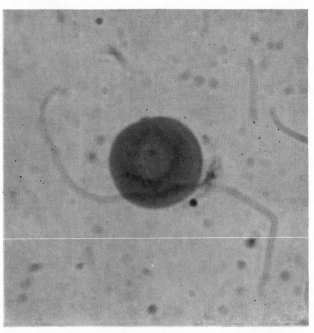

A SPOKED HEXAGON at right above, surrounded by a whitish halo, may be a fossil remnant of life from space. It was found in a new study of a meteorite that fell a century ago.

A CELL-LIKE BALL is one of 26 different shapes resembling earth forms that were found in studies of several meteorites. Its color is from stains used in microscopic examinations.

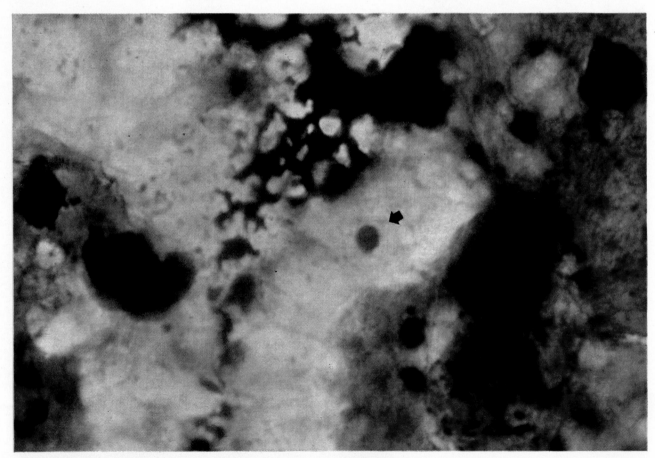

A PLANTLIKE SPHERE, shown here in its natural color (arrow), was discovered in a meteorite that fell in Tanganyika in 1936. Under higher magnification it has a band around its middle and is covered with short spines, like many terrestrial algae. Surrounding the sphere is a mass of whitish magnesium sulphate, which is embedded in iron and rock.

Clues to Life's Beginnings

How did the profusion of life on the earth begin? Two recent series of experiments have suggested two possible answers. One group of scientists has examined small particles chipped from meteorites and has found infinitesimal fossils (*opposite*) of what is cautiously described as "organized" material. This implies that life on earth could be a transplant from another planet. Another group of scientists, among them Dr. Stanley Miller (*right*), has conducted experiments which demonstrate that life could have developed here spontaneously when the elements on the primitive earth combined to form the amino acids which are the basis of the proteins of life. After eons of futile combination and recombination, these amino acids might have formed a complex "Adam molecule," which could grow and reproduce, a spark of life struck off from an infinity of inanimate matter.

MIXING GASES to simulate the earth's early atmosphere, Dr. Stanley Miller shows that this ancient air could produce organic material as a possible precursor to life itself.

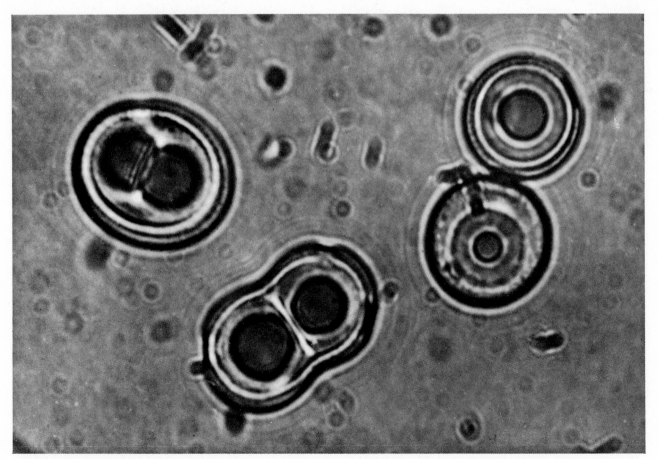

"ORIGIN OF LIFE" experiment sets out to duplicate conditions under which primordial amino acids may have turned into proteins, the basic ingredient of life. Here, a laboratory solution containing amino acids has been heated and then cooled. In the process, a few tiny droplets (*above*) of a simple proteinlike substance are created from the amino acids.

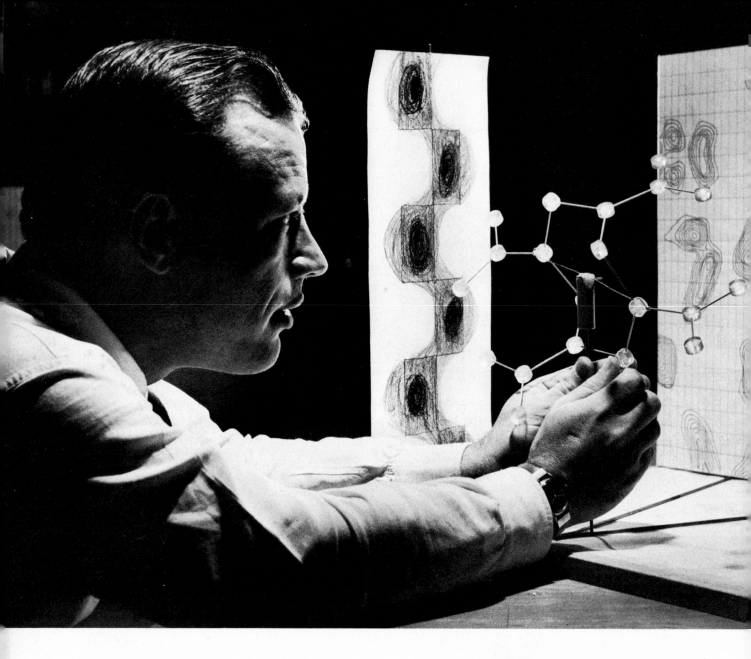

DNA, Protector of Species

Using a vast variety of tools, from electron microscopes to massive computers, scientists in the past few years have been probing deeper and deeper into the living cell. At last, within the chromosomes of the cell's nucleus, they have identified molecules of desoxyribonucleic acid, called DNA for short, which is central to all life.

DNA forms an exact pattern determining how a plant or animal looks and functions. Each species has a different complement of DNA molecules; hence each looks and functions like no other. Further, the arrangement of DNA molecules is passed from parents to offspring. Thus there is continuity in the species, dogs always giving birth to dogs, and humans to humans.

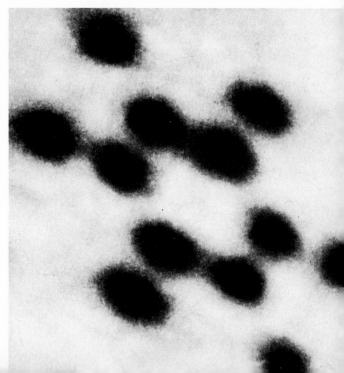

A MOLECULE MODEL is built up from a map of its atomic structure (*above*). Molecules can only be seen indirectly, in the patterns X rays make on a photographic plate when deflected by atoms.

A MOLECULE PORTRAIT shows an early attempt to map an atomic structure (*opposite*). This is a reconstruction of the atoms of a simple, ringed molecule which is in fact 235 million times as small.

A MOLECULE OF DNA has clusters of atoms which take a spiral shape (*right*). This model of DNA was based on X-ray photographs and other techniques that reveal otherwise invisible atomic structures.

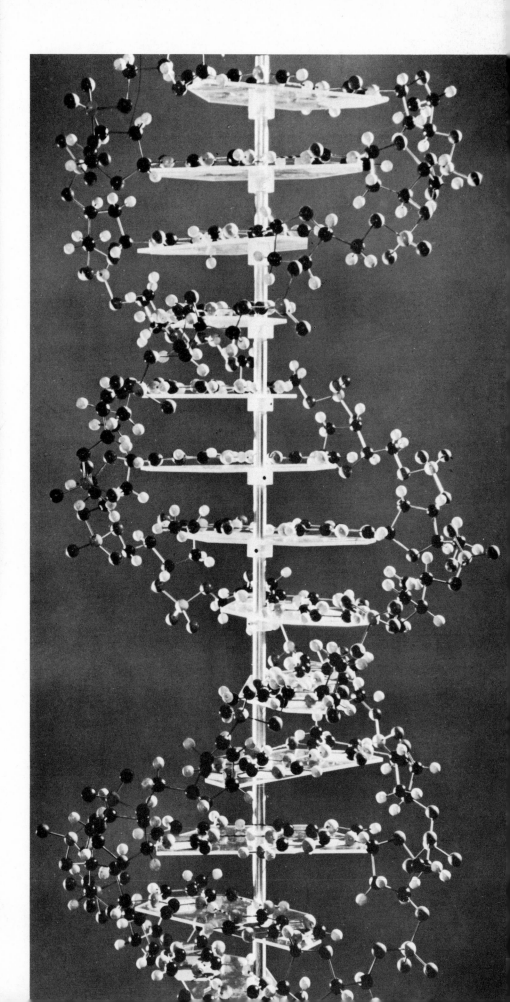

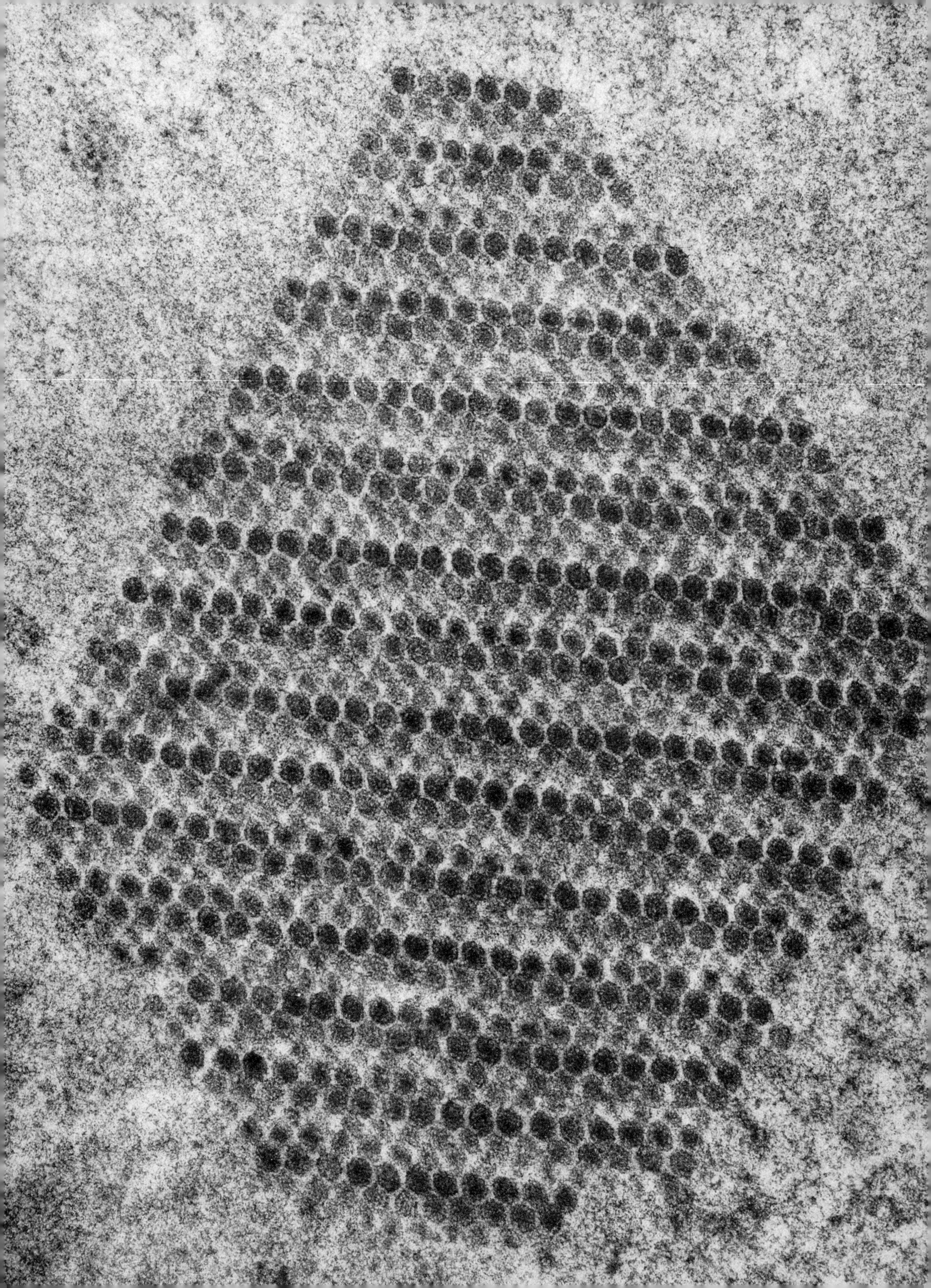

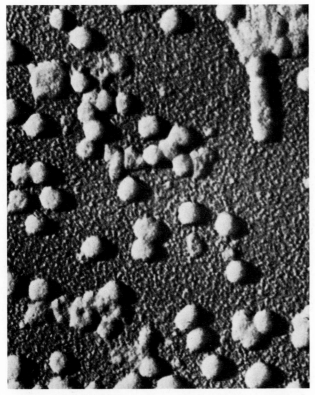

FLU VIRUSES, magnified 35,000 times, appear as irregular balls. Each ball is composed of molecules too small to be photographed by the most powerful electron microscope.

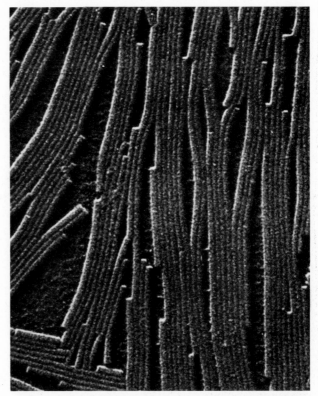

GIANT PLANT VIRUSES cling tightly together like sticky strands of spaghetti. Each long, thin strand forms a virus particle of the type which causes mosaic disease in tobacco.

The Resurrecting Viruses

When life began, it probably flickered uncertainly. An organism might show a spark of life, then revert to the state of inert matter—and, under some stimulus, come to life again. Viruses lead the same flickering existence and are probably much like the earliest life forms in this respect. Viruses can be inert crystals, with no more sign of life than so much table salt, or become living particles (*above*). Composed of a core of nucleic acids in a protein envelope, a virus apparently does not reproduce out of its own matter but makes the cell it attacks turn into a factory producing more virus. An apparently inert virus will assume the properties of life if it encounters fresh cells it can invade. A tiny example of the evolutionary process is shown by the influenza virus, which suddenly developed strains resistant to a vaccine that had been effective against it.

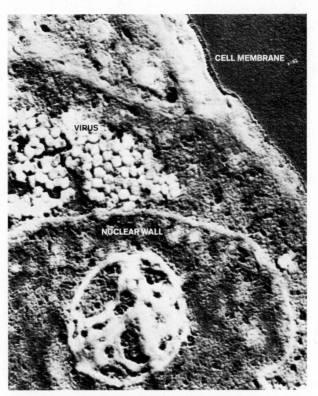

A CLUSTER OF VIRUSES photographed deep within a living cell gathers threateningly outside the nuclear wall. This is the globular fowl-pox virus, enlarged 10,800 times.

A CRYSTAL LATTICE is formed by a virus (*opposite*) which has penetrated the nucleus of a living cell. This honeycomb of crystallized virus has been magnified 94,000 times.

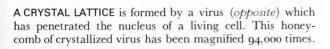

151

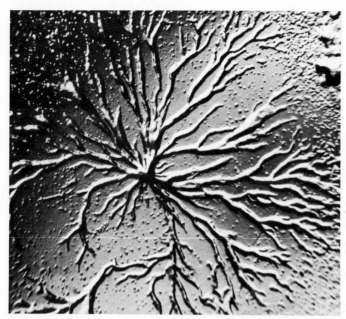
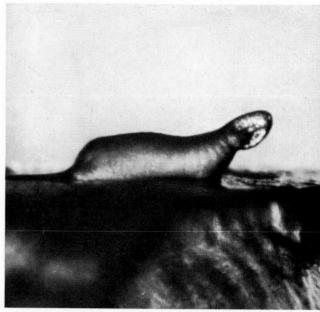

STAGES IN A SLIME-MOLD LIFE CYCLE SHOW (FROM LEFT) THOUSANDS OF AMOEBAS FLOWING TOGETHER TO FORM A SLUGLIKE BODY WHICH

Two Microcosmic Miracles

One of the wonders of life is how primitive living cells first banded together to form larger organisms. In what ways did these early organisms survive, reproduce and grow in complexity? To investigate such questions, scientists have studied some of the simple life forms that still abound on the earth. Two are shown on these pages, a slime mold (*above*) and a hydra (*below*). The slime mold repeatedly goes through a strange metamorphosis in which it takes on characteristics of both the plant and animal kingdoms. First, large numbers of amoebalike creatures band together to form a new organism which behaves like a worm crawling along on its belly. Then, for some reason, it halts and starts growing like a plant, raising its spore mass on a thin stalk.

A CLUMP OF CELLS FROM A MINCED-UP HYDRA REGENERATES TWO NEW ANIMALS IN THE SEQUENCE BELOW. STUBBY NEW TENTACLES

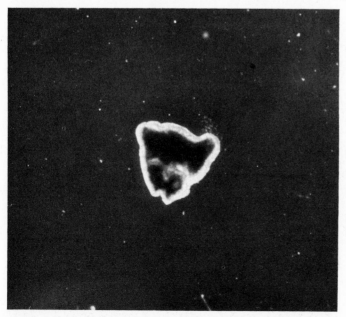
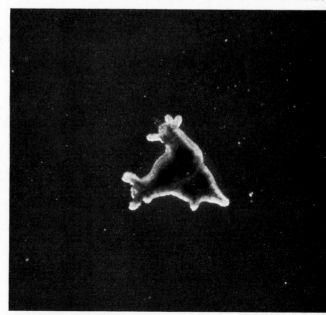

THEN BECOMES A PLANT WITH A STEM AND A SPORE CASE ON TOP. LIBERATED SPORES BECOME AMOEBAS, AND THE CYCLE IS REPEATED

Abruptly, and just as strangely, the stalk bends and the spore ball bursts, releasing the individual amoebas to start swarming again as the life cycle of the cell community repeats.

The tiny hydra is remarkable in a different way. Named for the Greek mythical monster that could sprout new heads when one was cut off, it can regenerate itself, perfect and whole, even after it is cut in pieces. Biologists have taken hydras and diced their bodies into microscopic mincemeat. Somehow these scrambled bits of hydra are able to produce complete organisms again. Investigation of this indomitable growth mechanism may provide clues not only to the nature of primitive animals but also to the ability of the cells of higher animals to regenerate damaged tissue.

START TO BUD AT THE CORNERS OF THE CELL MASS, WHICH THEN SLOWLY PULLS APART TO FORM A PAIR OF INDEPENDENT·HYDRAS

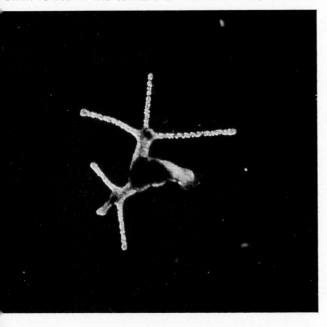

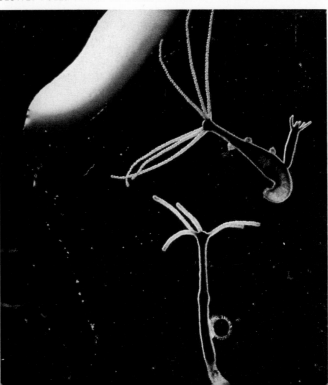

A MODEL OF A HUMAN CELL at the Museum of Science and Industry in Chicago is big enough for visitors to walk around in. Twelve feet high and 24 feet in diameter, it enlarges the cell more than one million times. The plastic rods simulate the structures under the cell's outer membrane, which is also full of punctures and protuberances.

The World within the Complex Human Cell

All living creatures are made up of one or more microscopic compartments called cells. Amoebas consist of just one. Adult man has about 1,000 billion of them. The jumbling of plastic tubes and globes on these pages is the world's largest, most accurate model of a human cell, the first to show its key structures in their proportionate sizes. This is a generalized cell; the specialized cells vary greatly in appearance.

In the center of the model (*opposite*) are the cell's centrosome and nucleus. The spiked centrosome triggers cell division; the process of growth requires that the cell reproduce by dividing in two. The nucleus contains chromosomes —the twisted, ropelike objects—which in turn contain DNA, the hereditary "code." Before a human cell divides, the chromosomes double so that each of its two "daughter" cells will have a set of 46, like its parent. At the nucleus' center is the nucleolus, where the ribonucleic acid, called RNA (shown as red globules), is stored. RNA apparently acts as a pattern for the making of new protein. Suspended above the nucleus are two perforated shapes, part of the cell's protoplasm. In a real cell, protoplasm fills most of the space between the nucleus and the cell surface. The protoplasm also contains fat globules which are the storehouse of food and fuel in the cell.

THE HEART OF A CELL consists of the nucleus and a spiky centrosome (*opposite*). They regulate the cell's protein synthesis, heredity and the process that starts cell division.

154

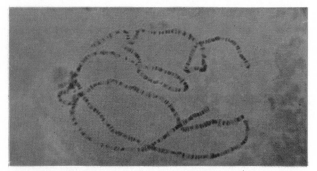

TANGLED CHROMOSOMES, found in the nuclei of living cells, entwine in a beaded pattern. Molecules of DNA, arranged within the beads, are largely responsible for heredity.

The Coils of Heredity

Earth's vast variety of life has evolved, over an immense time, from one or a very few simple living specks. Such diversity is possible because an organism is never an exact duplicate of its parents. Thus tiny variations are fed into the stream of life with each generation. Occasionally a very different individual, or mutation, crops up. Most mutations are failures, but rare ones produce a being better adapted to the struggle for existence.

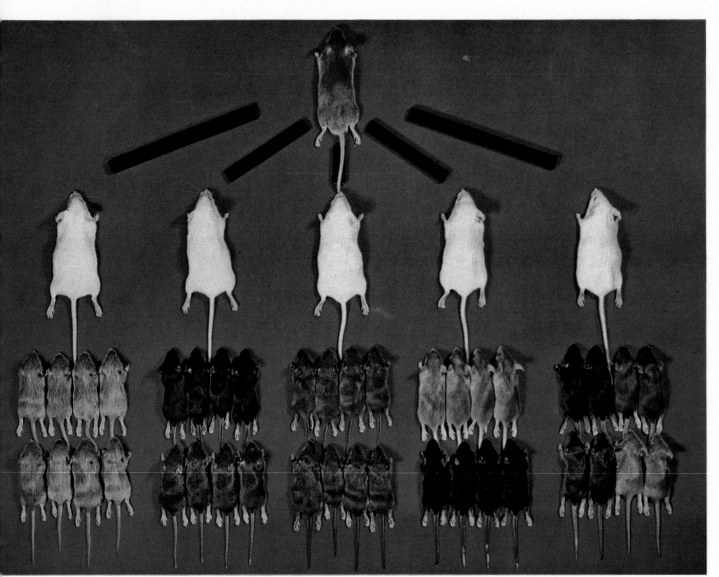

A FAMILY OF MICE shows how offspring can vary from their parents. One gray-colored father (*top*) and five white mothers (*second row*) have produced young (*bottom rows*) of six different colors. Such simple variations are caused by the pairing of parental chromosomes and are not new mutations.

MUTANT AFRICAN VIOLETS offer evidence of the effects of radiation on living things (*opposite*). A violet plant having normal leaves and flowers, like those shown at center, was exposed to ordinary X rays. All of the different leaves and flowers around it are mutations resulting from this radiation.

7

An Uncertain Destiny

No sibyl or oracle of ancient times ever performed such prodigies of prediction as today's scientist does when he foretells the swaying of an unbuilt skyscraper in a hurricane, the spiraling orbits of an unlaunched astronaut, the qualities of an untried alloy, the vitality of an uncrossed hybrid or the power of an undetonated weapon. Yet these feats are mere child's play compared with the attempts of modern earth theorists to forecast the global trends taking place in the land, sea and air of man's planet. What may happen to a skyscraper, bomb or rocket is a nearly self-contained chain of cause and effect. But many natural earth processes are not self-contained, and the number of outside forces which may shape their outcome is legion. Weather over Los Angeles, for instance, cannot be exactly forecast except as a part of the total behavior of the earth's atmosphere. And this behavior is delicately modified by faint forces and subtle effects from an incredible variety of sources: the amount of carbon dioxide released by chimneys, the number of fragments of disintegrated comets which the earth sweeps up in its path through interplanetary space, the sudden increase in friction between wind and land when the trees leaf in spring.

Such an intricate mechanism as the atmosphere or the oceans or the crust of the earth is known by mathematicians as a "complex system." And the entire earth, embodying as it does gases, liquids and solids, is about as complex as a system can be. The purely gaseous sun, though 10 million times as large as the earth, is far simpler mechanically. Even the universe is simpler, though it undoubtedly contains many billions of planets like the earth. The reason this can be so is that the complexities of an earth, a sun or even a galaxy have no effect whatsoever on the forces shaping the universe at large. Nothing that happens on earth can influence the future evolution of the sun and nothing that happens on the sun can influence the evolution of the galaxy, the assemblage of 100 billion-odd stars in which the sun has membership. But the evolution of the universe does affect the galaxy, the evolution of the galaxy does affect the sun and the evolution of the sun does affect the earth. The ultimate fate of the earth can be foretold with absolute certainty because it depends on the mathematically simple system of the universe at large. The short-term future, however, is rich with possibilities which cannot be either denied or definitely predicted.

SCIENTISTS hope and expect that their crystal balls will not always be so cloudy. At Suitland, Maryland, a contingent of government meteorologists, armed with computers, is already calculating the day-to-day weather on the basis of the first crude but comprehensive mathematical models of the entire atmosphere. Moreover, they are constantly improving their equations and their results as they learn to use the over-all global information coming in from orbiting weather satellites. Eventually they hope to gain insight from their studies which will enable them to understand long-term climates as well as short-term weather—to look months, years and perhaps even centuries ahead, and predict world-wide changes in temperature, ocean level and glaciation. If they are successful and can learn to forecast floods and famines well ahead of time, it may take some spice out of life but it will permit nations to forearm themselves against natural disasters and perhaps even to participate in wholesale international weather control programs.

Since weather is vitally important to trade and commerce, it has been studied more intensively than most earth processes. But man's small, hard-worked cadre of earth scientists is also busy measuring, analyzing and correlating the other forces of change which mold the earth's future. Hardly a month goes by in which some scientist somewhere does not uncover neglected factors to refresh the mystery and refine the explanation of some earthly phenomenon which already was thought to be understood. To the oceanic tides of Newton, latter-day physicists have added aerial tides raised in the atmosphere by both moon and sun, and even land tides, two or three inches high, raised in the solid rock of the earth's crust. To the earth's simple axial rotation they have added half a dozen wobbles and precessions. To visible sunlight and starlight they have added a whole spectrum of incoming cosmic energy: radio and infrared waves, ultraviolet, X and gamma rays, even cannon-balling motes of matter coming from stars which have exploded in the depths of space.

It may well take decades to fit together all the puzzling pieces of evidence into a true portrait of the dynamic earth. No field of science encompasses such a wealth of unexplained facts. The oxygen content of the oceans may have decreased 12 per cent since 1920. No one knows why. The ocean levels in the Northern Hemisphere drop eight inches every spring without any compensating rise south of the equator. No one knows where the water goes. All in all, geophysics is a young science with a tremendous number of exciting discoveries lying ahead of it. Until as recently as 1948 the local curvature of the earth in Europe was so little known that the maps of different countries did not join properly. Maps made in Sweden differed from maps made in Denmark by 300 feet. English and French maps were out of mesh by 600 feet. Even today, when space satellites have vastly improved the precision of earth measurements, American missilemen still do not know exactly the direction of the Kremlin. If they ever have to aim and fire they will start—even before the vagaries of their propulsion systems take effect—with built-in uncertainties of hundreds of feet.

Limited as modern geophysicists are by quantitative doubts and analytic dilemmas, they can still make a number of confident qualitative predictions about the immediate future of the earth. The continents which have grown out of the ocean from nuclei like the Canadian and north Brazilian shields will continue to grow. The volcanic "ring of fire" which surrounds the Pacific Ocean, pushing up new island arcs and joining them gradually with the mainland, will continue to narrow. California and Mexico will probably continue to expand southwestward, building on the drowned peaks and plateaus of the East Pacific Rise. Siberia and Alaska, aided by the Aleutian volcanoes, may rejoin permanently and the ancient land bridge of the Eskimos, Indians and mastodons may emerge from the sea once and for all. Britain may be indivisibly added to the Common Market. Patagonia and Tierra del Fuego may fuse with Antarctica to cut off the channel between the Atlantic and Pacific Oceans. On the other hand, the Panamanian Isthmus might sink, creating a new channel. If the islands of the West Indies continue to rise, the Caribbean could become an enclosed sea. The Asiatic land mass may annex Indonesia and possibly even Australia, re-creating the land bridge over which the ancestors of kangaroos and platypuses first migrated Down Under some hundred million years ago.

As the continents grow, and as their granite spreads out over the ocean bottoms, mountain-building will inevitably slow down. The radioactive heat which mainly powers the earth's orogeny today cannot last forever. Already the short-lived radioactive elements which were present in the primordial earth have decayed and grown cold. Long-lived thorium, uranium and potassium still supply enough heat to keep the crust restless, but since their combined half-lives work out at about five billion years, they should be building roughly half as many mountains in A.D. 5,000,-000,000 as they are today. This should give erosion longer intervals to do its work between successive epochs of mountain-building and should make the average terrestrial landscape a good deal flatter and duller than it is now. The oceans meanwhile will become pent up in ever deepening abysses from which they will spill over as shallow seas onto the broad continental shelves. Of course, if there are descendants of Homo sapiens living then, they may restrict the ocean entirely to its abysses by walling the continental shelves with massive dikeworks.

Over the ages, as the inequalities in the earth's structure are gradually ironed out, men and beasts will be plagued periodically by glacial periods. At present the human race is thriving either at the end of the Pleistocene ice ages or in a brief respite between the fourth and fifth glaciations. The balance of evidence seems to indicate that modern times are interglacial, but the picture is still somewhat confused. Until recently glaciologists had to rely on such imprecise local gauges as the movements of ice rivers near Swiss hotels or the depths of clay layers at the bottoms of lakes. Now, with the advent of radioactive dating, they have begun to sort out facts from fallacies and assemble a true chronology of ice-age history.

The most extraordinary piece of isotope detective work bearing on the ice ages has been done by Nobel prize chemist Harold Urey and a group of his students and associates at the University of Chicago. By measuring the relative abundance of two isotopes of oxygen in fossil sea shells, the Urey group found they could determine the precise temperature of the sea water in which ancient mollusks and protozoa built their hard-hat homes. So delicate is the measurement that developing the instruments to make it took Urey four years. So exact is the perfected technique that it can pin down the season of year in which an ancient oyster was born and the number of years it lived. Using the method on fossil shells of the last 300,-000 years, Urey's colleagues found that ocean temperatures throughout the recent ice ages have varied by about 10° F. in a 40,000-year cycle which exactly corresponds to the ebb and flow of the glaciers on land.

The temperature cycle discovered by the Urey team tends to support an old theory of the ice ages proposed by the Serbian physicist Milutin Milankovitch in the 1920s. Milankovitch calculated the effect of the earth's many rotational wobbles and orbital deviations on the sequence of its seasons. He found that every 40,000 years circumstances should combine to give the higher latitudes of earth cool summers and mild winters—summers in which glaciers would not melt much, and winters in which snowfall would be heavy over the arctic regions and high mountains where glaciers form.

The Milankovitch theory explains why temperatures have fluctuated during the ice ages but it does not explain why the ice ages first began. During most of geologic time the temperate regions have enjoyed balmy, subtropical climates, enabling palm trees to flourish and leave fossils within a thousand miles of the North Pole. Within the past 30 million years, according to the Urey group, the bottom waters of the ocean began decreasing steadily in temperature, falling from 70° F. at the end of the era of dinosaurs to a mere 36° at the onset of the ice ages a million years ago.

Two theories exist to explain the creeping chill which has brought earth's temperate zones to the edge of iciness. The minority view is that the sun has been shedding less heat these last 30 million years. But astronomers generally deny this possibility. A number of geophysicists feel that the great cooling must be connected with a second, equally dramatic event for which they have found good evidence in the earth itself: the shifting of the earth and its geography in relation to the closely coupled magnetic and geographic poles. The fossil crystalline compass needles in the earth's crust indicate that 500 million years ago the North Pole was near Hawaii, 350 million years ago near Japan, and since then at various points across the North Pacific until it became ensconced in the ocean now known as Arctic. At the same time the South Pole moved out of the Atlantic onto Antarctica, converting it from a subtropic continent of lush vegetation and coal deposits into a glacial wasteland.

This so-called polar wandering—in which the earth's axis actually remains fixed in its direction in space while the earth's matter moves around it like so much taffy apple on a stick—has been explained by one group of theorists as a necessary readjustment which the earth makes whenever upheavals raise new mountain chains north or south of the equator. The mountains cause top-heaviness, which is only stabilized when the earth has reoriented itself so that the new mountains come into better equilibrium with the distribution of masses in the opposite hemisphere.

The way polar wandering may have brought on ice ages is by reducing earth's energy intake: by changing dark, heat-absorbing areas of the land into snow-covered, reflective areas. As long as the poles were at sea in the Atlantic and Pacific, their ice packs must have been held in check by the moderating warmth and dispersing currents of the ocean. But when Antarctica, Canada, Siberia and Greenland turned frosty white, the earth must have taken in less of the sun's heat every year, and gradually the whole earth, including the heat reservoir of the oceans, must have grown colder. When the oceans were no longer able to supply enough heat to counteract the trends on land, the glaciers were presumably free to advance and retreat in response to the Milankovitch cycle.

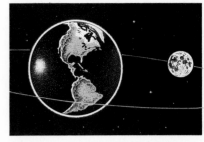

The future of the moon, according to one theory, is shown in these drawings. Above, the moon is still in its accustomed orbit around earth and looks as it does today.

For several billion years, the moon will spiral farther out into space, increasing its orbit to compensate for the decrease in the speed of the rotation of the earth.

IF the polar-wandering theory of ice ages is correct, it seems unlikely that the ice ages will end and the earth return to its normal equable climate until new mountain chains in the far north and south have forced the poles to put to sea again. The best evidence of the oxygen-isotope shell thermometers indicates that the interglacial climate reached its warmest about 8000 B.C. and has been intermittently cooling down since then. Its fluctuations seem to have coincided with several great historical events. The warm era some 10,000 years ago probably dried up the Sahara and forced the people of North Africa into the oases of the Nile, where they founded civilization. Prolonged cold snaps in preclassic times and again in the early centuries of the Christian era may have helped propel barbarian hordes southwestward out of Central Asia against the walls of Knossos, Troy, Rome and Byzantium. A balmy spell about A.D. 1000 probably enabled the Vikings to discover Iceland, Greenland and America. Since about 1720 the ocean temperature has risen slightly but there is no reason to believe that it will not shortly turn down again. It may merely dip by a fraction of a degree or drop several degrees in the first of a series of plunges like those which have characterized the gradual onsets of past glacial periods.

The moon, spiraling back to earth later in response to the earth's faster rotation, caused by the gravitational pull of the sun, may come close enough to shatter.

In the event that the glaciers do grind slowly south again over the next few thousand years, man will either have to migrate into the tropics and the no-longer-dry desert zones of the earth or he will have to spend considerable power and ingenuity diverting the streams of ice away from his northern cities. If, on the other hand, the poles shift or the sun burns hotter, the ice ages will come to an end and the tremendous volume of water locked in the icecaps of Greenland and Antarctica will be released to raise the level of the oceans by an estimated 200 to 300 feet. In this event, also, man will either have to move or expend enormous energy and intellect. Either he will have to abandon his present coastlands and great port cities or, if he has gone on improving his technological proficiency, wall the entire seaboards of Europe and America with dikes thousands of miles long.

It is highly likely that industrial man by his very existence will artificially

In the final stage, billions of the moon's fragments would circle the earth as tiny satellites, creating a ring similar to the ones now seen around the planet Saturn.

The burning-out of the sun will take many billions of years. Above, the sun is at the strength it has held for six billion years and will retain for six billion more years.

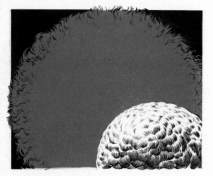

Helium is forming at the sun's core. Expanding over six billion years, it will transform the sun into a red giant, turning the earth's oceans to clouds of steam.

After about a billion years as a red giant, the sun will begin to shrink back to modest size, but it will be in its death throes by then and its brightness will slowly fade.

Fifteen billion years from now, the sun will be a white dwarf, its fires almost out. As it contracts more and more, the earth in time will be a dark, frozen mass.

164

modify the cycles of the ice ages or abolish them. Over the last 100 years, factory chimneys have poured 360 billion tons of carbon dioxide into the atmosphere and almost an equal amount has been released by soil cleared of forest for farming. Almost half of the gas has been quickly captured by dead leaves, living things and other organic material. The rest has risen into the air, increasing its carbon dioxide content by about 13 per cent. Since carbon dioxide in the atmosphere prevents the escape of heat from the earth into space, this change in the content of air has raised earth temperatures by about 1° F. In A.D. 2000 a possible trillion tons of industrial CO_2 in the air will increase earth's average temperature by 3.6°. By A.D. 3000 man's industrial exhaust may have increased the atmosphere's CO_2 eighteenfold; even after the oceans have absorbed all of the fumes they can, enough may remain aloft to raise earth's average temperature by 12.5°. At this point the ice ages, naturally or not, will almost certainly end and man will have to contend willy-nilly with the floods of melted glaciers.

THE Herculean labors which the dynamic earth may exact of the human race during future floods and glaciations are as nothing compared to the challenges which will come from outside the earth. The first and least serious threat will come from the moon. The tides it raises in the land, sea and air are gradually slowing down the earth's spin. At present the rotation period is lengthening at the rate of about 25 billionths of a second each day. This seems like little, but after five billion years it will give the earth roughly a 36-hour day. Man and his crops should be able to adjust themselves to broiling 18-hour days and equally long cold nights but the effect on the atmosphere—especially on the creation of tornadoes and tropical hurricanes—may well be catastrophic. The earth's slowing rotation will be accompanied by a second phenomenon: the energy of spin which the earth loses will be picked up by the moon through gravitational linkage and as a result the moon will move faster through space, spiral outward from the earth and shine more faintly in the sky. At present it is departing from the earth by about one foot every 30 years. But this rate will be decreased the farther out it goes because of competitive effects caused by the sun. The alternate heating and cooling of the earth's atmosphere by sunlight works to speed up the rotation of the earth. When the moon's pull on earth becomes weakened because of its increasing distance, the sun's speeding of earth rotation will overcome the moon's slowing of earth rotation. The earth will turn more quickly again and will begin to pull the moon inward once more. This will probably happen in about five billion years, when the moon is nearly half again as far from the earth as it is today. At that point in the moon's future the sun itself will change, quickening the moon's return toward earth and intervening in earth's evolution so dramatically that for a while further lunar developments will seem inconsequential.

Astronomers know how the sun will evolve because they have studied sunlike stars, older than the sun, and have seen how they behave as they begin to run out of the nuclear fuel which makes them burn. When a star of the sun's mass has converted 15 per cent of its original hydrogen into helium by the H-bomb fusion reaction, the helium ash at its core lights up in a second nuclear reaction which is far hotter. As a result the star begins to pour out energy at an increasingly profligate pace, swelling and turning blood red as it does so.

Between about five and six billion years from now the sun will bloat up from its present size until it fills most of the volume between itself and the innermost planet, Mercury. At the prodigal height of its power, its width will cover a full twelfth of the arc from one earth horizon to another and its outpouring of energy will raise the terrestrial temperature to about 1,000° F., a heat so grilling that lead will ooze molten out of the crevices of the earth and the oceans will—if unprotected—boil away into an enveloping shroud of steam.

After the lethal climax of its life the sun will swiftly shrink again and the waters of the firmament will fall back on earth in a second deluge. For a few hundred million years the sun will burn blue as it converts the last of its nuclear fuels into metallic elements. During the course of its senescence it will possibly go through unstable stages in which eruptions in its outer layers will lay bare its blazing interior and expose the earth to devastating doses of X and gamma rays. Finally it will consume the last of its nuclear energy and lapse into permanent quiescence. The waters of the earth will then freeze into a permanent mantle of ice. As the sun cools further, it will continue to shrink under its own weight and will glow feebly for a long, long time. The shrinkage will not affect the orbit of earth because the sun's mass will not decrease: its matter will simply grow more dense. Altogether, in the entire span of its life, the sun will have turned only about one thousandth of its matter into energy, and this will represent a loss of mass far too small to loose the bonds of gravity binding the earth in its ceaseless round of the heavens. Ultimately, after several hundred billion years, the sun will go out completely and course onward through space only as a black corpse of a star, shrunken to incredible density and taking up no more room than a planet. In its final state of inert self-compression it will actually be smaller than the earth, but its huge mass will still keep the earth locked in orbit around it.

WHILE the sun is dying, the moon will probably be spiraling in toward the earth. As long as the sun remains hot, the inward movement should continue. Conceivably it could bring the moon so close to the earth that the difference in pull of the earth's gravity on its near and far faces would finally shatter it into fragments. The fragments, grinding themselves smaller and smaller by constant collisions with one another, would eventually form into rings like Saturn's, girdling the earth's equator in a washer-shaped disk of debris. But modern theorists have begun to doubt that the sun will remain hot enough long enough for this to happen. They suggest that the sun will go through its final phases too quickly for its heat to bring the moon within shattering distance. Instead, the moon's tidal effects will take over again and the moon will once more pull away from the earth. As it drifts off it will have little light to reflect and the nights will become darker and darker until it is no longer visible at all. As for the days of that bleak, remote epoch, lit only by the wan and watery light of the fast-fading sun, they will be little brighter than modern moonlight nights.

Scientists generally assume that the human race will not live long enough to suffer in the fiery swelling of the sun or the dark doom of the moon. The average life of any one animal species revealed by the geologic record in the rocks of earth is only about one million years—one million years compared to five billion years before the sun even begins to swell and embark on the last apocalyptic violences of its career. Even though it is logical to conclude that man will fare no better, he just might. Some species have survived unchanged on earth for hundreds of millions of years. What is more, the human species is not subject to the same laws of evolution that have operated up to now. Already man so dominates his planet that the natural evolution of most land plants and large animals has been drastically altered. Man's own evolution has also escaped from the natural channels. On the debit side, it no longer encourages fitness through survival since it no longer prevents the reproduction of individuals with weaknesses like congenital diabetes or low intelligence. On the credit side, it has ceased to be a physical evolution at all and has gradually become a cultural and social one.

UNDER the circumstances no scientist, when pressed, will insist that the human race is subject to the same inglorious laws of survival as those which determined the course of prehuman evolution. Nonetheless, most scientists persist in taking a gloomy view of man's ability to survive his own predatory nature. Whether this pessimism is justified remains to be seen, but if the human race does outlive its warlike proclivities and murderous instincts, it may well plan to outlive the sun as well. Colonizing other planets around stars burning more slowly than the sun may possibly provide a temporary escape for a few fortunate astronauts and astronautrixes. For the entire race of human descendants remaining on earth, however, there conceivably would be a more democratic and economical escape.

At its worst, the sun will not scald the earth with heat and cosmic rays so lethal that human intelligence could not devise shielding against them. It may be that when the heat-death approaches on earth some five billion years from now, some human form of big-headed, small-limbed intelligent life will already have gone underground, taking with it as much of the earth's air and water as possible and coating the outside of its single huge planetary survival shelter with pyroceramic mirrors which will deflect most of the sun's scorching heat back out into space.

Thereafter, as the sun cools, Homo futurus may be able to come out of his artificial caves into the open again and finish his preparations for the eternal night and cold ahead. If he has been able to preserve one half the earth's present water, he will have enough hydrogen fuel so that his thermonuclear reactors will be able to power the earth as liberally as it is now powered by the sun for a period of 10 billion years. Since most solar energy today is wasted, he should be able to eke out his reserves still further, perhaps for 10 trillion years, giving himself a future on earth 1,000 times as long as the entire history of the earth previously. Nor would that be the end of his resources. The planet Jupiter contains about a thousand times as much hydrogen as the earth, and if he could build power reactors on Jupiter, he could beam energy back to earth so frugally that almost none would be lost. The engineering difficulties would be stupendous and, of course, the entire possibility at this great distance in time and civilization—when man has existed for a mere million years—is entirely speculative. The fact remains, however, that science has found no reason yet why Homo futurus should not extend his spiritual evolution almost indefinitely far into the future, if he can once make up his mind to live as a purely intelligent creature instead of a half-intelligent, half-instinctive semibrute.

A MOB OF CHINESE JAMS A STREET IN SHANGHAI. WITH 700 MILLION NOW, CHINA WILL HAVE A BILLION MOUTHS TO FEED BY 1981

The Crowded Future

Billions of years before the world ends in some celestial disaster, man must learn to manage it better, lest he manage his own premature extinction. Pressing problems confront the race—not the least of them the problem of finding standing room. The past saw a squandering of resources; the present is witnessing a search for new ones. The future will reveal whether they are found in time.

167

CROWDING EVERY BIT OF LAND, THIS PUERTO RICAN SLUM, KNOWN AS "THE MUD PUDDLE," PUSHES OUT INTO THE WATER AT SAN JUAN.

The Goad of Overpopulation

Ever since 1798, when Thomas Malthus propounded that the world's population would outstrip the world's food supply, pessimists have been saying that mankind is breeding for disaster. Where there were four of us 10 years ago, there are now five; and the earth's population of two and a half billion in 1950 will swell to over six billion by 2000. But the Malthusian arguments are based on the premise that the earth has a fixed capacity to support mankind. That capacity, however, has proved most flexible.

Today a densely populated but scientifically cultivated Holland provides every Dutchman with a good and varied diet, produced on only two thirds of an acre. If Dutch efficiency could be applied to agricultural methods in needy areas, there would be enough food for 30 billion people, 10 times the world's present number. In Japan, where population has increased around 134 per cent since 1885, food production has gone up by more than 300 per cent. Taking Japanese standards of diet and agriculture, food could be provided for 90 billion people. Thus, while it holds the seeds of disaster, population growth can also be a goad—perhaps the only one that can force man from old, earth-wasteful ways.

TERRACED FIELDS in overcrowded Japan (*right*) are divided among the 11 families shown here, each tilling three acres. Japan has only one tenth of an arable acre per person.

168

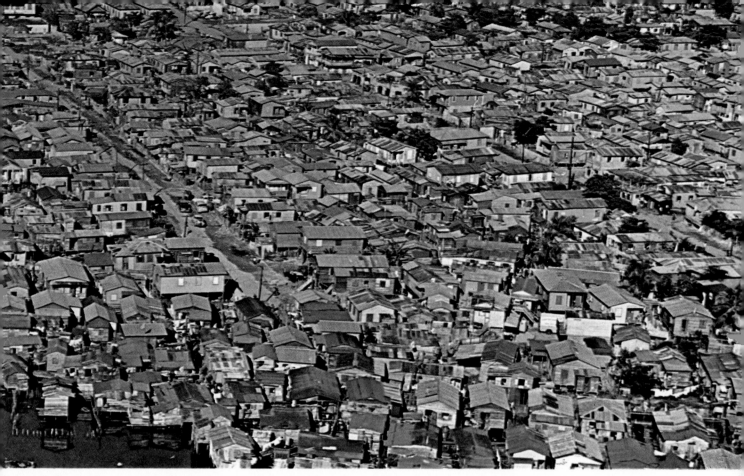

UNLESS POPULATION GROWTH CAN BE CONTROLLED, NEW HOUSING PROJECTS ARE SHORT-RANGE SOLUTIONS TO SUCH URBAN CONGESTION

EVISCERATED LOOK of the world's largest open-pit iron mine in Minnesota testifies to the depletion of mineral resources. Once considered an inexhaustible supply of high-grade ore, the Hull-Rust-Mahoning mine now yields low-quality ore refined from taconite, the hardest rock quarried in the world. New methods make this economically feasible.

NEW TECHNIQUE FOR MINING LOW-GRADE IRON ORE INVOLVES USING A 4,500° FLAME TO PIERCE HARD ROCK

The Irreplaceable Ores

The world's mineral wealth is running out. Even the United States, one of the richest natural storehouses of minerals on earth, is facing shortages. Between 1900 and 1950, when its population doubled, its consumption of minerals went up by six times, and by 1975 that rate will probably double. Already, world reserves of such essentials as copper, lead and zinc are considered inadequate. As the search for new sources goes on, it is clear that methods of exploration and ore extraction must be vastly improved to keep costs from soaring. But as high-quality ore in Minnesota neared exhaustion a few years ago, production of iron from taconite, a hard rock containing ore (*above*), was achieved. What happens when all the iron in the world is used up? Substitutes may be found, or perhaps men will be able to fish nickel-iron asteroids from space to supply earth with ore.

...And Not a Drop to Drink?

Water, man's most precious resource, is the one he has most recklessly squandered. In the U.S. the consumption of water per person is a staggering 60 gallons a day, a figure that will probably rise to 85 in the next 30 years. Already, the city of Los Angeles has drunk a 25-by-20-mile lake dry. Industrial wastes increasingly contaminate rivers and harbors (*left*), killing fish. Sewage does its dirty work too: in 1961 it added twice as much pollution to U.S. waterways as was considered a permissible limit in 1951.

Conservation and re-usage of water are partial answers to the problem. But the world's real hope lies in making salt water fresh. Efforts range from small solar stills to the world's largest distillation plant, in Kuwait, which produces nearly five million gallons a day. Costs in many areas are prohibitive, but when they are reduced —perhaps by use of some new cheap fuel—the double threat of drought and famine may vanish.

SCUMMY WATERS of a harbor in Washington State are polluted with wastes. Pollution is a growing menace everywhere, even though millions are being spent to combat it.

A HOARDED RESERVE of water in India, for use during the drought season, is enlarged by deepening its bed (*above*). The scores of workers are volunteers from nearby villages.

A VAST SUPPLY of water for the American Southwest will be held by the Glen Canyon Dam (*opposite*) on the Colorado River. A 700-foot-high wall will make a 185-mile lake.

Where the Water Is—and Is Not

in the Thirsty United States

A water map of the continental United States shows areas where water is plentiful and where it is scarce. Twenty basins are indicated, each based on river flow and topography. The basins are numbered in the order of water scarcity: thus Basin 1, the upper Rio Grande and Pecos region, has the least water; and Basin 20, the Southeast, the most. The regions colored white, yellow, orange and brown are water-

poor areas; those colored blue are water-rich—the deeper the blue, the more plentiful the water. The average yearly rainfall in the United States as a whole is a substantial 30 inches (4,300 billion gallons a day), but rainfall varies from 140 inches in the Pacific Northwest's Olympic rain forest to two inches in Death Valley. Nearly a fourth of the average rainfall is carried off by the country's rivers. On this map,

the width of a river indicates its comparative rate of flow. The Mississippi carries 360 billion gallons a day into the Gulf of Mexico; the Colorado carries eight billion gallons a day to the Gulf of California. The East, with 75 per cent of the nation's water supply, uses only 2 per cent of that share. The thirsty West uses 65 per cent of its 25 per cent share; by 1980 Westerners may face an acute water famine.

175

POWER SOURCE OF THE FUTURE, a nuclear reactor submerged in a protective pool makes the water glow blue with its radiation. A chief advantage of nuclear power lies in the concentrated nature of its enriched uranium fuel, one pound of which can produce the energy released by burning the coal carried by approximately 25 railroad cars.

FOCUSED RAYS OF THE SUN MELT A HOLE IN STEEL

A Limitless Supply of Energy

Only 20 years ago men worried about world energy sources. There was only so much coal and petroleum in the earth, and while not all of these fuels had been located, they seemed bound to give out in time. Hydroelectric power could hardly turn the gears of civilization or run its automobiles. Today, the energy supply is unbounded. The breakthrough came on December 20, 1950, in a laboratory in the Idaho desert, when scientists generated electricity from atomic energy for the first time. The significance was that radioactive fuels contain much more energy than any others (*opposite*); and uranium reserves alone are 10 times those of coal, oil and natural gas in terms of extractable energy.

Since that historic advance, other new sources of energy have been tapped. The sun has been used to heat houses, melt steel (*above*) and power satellites. An atomic bomb in New Mexico produced an underground reservoir of hot (1,400° F.) liquid salt, into which water was injected to form steam which could run a turbine. Even bacteria have gone to work. Germs feeding on sugar in sea water have powered a radio transmitter, and conceivably bacteria-generated electricity could convert salt water into fresh, and nitrogen and phosphorus into fertilizers.

THE GIANT MIRROR of a solar furnace in France focuses the sun's rays into an oven, where temperatures go as high as 5,400° F., roughly half as hot as the sun's own surface.

WEATHER CONTROL is attempted in this early experiment. Dry ice scattered from a plane cuts a racecourse pattern in the moisture-laden clouds, forcing them to disgorge rain.

MAKING RAIN, Dr. Bernard Vonnegut demonstrates his early method of vaporizing silver iodide with a charcoal burner (*below*). The vapor condenses water from the clouds.

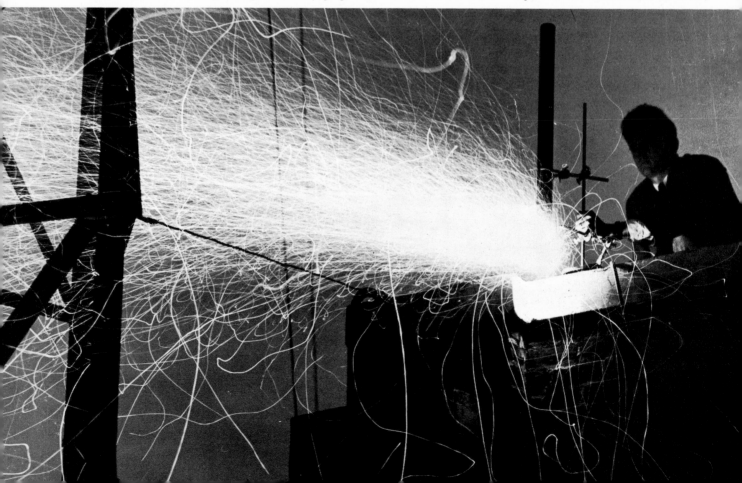

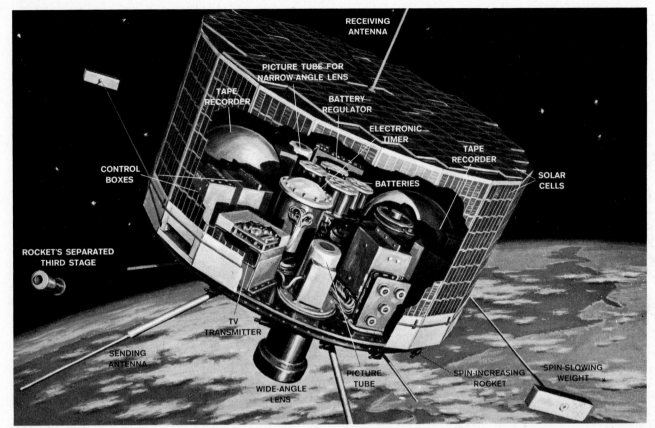

AN EYE FOR WEATHER, a sun-powered Tiros satellite spins through space in the drawing above, photographing cloud formations with two television cameras. From the pictures it transmits to earth (*below*, *right*) meteorologists can make long-range forecasts. Tiros IV helped check weather around the world prior to John Glenn's 1962 orbit of the earth.

First Steps to Weather Control

The new science of weather control was born nearly two decades ago when meteorologists seeded clouds with dry ice and silver iodide to induce rain (*opposite*) and dissipate clouds and fog. But real weather control is impossible until atmospheric processes are more fully understood. U.S. Tiros weather satellites (*above*) are beginning to provide such information. Tiros I, during 78 days of operation in 1960, produced about 14,000 good pictures of the earth and clouds (*right*). For the first time, meteorologists saw the large-scale cloud and storm patterns they had been drawing on their maps.

From such improved satellites as Nimbus and Aeros, weathermen will be able to keep better watch on weather and to follow storms in their early stages. This may lead to ways of diverting them. Now scientists are pondering a longer-range possibility—seeking ways to alter not merely local weather but whole regional climates.

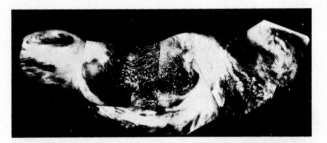

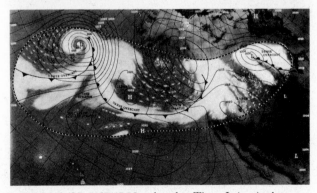

A MOSAIC OF PICTURES taken by Tiros I (*top*) shows a storm east of Japan (*left*), another over the American West and a third over Canada (*far right*). A weatherman superimposed a weather map (*bottom*) on the montage to demonstrate how Tiros can be used to forecast the paths of storms.

179

EAVESDROPPING ON SPACE with an 85-foot-wide dish antenna, a radio telescope in West Virginia, shown in a starstreaked time exposure, listens for radio signals from planets or stars during 1960's Project Ozma. Though the results were negative, the experiment pointed to the day when improved equipment will permit communication by radio with

A "COCKPIT" RUNS THE LARGEST RADIO TELESCOPE, IN ENGLAND

Is Anyone Talking Out There?

In reaching for the stars, man finds himself humbled by them. The astronomers estimate that the Milky Way, only one among billions of galaxies, has at least 100,000 habitable planets and concede that the intelligence of beings on them could equal or exceed our own. Until a few years ago, there was no hope of communicating with the stars. Now the huge mesh ears of radio telescopes permit man to hear the electric impulses that bombard the earth from space. Out of this stellar static may one day come a message, perhaps only a simple mathematical equation like the ones below, to end man's loneliness in the universe.

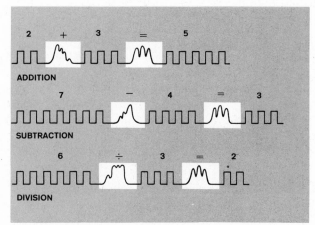

other worlds. A new device, called a laser and employing a synthetic ruby to produce a pencil-thin beam of light, opens up the possibility of sending messages with pulses of light.

INTERSTELLAR TALK could start off with mathematics, as shown above. Numbers would be counted out with electronic blips; other signals would stand for arithmetical symbols.

181

Countdown to the Future

Man's achievements in space are already beginning to catch up with science fiction. In the last decade he has sent instruments, animals, and now humans, whizzing around the earth. Next comes the infinitely more difficult job of freeing a rocket from the gravitational drag of the earth and penetrating the wastes of space. This should occur by 1967, when a Nova rocket as tall as a 25-story building is expected to take U.S. astronauts to the moon and back. Flights to Mars and Venus should follow within three decades. Trips outside the solar system are conceivable in the next 100 years.

THE SATURN BOOSTER, capable of hurling a 10-ton pay load into space, dwarfs the men working on its cluster of eight engines. They were successfully flight-tested in 1961.

A FIERY TRAIL is traced in the Florida sky in this rocket launch of a U.S. moon probe (*opposite*). Plans exist for using the moon as a giant base for trips to deeper space.

Bibliography

Geology and Geography

Brown, Lloyd A., *The Story of Maps*. Little, Brown, 1949.

Dunbar, Carl O., *Historical Geology* (2nd ed.). John Wiley, 1960.

Eardley, A. J., *Structural Geology of North America*. Harper & Brothers, 1951.

Emmons, William H., Ira S. Allison, Clinton R. Stauffer and George A. Thiel, *Geology: Principles and Processes* (5th ed.). McGraw-Hill, 1960.

Longwell, Chester R., and Richard F. Flint, *Introduction to Physical Geology* (2nd ed.). John Wiley, 1962.

Namowitz, Samuel N., and Donald B. Stone, *Earth Science* (2nd ed.). D. Van Nostrand, 1960.

Raisz, Erwin, *General Cartography* (2nd ed.). McGraw-Hill, 1948.

Shimer, John A., *This Sculptured Earth*. Columbia University Press, 1959.

Strahler, Arthur N., *Physical Geography* (2nd ed.). John Wiley, 1960.

Trewartha, Glenn T., Arthur H. Robinson and Edwin H. Hammond, *Fundamentals of Physical Geography*. McGraw-Hill, 1961.

Von Engeln, O. D., *Geomorphology*. Macmillan, 1942.

Wyckoff, Jerome, *The Story of Geology*. Golden Press, 1960.

Zeuner, Frederick E., *Dating the Past: An Introduction to Geochronology* (4th ed.). Longmans, Green, 1958.

Geophysics

Bullen, K. E., *Seismology*. John Wiley, 1954.

Chapman, Sydney, *The Earth's Magnetism* (2nd ed.). John Wiley, 1951.

Gutenberg, Beno, *Physics of the Earth's Interior*. Academic Press, 1959.

Howell, Benjamin F. Jr., *Introduction to Geophysics*. McGraw-Hill, 1959.

Jacobs, J. A., R. D. Russell and J. Tuzo Wilson, *Physics and Geology*. McGraw-Hill, 1959.

Jeffreys, Harold, *The Earth* (4th ed.). Cambridge University Press, 1959.

Kuiper, Gerard P., ed., *The Earth as a Planet* (The Solar System, Vol. II). University of Chicago Press, 1954.

Landsberg, H. E., and others, eds., *Advances in Geophysics* (8 vols. to date). Academic Press, 1952-1961.

Munk, Walter H., and G. H. F. Macdonald, *The Rotation of the Earth*. Cambridge University Press, 1961.

Parasnis, D. S., *Magnetism*. Harper & Brothers, 1961.

Richter, C. F., *Elementary Seismology*. W. H. Freeman, 1958.

Upper Atmosphere

Beiser, Arthur, and Germaine Beiser, *The Story of Cosmic Rays*. E. P. Dutton, 1962.

Chamberlain, J. W., *Physics of the Aurora and Airglow*. Academic Press, 1961.

Hooper, J. E., and M. Scharff, *Cosmic Radiation*. John Wiley, 1958.

Massey, H. S. W., and R. L. F. Boyd, *The Upper Atmosphere*. Philosophical Library, 1959.

Ratcliffe, J. A., *Physics of the Upper Atmosphere*. Academic Press, 1960.

Mining and Minerals

Dobrin, Milton B., *Introduction to Geophysical Prospecting* (2nd ed.). McGraw-Hill, 1960.

Kraus, Edward H., Walter F. Hunt and Lewis S. Ramsdell, *Mineralogy* (5th ed.). McGraw-Hill, 1959.

* Pearl, Richard M., *How to Know the Rocks and Minerals*. McGraw-Hill, 1955.

Witcombe, Wallace H., *All About Mining*. Longmans, Green, 1937.

Weather and Climate

† Battan, Louis J., *The Nature of Violent Storms*. Doubleday, 1961.

Byers, Horace Roberts, *General Meteorology* (3rd ed.). McGraw-Hill, 1959.

† Clausse, Roger, and Léopold Facy, trans. by J. Ferrante, *The Clouds*. Grove Press, 1961.

Fairbridge, Rhodes W., ed., *Solar Variation, Climatic Change, and Related Geophysical Problems*. New York Academy of Sciences, 1961.

† Fisher, Robert Moore, *How to Know and Predict the Weather*. New American Library, 1960.

Kendrew, W. G., *The Climates of the Continents* (4th ed.). Oxford University Press, 1953.

* Lehr, Paul E., R. Will Burnett and Herbert S. Zim, *Weather*. Golden Press, 1957.

Loebsack, Theo, *Our Atmosphere*. Pantheon, 1959.

Orr, Clyde, Jr., *Between Earth and Space*. Macmillan, 1959.

Petterssen, Sverre, *Introduction to Meteorology* (2nd ed.). McGraw-Hill, 1958.

Shapley, Harlow, ed., *Climatic Change: Evidence, Causes, and Effects*. Harvard University Press, 1954.

Fossils and Evolution

Aitken, M. J., *Physics and Archeology*. Interscience, 1961.

* Colbert, Edwin H., *Evolution of the Vertebrates*. John Wiley, 1955.

Fenton, Carroll Lane, and Mildred Adams Fenton, *The Fossil Book*. Doubleday, 1958.

Libby, Willard F., *Radiocarbon Dating* (2nd ed.). University of Chicago Press, 1955.

† Matthews, William H., *Fossils: An Introduction to Prehistoric Life*. Barnes & Noble, 1962.

Romer, Alfred S., *Vertebrate Paleontology* (2nd ed.). University of Chicago Press, 1945.

Shrock, Robert R., and William H. Twenhofel, *Principles of Invertebrate Paleontology*. McGraw-Hill, 1953.

Stirton, R. A., *Time, Life, and Man: The Fossil Record*. John Wiley, 1959.

Young, J. Z., *The Life of Vertebrates*. Oxford University Press, 1950.

General

Academy of Sciences of the U.S.S.R., trans. by J. B. Sykes, *The Other Side of the Moon*. Pergamon Press, 1960.

* Adams, Frank Dawson, *The Birth and Development of the Geological Sciences*. Peter Smith, 1954.

Asimov, Isaac, *The Intelligent Man's Guide to Science* (Vol. 1, The Physical Sciences). Basic Books, 1960.

Baker, Robert H. *Astronomy* (7th ed.). D. Van Nostrand, 1959.

Bascom, Willard, *A Hole in the Bottom of the Sea*. Doubleday, 1961.

* Bates, D. R., ed., *The Earth and Its Atmosphere*. Basic Books, 1957.

† Crombie, Alistair C., *Medieval and Early Modern Science* (2nd rev. ed., 2 vols.). Doubleday, 1959.

† Dury, G. H., *The Face of the Earth*. Penguin Books, 1959.

* Fenton, Carroll Lane, and Mildred Adams Fenton, *Giants of Geology*. Doubleday, 1952.

† Hurley, Patrick M., *How Old Is the Earth?* Doubleday, 1959.

Kendrick, T. D., *The Lisbon Earthquake*. J. B. Lippincott, 1957.

Krauskopf, Konrad, and Arthur Beiser, *The Physical Universe*. McGraw-Hill, 1960.

Larousse Encyclopedia of the Earth. G. P. Putnam's Sons, 1961.

LIFE Editorial Staff and Lincoln Barnett, *The World We Live In*. Time Inc., 1955.

Moore, Ruth, *The Coil of Life*. Alfred A. Knopf, 1960.

The Planet Earth. A Scientific American book. Simon and Schuster, 1957.

Richardson, Robert S., and Chesley Bonestell, *Man and the Moon*. World Publishing, 1961.

* Stumpff, Karl, *The Planet Earth*. University of Michigan Press, 1959.

Sullivan, Walter, *Assault on the Unknown: The International Geophysical Year*. McGraw-Hill, 1961.

Thompson, William L., and others, eds., *Man's Role in Changing the Face of the Earth*. University of Chicago Press, 1956.

True, Webster P., ed., *Smithsonian Treasury of Science* (3 vols.). Simon and Schuster, 1960.

* Whitrow, G. J., *Structure and Evolution of the Universe*, Hillary House Ltd., 1959.

Wilkins, Hugh Percival, and Patrick Moore, *The Moon*. Macmillan, 1955.

Wilson, J. Tuzo, *IGY: The Year of the New Moons*. Alfred A. Knopf, 1961.

* Also available in paperback edition.

† Available only in paperback edition.

Where the Earth's Landforms May Be Seen

Many of the earth's most striking geologic formations lie within the borders of the United States and can be examined firsthand in the various National Parks and National Monuments and along the National Seashores (abbreviated below, respectively, NP, NM, and NS). This is a brief guide to the wonders on view in these public lands. The most unusual formations are singled out and described; less spectacular examples are listed at the end of each section.

Volcanoes

Active volcanoes are to be seen only in Hawaii, Alaska and the younger mountain ranges of the West, but the surrealistic effects of volcanic activity—cones, shields, lava flows, "calderas," dikes, sills, necks and so on, many bared by erosion—are on display in a variety of places, ranging from the Rio Grande to Maine.

HAWAII NP, HAWAII: Occupying more than 300 square miles on the islands of Hawaii and Maui, the park includes the 13,680-foot active shield volcano Mauna Loa; the nearby crater of Kilauea, which last erupted in 1960; active spatter cones; many-colored lava fields; black obsidian beaches; cinder cones and lava tubes on Hawaii. Maui's outstanding feature is the vast dormant crater of Haleakala.

KATMAI NM, ALASKA: Within this volcanic range, some 90 miles long, are fumaroles in the Valley of 10,000 Smokes; crater lakes; cones; and Katmai's giant *caldera*, the basin formed when the volcano erupted and collapsed in 1912.

LASSEN VOLCANIC NP, CALIF.: Lassen Peak, last active in 1917, cinder cones, *caldera*, lava flows, hot springs, plugs.

CRATER LAKE NP, ORE.: One of the world's greatest *calderas*, filled by a lake, the deepest in the U.S. (1,996 feet).

YELLOWSTONE NP, IDAHO-MONT.-WYO.: This is a park of volcanic superlatives. It has the world's largest and most spectacular collection of geysers (about 200), thousands of hot springs, mud volcanoes and fumaroles, Obsidian Cliff, and petrified trees.

Acadia NP, Me.; Bandelier NM, N. Mex.; Big Bend NP, Texas; Capulin Mtn. NM, N. Mex.; Craters of the Moon NM, Idaho; Death Valley NM, Calif.-Nev.; Devils Postpile NM, Calif.; Devils Tower NM, Wyo.; Grand Canyon NM & NP, Ariz.; Great Smoky Mtns. NP, N.C.-Tenn.; Isle Royale NP, Mich.; Lava Beds NM, Calif.; Mt. Rainier NP, Wash.; Pinnacles NM, Calif.; Sunset Crater NM, Ariz.

Faults and Folds

The results of diastrophism, the processes that thrust the earth's crust up and down along fractures, or faults, squeeze the surface into folded layers, and wrench entire areas askew, are magnificently evident in the Western U.S.

JOSHUA TREE NM, CALIF.: The entire area—870 square miles—reveals how mountain blocks are separated by shifting along faults. Salton View offers an excellent, 5,185-foot-high vantage point from which to see the famous horizontal San Andreas Fault, which runs along the Coachella Valley.

GRAND TETON NP, WYO.: Teton Range, a classic example of block faulting, rises abruptly from the valley of Jackson's Hole to an altitude of 13,766 feet.

COLORADO NM, COLO.: A vertical displacement, hundreds of feet high, is made more impressive by vivid layers of sandstone. The ends of the fault—bent rather than broken—can be seen in Fruita and No Thoroughfare Canyons.

ZION NP, UTAH: Practically no other area in the U.S. offers more vivid proof of the mobility of the earth's crust. Disrupted by the great Hurricane Fault, the brilliantly colored canyons along Kolob Terrace dramatically illustrate the effects of uplifting, faulting and erosion.

DEATH VALLEY NM, CALIF.-NEV.: An enormous graben, or rift valley, between two fault breaks.

CAPITOL REEF NM, UTAH: The wonders here range from a section of the 150-mile Waterpocket Fold, exposed in a many-colored cliff, through striking examples of rock erosion, to dinosaur tracks and petrified wood.

Big Bend NP, Texas; Bryce Canyon NP, Utah; Dinosaur NM, Utah-Colo.; Glacier NP, Mont.; Grand Canyon NM & NP, Ariz.; Mesa Verde NP, Colo.; White Sands NM, N. Mex.; Yellowstone NP, Idaho-Mont.-Wyo.

Sedimentation

The accumulated layers of sediment laid down by oceans, lakes and rivers form the stone records from which geologists read the past. The national parks and monuments are rich in these, but the most outstanding sequences of sedimentary rock, covering a billion and a half years of the earth's history, are found in the first three, within 75 miles of each other.

GRAND CANYON NM & NP, ARIZ.: The earth's timetable is revealed here. The canyon contains 1,270 million years of stratification; the deepest layer dates from 1,500 million years ago, and the most recent from the Mesozoic era.

ZION NP, UTAH: Sharply defined, these strata were formed during the Mesozoic, 230 to 63 million years ago.

BRYCE CANYON NP, UTAH: The exposed layers show geologic history dating back 63 million years.

CAPE HATTERAS NS, N.C.: A depositing seashore, where banks and islands are being formed by ocean currents.

Badlands NM, S. Dak.; Cape Cod NS, Mass.; Capitol Reef

NM, Utah; Cedar Breaks NM, Utah; Colorado NM, Colo.; Dinosaur NM, Utah-Colo.; Everglades NP, Fla.; Mesa Verde NP, Colo.; Shenandoah NP, Va.; Virgin Islands NP, V.I.; Yellowstone NP, Idaho-Mont.-Wyo.

Erosion

The forces of water and ice, weather and wind, constantly wearing away the earth, have created all sorts of odd and beautiful effects in the national parks and monuments and along the shores. Among these are the world's greatest canyon and largest natural bridge, castellated spires, vast caves and beautifully sculptured coast lines.

GRAND CANYON NM & NP, ARIZ.: The canyon without equal, cut by the Colorado River, is four to 18 miles wide, 217 miles long, and 4,000 to 6,000 feet deep.

RAINBOW BRIDGE NM, UTAH: The record 309-foot span soars 278 feet above the stream that scooped it out.

BRYCE CANYON, NP, UTAH: Small streams, rain and frost conspired here to create fantastic spires and pinnacles.

ARCHES NM, UTAH: The corrosive effect of freezing winter rains chipped away fragments of rock to produce these 88 arches on a streamless plateau.

MAMMOTH CAVE NP, KY.: No one is certain how big this eroded limestone cave really is, but 150 miles have been explored. Distributed over its five levels are three rivers, eight waterfalls, two lakes.

ACADIA NP, ME.: The cliffs and caves have been carved and undercut by pounding waves.

Badlands NM, S. Dak.; Big Bend NP, Texas; Black Canyon of the Gunnison NM, Colo.; Capitol Reef NM, Utah; Carlsbad Caverns NP, N. Mex.; Cedar Breaks NM, Utah; Colorado NM, Colo.; Dinosaur NM, Colo.-Utah; Jewel Cave NM, S. Dak.; Lehman Caves NM, Nev.; Natural Bridges NM, Utah; Olympic NP, Wash.; Oregon Caves NM, Ore.; Scotts Bluff NM, Neb.; Timpanagos Cave NM, Utah; Wind Cave NP, S. Dak.; Yellowstone NP, Idaho-Mont.-Wyo.; Yosemite NP, Calif.; Zion NP, Utah.

Glaciation

Live glaciers occur in the United States only in Alaska and on the high peaks of the Northwest, but the results of both alpine and continental glaciation—cirques, faceted peaks and saw-toothed ridges, moraines, scouring, polishing, striations, scratches and lakes—are widespread in the northern part of the country.

GLACIER BAY NM, ALASKA: In an area of nearly 3,600 square miles, there are more than 20 giant glaciers and scores of smaller ones. These show glaciation in various stages, from the rapid flow of Muir Glacier (20 or 30 feet a day) through stagnant ice masses to fiords.

MOUNT McKINLEY NP, ALASKA: The continent's highest mountain (20,320 feet) feeds glaciers into every valley. The largest and most spectacular is the Muldrow Glacier.

GLACIER NP, MONT.: There are about 60 small remnant glaciers here, and examples of alpine glacial carving.

MT. RAINIER NP, WASH.: Twelve major and 14 minor glaciers flow down the sides of this extinct volcano.

Acadia NP, Me.; Cape Cod NS, Mass.; Devils Postpile NM, Calif.; Grand Teton NP, Wyo.; Isle Royale NP, Wis.; Katmai NM, Alaska; Kings Canyon NP, Calif.; Olympic NP, Wash.; Rocky Mountain NP, Colo.; Sequoia NP, Calif.; Yellowstone NP, Idaho-Mont.-Wyo.; Yosemite NP, Calif. Also Wisconsin's proposed Ice Age NP.

Fossils

The fossil remains and imprints of plants and animals that lived as long ago as 500 million years are clearly visible in rocks in the following national parks and monuments:

DINOSAUR NM, UTAH-COLO.: This is the finest dinosaur-fossil deposit in the world. The specimens range from the 84-foot diplodocus through the brontosaurus and allosaurus to the relatively small (six-foot) laosaurus. A Visitor Center has been built so that one of its walls consists of a huge section of fossil-bearing rock. Here visitors can observe the excavation and preparation of fossil skeletons.

BADLANDS NM, S. DAK.: This virtual zoo of the Oligocene period, 36 to 25 million years ago, contains remains of the saber-toothed cat, the three-toed horse, and of ancestors of the rhinoceros, hog and camel.

GRAND CANYON NM & NP, ARIZ.: In the rocks of the canyon lie the fossils of crablike trilobites, dating back more than 500 million years; also plants, insects and fish.

PETRIFIED FOREST NM, ARIZ.: This is the world's largest and most colorful collection of fossilized wood, dating from the Triassic period, 230 to 200 million years ago.

COLORADO NM, COLO.: Many dinosaur fossils have been found here, including pieces of a 74-foot brachiosaur.

BIG BEND NP, TEXAS: The marine fauna and flora of 200 million years ago are preserved in the rocks. Dinosaur and crocodilian remains have been uncovered here, too, including the six-foot skull of the largest known extinct crocodile.

Bryce Canyon NP, Utah; Channel Islands NM, Calif.; Capitol Reef NM, Utah; Carlsbad Caverns NP, N. Mex.; Death Valley NM, Calif.-Nev.; Glacier NP, Mont.; Joshua Tree NM, Calif.; Scotts Bluff NM, Neb.; Walnut Canyon NM, Ariz.; Wind Cave NP, S. Dak.; Yellowstone NP, Idaho-Mont.-Wyo.; Zion NP, Utah.

Gems and Minerals

Most of the gem and mineral deposits in government-owned parks and monuments are either too low-grade to be worth mining or have been depleted. Many prime examples of the raw wealth of the earth, however, are on exhibit in natural history museums all over the country. There are remarkable displays at the Smithsonian Institution in Washington, D.C., and at the Museum of North Carolina Minerals on the Blue Ridge National Parkway.

For the indefatigable few who insist on doing their own gold-digging, the superintendent of Mount McKinley National Park, Alaska, is empowered to issue special prospecting permits.

Credits

The sources for the illustrations in this book are shown below. Credits for pictures from left to right are separated by commas, top to bottom by dashes.

Cover—Ray Manley from Shostal
8—Frank J. Scherschel
10, 11—Joseph Bertelli
12, 13—Joseph M. Sedacca courtesy American Museum of Natural History
14—Matt Greene
15—Joseph M. Sedacca courtesy American Museum of Natural History
17—George Solonevich
18 through 21—Antonio Petruccelli
22—Herman Eisenbeiss from Photo Researchers, Inc.
23—Don Moss, Emil Schulthess from Black Star
24—Top Lewis C. Thomas and Joseph F. Ossanna Jr. from The Bell Telephone Laboratories, Inc., Murray Hill, New Jersey; bottom Don Moss
25—Emil Schulthess from Black Star
26, 27—Mel Hunter—Lunar and Planetary Laboratory, University of Arizona
28—U.S. Air Force
29—Courtesy *Atlas of the Other Side of the Moon*—Ralph Morse
30—William A. Cassidy-Lamont Geological Observatory—The Smithsonian Institution—Jack Birns
31—The Smithsonian Institution, courtesy American Museum of Natural History (2)—Albert Fenn
32, 33—Left Jay Leviton; right Professor L. Kulik—J. R. Eyerman
34—Andreas Feininger
36, 37—Joseph M. Sedacca courtesy American Museum of Natural History
39—Adolph E. Brotman
40, 42—Adolph E. Brotman
45—Mel Hunter
46, 47—Left Charles W. Halgren courtesy Caru Studios—Camera Hawaii from Alpha Photo Associates, Inc.; right Eliot Elisofon
48—New York University Engineering Research Division
49—J. R. Eyerman
50, 51—*The New York Times*, courtesy International Seismological Summary—Joseph Lynch S.J.

52, 53—Left Hugo Benioff courtesy California Institute of Technology-Seismological Laboratory—Carnegie Institution of Washington; center Carl Mydans; right N. R. Farbman—Mainichi Shimbun
54, 55—Fritz Goro
56—Mel Coston for Humble Oil and Refining Company
58, 59—Dan Todd
60—Dan Todd—Matt Greene
61—Dan Todd—Matt Greene
65—Roland B. Bourne
66—Max Gschwind for FORTUNE
67—N. R. Farbman
68, 69—D. J. K. O'Connell
70, 71—The Reverend Frank Dinwiddie, C. R. Rouillon © World Meteorological Organization, Ruth Galaid from Photo Researchers, Inc., Russ Kinne from Photo Researchers, Inc.—Eliot Elisofon
72—Richard Jepperson from Alpha Photos
73—Ewing Galloway
74, 75—Left U.S. Naval Ordnance Laboratory—Horace S. Benson courtesy General Electric Corporation; center Ted Bank from Monkmeyer Press Photos; right Wide World Photos
76, 77—Left Bill Burkett—United Press International; right George Yates for *The Des Moines Register*
78, 79—Air Force Cambridge Research Laboratories, Charles W. Banks for Boston *Globe*
80—J. Allan Cash
83—Dan Todd
84, 85—Matt Greene
88—Adolph E. Brotman
89—Dan Todd
91—Margaret Bourke-White
92—Stan Wayman—Andreas Feininger
93—Earl Palmer from Monkmeyer Press Photos
94—Margaret Bourke-White—Bob Landry
95—Margaret Bourke-White—Homer Page for FORTUNE
96—Margaret Bourke-White
97—Herbert Gehr
98—George Silk

99—J. R. Eyerman—Fritz Goro
100—Courtesy American Museum of Natural History, Dmitri Kessel—Dmitri Kessel, courtesy American Museum of Natural History—Dmitri Kessel
101—Dmitri Kessel, courtesy American Museum of Natural History—courtesy American Museum of Natural History, Russ Kinne from Photo Researchers, Inc.—Floyd R. Getsinger, Dmitri Kessel
102—Andreas Feininger—Ultra-Violet Products, Inc. courtesy Gemmological Institute of America, Floyd R. Getsinger
103—Floyd R. Getsinger
104—Cole Weston from Rapho-Guillumette
109, 111—Matt Greene
113—David Muench
114—Andreas Feininger
115—Josef Muench—Nino Carbe
116, 117—Ansel Adams from Magnum
118, 119—Ernst Haas from Magnum, George Leavens from Photo Researchers, Inc.—Paul Jensen, Josef Muench (3)
120—Ansel Adams from Magnum
121—A. Y. Owen—Andreas Feininger
122, 123—Ned Haines from Rapho-Guillumette
124—Margaret Bourke-White
125—KLM Royal Dutch Airlines
126, 127—N. R. Farbman, Fritz Goro
128, 129—Royal Canadian Air Force and The Arctic Institute of North America, William M. Lee
130—John H. Gerard from Monkmeyer Press Photos
132, 133—Adolph E. Brotman
134, 135—Mark A. Binn
138, 139—Maps by Adolph E. Brotman
141—Carroll Lane and Mildred Adams Fenton
142—National Park Service
143—Carroll Lane and Mildred Adams Fenton—courtesy F. M. Carpenter
144, 145—Antonio Petruccelli
146—Dr. George Claus and Dr. Bartholomew Nagi

147—United Press International—Shuhei Yuyama courtesy Dr. Sidney Fox
148, 149—Left Albert Fenn—Kodak Research Laboratories; right Ezra Stoller for Sloan-Kettering Institute
150—Councilman Morgan, M.D.-Department of Microbiology, Columbia University
151—From *Electron Microscopy* by Dr. Ralph W. G. Wyckoff © 1949 by Interscience Publishers Division of John Wiley and Sons, C. E. Hall—courtesy Dr. Ralph W. G. Wyckoff and The Upjohn Company, Kalamazoo, Michigan
152—Dr. Roman Vishniac—Fritz Goro
153—Dr. Roman Vishniac—Fritz Goro
154—Dmitri Kessel
155—Ezra Stoller courtesy The Upjohn Company, Kalamazoo, Michigan
156—Argonne National Lab—Hansel Mieth
157—Dr. Arnold H. Sparrow and Robert F. Smith-Brookhaven National Laboratory, Upton, Long Island
158—Mel Hunter
163, 164—Ibex Ebel
167—Marc Riboud from Magnum
168, 169—Thomas E. Benner from Shostal—John Dominis
170, 171—Laurence Lowry from Rapho-Guillumette, Jerry Cooke
172—Marshall Lockman from Black Star—Howard Sochurek
173—A. Y. Owen
174, 175—Map by Fred Freeman
176—Albert Fenn
177—Joe Scherschel, N. R. Farbman
178—U.S. Signal Corps—George Burns courtesy General Electric Company
179—Ray Pioch—U.S. Department of Commerce, Weather Bureau (2)
180, 181—Left Andreas Feininger; top right Larry Burrows
182—Don Uhrbrock
183—United Press International
186, 187—Matt Greene

Acknowledgments

The editors of this book are particularly indebted to Wallace S. Broecker, Associate Professor of Geology, Lamont Geological Observatory, Columbia University, who read the text of the entire book and criticized the chapters in his own area of study. The editors are also indebted to Hugo Benioff, Assistant Professor of Seismology, California Institute of Technology; Cesare Emiliani, Research Associate Professor of Marine Geology, Marine Laboratory, University of Miami; William R. Farrand, Assistant Professor of Geology, and Councilman Morgan, Associate Professor of Microbiology, College of Physicians and Surgeons, Columbia University; Gerard P. Kuiper, Director, W. J. McDonald Observatory, University of Texas; the Reverend J. Joseph Lynch, head of the Seismic Station, Fordham University; Gordon J. F. MacDonald, Professor of Geophysics, University of California; Brian Mason, Curator, Physical Geology and Mineralogy, and Norman D. Newell, Curator, Invertebrate Fossils and Historical Geology, American Museum of Natural History; Brian J. O'Brien, Assistant Professor of Physics and Astronomy, University of Iowa; Robert H. Rose and Howard R. Stagner, National Park Service, U.S. Department of the Interior; Jerome Spar, Associate Professor of Meteorology, and Herbert Becker, Senior Research Scientist, New York University; Erling Dorf, Professor of Geology and Paleobotany, Princeton University; Melvin Calvin, Professor of Chemistry, University of California at Berkeley; Sidney Fox, Professor of Chemistry, Florida State University; Thomas Gold, Professor of Astronomy, Cornell University; J. Lamar Worzel, Assistant Director, and J. Laurence Kulp, Professor of Geochemistry and Director of the Geochemistry Laboratory, Lamont Geological Observatory, Columbia University.

Index

Numerals in italics indicate a photograph or painting of the subject mentioned.

Achondrites, 16
Adriatic Sea, 63
Aeolian erosion, 109
Aeros weather satellite, 179
African violets, mutant, *157*
Agadir earthquake, 53
Air, 57; carbon dioxide content of, 58, 159, 164; composition of, 58; currents, 60-64, 67, *76-78;* temperature, 58. *See also* Atmosphere
Air glow, 67
Airy, George B., 87
Algae, 137; fossils of, 133, *144*
Allosaurus, 138
Alpha Cephei, 14
Alpha Draconis, 13, 14
Alpha Ursa Minoris, 13
Alphonsus, lunar crater, 26, *27*
Altostratus clouds, 61
Aluminum resources, in rock, 83, 112
Amazonian shield, 133, 161
Amethyst, *101*
Amoebas, *152*, 153, 154
Amphibians, 134; early, 137, 138, 139
Animals: Cambrian, 135-136; Carboniferous, 137-138; Cenozoic, 139; classification of, 134-135; Cryptozoan, 133; Devonian, 137; evolution of, *table* 137; first land, 137; first warm-blooded, 139; fossils of, *134, 141-144;* Mesozoic, 138-139; Ordovician, 136; Permian, 138; Silurian, 136-137
Antarctica: coal deposits of, 88, 162; ice sheet of, 108, 163
Anticline, 84
Anticyclone, 61
Archimedes, 86
Arizona desert, 32, *72*
Arthropods, 134-135; early, 136, 137
Asbestos, *100*, 101
Ascension Island, 82
Asia: earthquake belts of, 38; loess deposits in, 109; weather features of, 62-63
Asteroids, 16, 36, 37, 171
Astronomical unit, 36
Atlantic Ocean, 63, 110, 162, 163
Atmosphere: beneficence of, 57, 65; composition of, 57; currents in, 60-64, 67, *76-78;* density of, 58; distortion of light by, *67-69;* future changes in, 164; heating of, 60, 164; layers of, 58, *diagram* 66, 67; pressure of, 58; source of, 47, 89-90; temperatures in, 58, 59, 66; tidal move in, 160; weight of, 57-58
Auroras, 21, *65, 66*
Australia, 76, 138
Australian shield, 133
Australites, *30*
Axis of earth: shift of, 13, *14, 18;* tilt of, 12, *diagrams* 12-13
Azores Islands, 82
Azurite, botryoidal, *100*

Babylonian concept of earth, 10
Baguios, 78
Baltic Sea, 110
Basalt, 38, 41, 82, 84-85, 86-87, 90; columns, *80*

Batholiths, 84
Benioff, Hugo, 49
Bering Strait, 88
Birds, 134, 139; first, 137, 139
Blind Cave Characin, *134*
Bode, Johann, 36, 37
Bode's Law, 36
Boloids, 15
Bora, 63
Bouguer, Pierre, 87
Bridalveil Falls, Can., *120*
Brontosaurus, 138
Brown, Harrison, 112
Bryant, William Cullen, 105
Bryce Canyon, Utah, *114*, 115

Calcite, *102, 103*, 108, 111
Calcium, 83
Calcium carbonate, 109, 110
Calcutta earthquake (1737), 53
California earthquakes, 38-39, 52
California Institute of Technology, 49, 112
Cambrian period, 135-136, 137; *map* 138, 144
Canada, 61, 163; effect of icecap on, 108, *128-129*
Canadian shield, 133, 161
Canyon Diablo Crater, *32-33*
Cape Cod, 110
Cape Hatteras, 110
Carbon dioxide, in atmosphere, 57, 58; industrial increase in, 159, 164; influence of, on temperature, 60, 164
Carbon 14 dating, 131, *diagram* 132
Carbonic acid, weathering by, 109, 110
Carboniferous period, 136, 137-138; fossil, *130*
Carlsbad Caverns, N.M., 109
Carnotite, *98*
Cavendish, Henry, 38
Caves, 109-110, *122-123;* hollowing of, *diagrams* 109
Celebes, 38
Cells, living: division of, 154; model of human, *154-155;* specialization of, 140; viruses in, *150-151*
Cenotes, 109
Cenozoic era, 135, *tables* 136-137, 139
Cephalopods, 136, *144*
Chalcanthite, *101*
Chemical weathering, 109-110, *122-123*
Chernozem soil, 124
Chicago, University of, 162
Chilean earthquake (1960), 53
Chimborazo, Mount, 87
China, earthquakes in, 53
China Sea, 62-63
Chondrites, 16
Chordates, 134, 135; first known, 136
Chromium, 112
Chromosomes, 148, 154, *156*
Chrysolite, *100*
Cirrocumulus clouds, 71
Cirrostratus clouds, 61, 70, 71
Cirrus clouds, 61, *66, 70,* 71
Clams, 134; early, 137, *144*
Clay, 83, 85, 110, 111
Clearwater National Forest, 74
Climate control, 179

Climatic changes: prediction of, 160; temperature rise, 164; theories on, 162-163; tied in with historical events, 163. *See also* Ice ages
Clouds, *58-59*, 61, 64, *66, 70-71*
Coal: deposits, *85*, 88, 89, 93; formation of, 93, 137; mining, *92-93;* peacock, *100*, 101
Cold front, 58, 61-62
Colorado Plateau, 108, 115, 117
Colorado River, *8*, 144, *173;* erosion by, 107-108, 115, 117, 120, *121*
Columbus, Christopher, 11
Comets, 16, 32-33
Conglomerate, 83, 111
Conifers, Permian, 138, *144*
Continental crust, 40-41, 54, 84-85, 86-87
Continental-drift theory, 88-89
Continental shelves, 82, 110, 161
Continents, 82, 86; average height of, 82, 86; depression of earth's mantle by, 86-87; distribution of, over earth, 81-82; formation of, theories, 87-90; growth of, 161; tidal move of, 23, 49, 160
Contraction theory, 89-90
Convection-current theory, 88, *diagram* 89, 90
Copper, 112, 171
Coral, 110; Paleozoic, 136-137, *144*
Core. *See* Earth core
Cosmic rays, 21, 59, 131
Cretaceous period, *tables* 136-137, *map* 139
Crossopterygii, 137
Crust. *See* Earth crust
Cryptozoic eon, 133, 135
Cumulonimbus clouds, 61, *66, 70-71*
Cumulus clouds, 61, *66,* 71
Cuss I, barge, *54-55*
Cyclones, 61; tropical, 63
Cygnus, constellation, 14

Darwin, Charles, 85
Day and night cycle, 12, 18
De Magnete, Gilbert, 43
Deforestation, 112
Descartes, 36
Devil's Garden, Utah, *118*
Devon Island glacier, *128*
Devonian period, 136, 137, *map* 138, 144
Dew, 73
Diamond pipe, *84*, 94, 95
Diamonds, 91, 94, *95;* luminescent, *102;* mining of, *94-95*
Diastrophism, 106, 111
Dikes, magma, 83-84
Dinosaur National Museum, *142*
Dinosaurs, 137, 138-139; fossils of, *142*
Diplodocus, 138
Dip poles, 43-44
Discontinuities, in interior of earth, 40, 41
DNA molecules, *148-149*, 154, 156
Dolomite, 83
Dripstone formations, 109, *122-123*
Drumlin, *diagram* 111
Dunite, 41
Dust-cloud hypothesis, 36-37

Earth: age of, 35, 131, 132; ancient concepts of, *10, 11;* density of, 15, 38, 41; dimensions of, 10-11; global concept of, 10-11; interior of, 37-38, 40-42 (*see also* Earth core; Earth mantle); layered structure of, 40-41, *46;* magnetic field of, 12, 20-21, 41, 42-44; mapping of, 161; motions of, 12-14, *18-19,* 160 (*see also* Nutation; Orbit; Precession; Rotation); origin of, 35-37, *45;* pressure inside, 41-42; pressure on, 58; shape of, 11; shift of axis of, 13, *diagram* 14, 18; "short-term" future of, 160-164; surface of, 40-41 (*see also* Earth crust); temperatures inside, 42, 46; tilt of axis of, 12, *diagrams* 12-13; ultimate fate of, *158,* 160, 164-166; uniqueness of, 10, 14, 36; views of, from space, 11-12, *17,* volume of, 38; warming of surface of, 42, 60; weight of, 38, 41
Earth core: inner, 41, 46, 49; outer, 41, 44, 46; properties of, 41-42; temperature of, 42, 46
Earth crust, 15, 46, 49, 51, 81-90, 131; composition of, 38, 41, 82-83; continental *vs.* oceanic, 40-41, 54, 82, 84-85, 86-87; cutaway profile of, *84-85;* faults in, 38, *52, 85;* folds in, *84;* origin of, 85-86; plan to bore shaft through, 42, *54-55;* shift of, 89; structure of, 84-87; theories on major changes in, 88-90; thickness of, 40-41. *See also* Continents; Landscape; Rock
Earth mantle, 46; depression of, under continents, 86-87; earthquakes in, 51; flow of material in, 88, 90; plan to drill shaft through, to, 42, *54-55;* properties of, 41
Earth-moon gravitational system, 12-13, *19*
Earth strain meter, *49*
Earthquakes, 38-40, 46, 49-53; determining epicenter and force of, *42,* 50, 51; effects of, *52-53;* examples of, 39, 53; give proof of earth's layers, 40-41; global zones, 38, *map* 51; shock waves of, 39, 40, 41; shock wave recording, *50-51;* shock wave simulation, *48;* U.S. zones, *map* 40; victims of, 53
East Pacific Rise, 161
Eclipses, *24-25*
Eclogite, 41
Egyptian concept of earth, *10*
Electromagnetic waves, 60
Elizabeth I, Queen, 43
Els Hams Cave, Majorca, *122-123*
Equatorial bulge, 11, 13
Equatorial circumference, 10
Equinoxes, precession of, 13, *18*
Eratosthenes, 10
Erosion, 57, 83, 106-110, 113; coastal, *104,* 110, *125-127;* vs. diastrophism, 106, 111; by frost, 107, 109; glacial, 108, *128-129;* man-made, 112; by rainwater, 106, 107, *114, 118-119;* resistance to, 118; by rivers, 106-108,

115, *117, 118, 120-121;* and soil-building, 110, 124; underground, 109-110, *122-123;* by wind, 109, *118-119. See also* Weathering
Esker, *diagram* 111
Ether, 58
Ethiopian shield, 133
Europe: earthquakes in, 38-39; effect of ice ages on, 128
Evaporation, 64, 106
Evergreens, early, 137, *144*
Evolution, 133-135, 139-140; first land animal, 137; influence of man on, 135, 140; of man, 132, 166; from one-celled to multicellular organisms, 140, 152-153; outlines of, 135-139; parallel, on different continents, 137; time scale, *table* 137; warm-bloodedness, 139
Exosphere, 58, 59, 66, 67
Expansion theory, 90
Explorer satellites, 12, 20

Faults, in crust of earth, 38, *52, 85*
Feldspar, 108
Ferns. *See* Seed ferns; Tree ferns
Fish, 134; Cenozoic, 137; fossils, *134, 141, 144;* Paleozoic, 136, 137
Flash phenomena of light, *68-69*
Fluorite, *102*
Fly fossil, *143*
Fog, *73*
Folds, in crust of earth, *84*
Fordham seismological observatory, *50*
Fossilization, 143
Fossils, 111, *134, 135, 141, 143,* 162; Cambrian, 135; Carboniferous, *130;* Cryptozoan, 133; dating of, 132, 133; Devonian, 137; of first land animals, 137; found in Grand Canyon, *144;* freeing of, from rock, *142;* in meteorites, *146,* 147; Miocene, *143;* Phanerozoan, 133; Project Mohole search for, 42, *54;* Silurian, 137; source of, 83
Frogs, 134, 137, 138
Frost, 73; erosion by, 107, 109
Fukui earthquake, *52-53*
Fungi, fossils, 133

Galaxies, 9, 14, *18-19,* 36, 160, 181
Ganymede, 14
Garnet, *101*
Geogonies, 37-38
Geographic poles, 89, 162-163
Geologic periods, 133, 135
Geology, 85, 111
Geomagnetic poles, 43
Geysers, *34,* 46
Giant's Causeway, Ireland, *80*
Gilbert, William, 43
Glaciers, 108; erosion by, 108, *diagram* 111, *128-129;* in Southern Hemisphere, 88, 89, 138. *See also* Ice ages
Glen Canyon Dam, *173*
Glenn, John, 179
Global concept of earth, 10
Glossopteris fossil, *135*
Gneiss, 83, 132
Goblin Valley, Utah, *119*
Gold, 96, *97;* mining, *91;* river deposits of, 107
Graben, *85*
Grand Canyon, 8, 107-108, 115, *116-117, 121;* fossil record of,

144; present animal and plant life of, *145*
Granite, 38, 41, 82, 83, 84-85, 86, 87, 90; minerals in, 112; weathering of, 109
Gravel, 107, 110, 111
Gravitation, universal, 38
Great Bear, 43
Great Lakes, 128
Greenland icecap, 108, 163
Guiana shield, 133

Hail, 64
Half-life of radioactive elements, 132
Hawaii, 47, 83
Hebgen Lake, Montana, *53*
Heezen, Bruce, 90
Hercules, constellation, 14
Heredity, 148, 154, 156
High-pressure cell, *61*
Hindu concepts of earth, *11*
Hipparchus, 13
Hodges, Mrs. Hewlett, *32*
Horst, *85*
Hot springs, 46
Hudson Bay, 110, 133
Hudson River, 84
Hull-Rust-Mahoning mine, *170-171*
Hurricanes, 63-64, *78*
Hutton, James, 106
Huxley, Julian, 138
Hydra, *152-153*

Ice ages: erosive effects of, 108, *128-129;* future, 161-162, 163; Permian, 138; Pleistocene, 128, 136, 161-162; temperature cycle of, 162; theories on origin of, 162-163
Icecaps, weight of, 87, 108
Igneous rock, 82, 83, 84-85, 111, 112
India, earthquakes in, 38, 53
Indian Ocean, 62-63
Infrared radiation, 60, 160
Insects, 134, 139; Carboniferous, 137; Devonian, 137; Permian, 137, *144*
International Geophysical Year, 11, 59
Interstellar communication, 180-181
Ionosphere, 58, 59, 66, 67
Iron: chief component of earth's core, 41; content in rock, 83, 112; in meteorites, 16; mining of, *170-171*
Isostasy, theory of, 87

Japan: earthquakes in, 52-53; overpopulation of, 168, *169*
Johannesburg, Robinson Deep in, *91,* 96
Jupiter, 11, 14, 16, 37, 166
Jurassic period, 136, 137

Kansas City, Mo., tornado destruction in, *76*
Kant, Immanuel, 36
Karsts, 109
Keller, Will, 62
Kilauea, *46-47*
Kilimanjaro, Mount, *71*
Kimberley diamond mines, *94,* 95
Krakatoa, 64
Kuiper, Gerard P., 36
Kuwait, water distillation plant in, *172*

Lagoon, building of, *127*
Lampreys, 134, 136
Land: distribution of, over earth, 81-82; first animals on, 137; first plants on, 137; reclamation, 112. *See also* Continents
Land breeze, 62
Landscape: of the future, 161; shaping of, 90, 105-106, 113. *See also* Erosion; Mountain-building
Laplace, Pierre Simon de, 36
Laurentide ice sheet, 108
Lava, 83, 84; cooled, *80;* flow, *47*
Lead: content in rock, 112; product of radioactive decay, 132; resources, 171
Lichens, 135
Life, 57; origin of, 132-133, 147, 151; other than on earth, 10, 146, 147, 181. *See also* Animals; Evolution; Fossils; Man; Plants
Light, 9, 60, 69
Lightning, 64, *74-75,* 110
Limestone, 83, 111; erosion of, 109, *122-123*
Limonite, *100*
Lisbon earthquake, 39
Little Bear, 13
Lizards, 134; Permian, *144*
Lobsters, 134; early, 137
Loess, 109
Low-pressure cell, *60,* 61
Lunar atlas, *28-29*
Lunar craters, 14-15, *26-27*
Lunar eclipse, 24
Lunik rocket, 14, 28, 29
Luray Cave, Va., 109
Lynch, Joseph, *50*

McCoy, Ralph, *54*
Magma, 46, 83-84
Magnesium, 83
Magnetic field of earth, 12, 20-21, 41, 42-44
Magnetic poles, 43-44, 89, 162-163
Magnetosphere, 12, *20-21,* 44, 59, 66, 67
Majorca, Els Hams Cave of, *122-123*
Malachite, *100*
Malthus, Thomas, 168
Mammals, 134, 139; first, 137, 139
Mammoth Cave, Ky., 109
Man, 57, 58; evolution of, 132, 166; future of, 140, 163, 165-166, 167; influence of, on erosion, 112; influence of, on evolution, 135, 140; overpopulation problems, 167-169
Manganese, 112
Mankind, The Story of, Van Loon, 132
Mantle. *See* Earth mantle
Marble, 83
Mars, 16, 36, 37; travel to, 182
Mead, Lake, 108
Medieval concept of earth, 11
Mediterranean, 63, *68-69*
Mene Rhombeus fossil, *141*
Mercury, 14, 36, 37, 165
Mesosphere, 58, 66, 67
Mesozoic era, 135, *tables* 136-137, 138-139
Metal resources in rock, 112
Metamorphic rock, 82, 83, 84-85
Meteorites, 15-16, 26, *30-31,* 32-33; dating of, 132; fossils in, *146,* 147
Meteoritic dust, 16, 30, 32
Meteoroids, 15, 16

Meteorology, 160; term, 15
Meteors, 15, 16, 59, 65, 67
Mica, 107, 108
Michell, John, 39
Microline, *100*
Mid-Atlantic Ridge, 82
Milankovitch, Milutin, 162, 163
Milky Way, 9, 14, 181
Millepedes, 134, 137
Miller, Stanley, 147
Minerals, 83, 85, *100-101;* and chemical weathering, 109-110, 122-123; depletion of resources of, 112, 170-171; identification of, 102; luminescence of, *102-103*
Mining, *91-99, 170-171*
Miocene period, *map* 139; tree fossil, *143*
Mississippi: delta, 111; erosion by, 106-107, 121
Mistral, 63
Mohole, Project, 42, *54-55*
Mohorovičić, Andrija, 40
Mohorovičić discontinuity, 40, 41, 90
Mollusks, 134, 135; early, 136
Monocline, *85*
Monsoons, 62-63
Montana, earthquakes in, 50, *53*
Monument Valley, Arizona, *113*
Moon, 10, 14-15, *22; maps* 28-29; density of, 15, 23; dimensions of, 14, 23; distance of, from earth, 11, 14, 23; eclipse of, *24;* future of, *163,* 164, 165; hidden side of, 14, 28, *29;* influence of, on movements of earth, 12-13, *18, 19,* 164; landscape, 14-15, *26-27;* motions of, 13, 14, *19, 23;* origin of, 36-37, *45;* phases of, *23;* as seen from space, 11, *17;* superstitions about, 23; temperatures on, 15; tidal effect of, on earth, 13, 23, 49, 160, 164, 165; travel to, *182-183;* uniqueness of, 14, 36
Moon-earth gravitational system, 12-13, *19*
Moraine, *diagram* 111
Mountain-building, 106, 111; Carboniferous, 137; future, 161; Ordovician, 136; Permian, 138; and polar wandering, 163
Mountains: depression of earth's mantle by, 87; types of, *84-85*
Multicellular organisms, evolution of, 140, 152-153
Mutation, 156; due to radiation, *157*

National Science Foundation, 42
Negev, terracing of, 112
Neptune, 36, 37
Neptunist school of geology, 85
Nevada, exposed fault in, *52*
New York University, 48
Newton, Sir Isaac, 11, 38, 160
Niagara Falls, erosion by, 105
Nickel: in crustal rock, 112; in earth core, 41; in meteorites, 16
Night and day cycle, 12, 18
Nile River, erosion by, *118*
Nimbostratus clouds, 61, 71
Nimbus weather satellite, 179
Nitrogen, 58, 75, 132; cycle, 110
Noctilucent clouds, *66,* 67
North America: earthquake belt of, 38-39; effects of icecap erosion on, 108, *128-129;* land and sea distribution in, over various periods, *maps* 138-139; in Ordovi-

cian period, 136; in Silurian period, 136; tidal heave of, 23; weather features of, 61, 76. *See also* United States
North Magnetic Pole, 44
North Pole, former location of, 162-163
North Star, 12, 43; change of, 13, *diagram* 14
Nova rocket, 182
Nuclear power, 91, 99, 177; reactor, *176*
Nutation, 13, *18*
Nyamlagira volcano, *47*

Obsidian, 84
Ocean: average depth of, 82; decrease of oxygen content of, 160; distribution of, over earth, 81-82; erosion by, *104*, 110, *125-127*; floor, 82, 110-111; future changes in, 161; land-building by, 110, *127*; level, changes in, 81, 160-161, 163; origin of, according to contraction theory, 89-90; primordial, 85; ridges and trenches, 82; salinity of, 122; storms, 63, *70-71*; temperature, fluctuation of, 162, 163; tides, 13, 23; waves, 78, *79*
Oceanic crust, 40, 42, 54, 84-85, 86-87
Oil deposits, *84-85*
Olivine, 16, 31
Orbit of earth, 12-13, 18, *19*
Orbits, planetary, 37
Ordovician period, 136, *map* 138
Ore resources, 112, 171
Overpopulation, *167-169*
Overthrust fault, *85*
Oxygen: content in air, 58; content in oceans, 160; content in rock, 83; heavy, 58; importance of, to life, 57; in ionosphere, 59
Oxygen-isotope shell thermometer, 162, 163
Ozma, Project, 180
Ozone layer, 57, 58, 60, 67

Pacific earthquake belt, 38, 39, 161
Pacific Ocean, 63, *67*, *70-71*, *104*, 162, 163
Paleontology, 111
Paleozoic era, 135-138; time scale, *tables* 136-137
Palomar, Mount, observatory, 26
Pangaea, 88
Panthalassa, 88
Peacock coal, *100*, 101
Pele's Hair, *101*
Pennsylvanian period, *map* 139
Peridotite, 41
Permian period, 136, 138, 144
Phanerozoic eon, 133, 135
Pioneer satellites, 20
Planetesimals, 30
Planets, 14; distances of, from sun, 36, 37; gravitational forces of, on earth, 13; orbits of, 37; origin of, 36-37, *45*; outside solar system, 181
Plants, 110, 134; Cambrian, 135; Carboniferous, 137, 138; Devonian, 137; evolution of, *table* 137; first land, 137; fossils of, *130*, *135*, *143*, *144*; Permian, 138
Platanus tree fossil, *143*
Pleistocene, 137; ice ages, 161-162
Pluto, 36, 37
Plutonist school of geology, 85

Polar diameter, 11
Polar wandering, theory of, 162-163
Polaris, star, 13, 14, 43
Poles: geographic, 89; geomagnetic, 43; magnetic (dip), 43-44, 89
Potassium, 83; radioactive isotope of, 42, 132, 161
Power sources and supply, 91, 93, 99, 177; future, 166, *176*, 177
Precambrian period, 136, 144
Precession, 13, *18*
Precipitation, 60, 61, 63, 64, 70-71; and erosion, 106; in United States, 175
Pressure: atmospheric, 58; inside earth, 41-42
Pteranadon, 139
Ptolemaeus, lunar crater, *27*
Pyrite, *100*
Pyroxene, 16

Quartz, *100*, 107, 108
Quartzite, 83

Radiation, space, 12, *20-21*, 60, 65, 160; cosmic, 21, 59, 131; future solar, 165, 166; mutation by, *157;* solar, 37, 44, 57, 58, 59, 60, 67
Radioactive dating, 131-132, 162
Radioactive elements, 42, 132, 161
Radiocarbon dating, 131, *diagram* 132
Radiotelescopes, *180-181*
Rain, 64, *70-71;* average annual, in U.S., 175; erosion by, 106, 107, *114*, *118-119*
Rainbow, *72*, 73
Reforestation, 112
Reptiles, 134, 139; first, 137-138; flying, 139; Mesozoic, 137, 138-139; Permian, 137, 138
Rhone Valley, 63
River deltas, 110-111
Rivers, erosion by, 106-108, 115, *117*, *118*, *120-121*
RNA, 154
Rock, 82; average density of, 38; basic types of, 82-83, 84; composition of, 83; Cryptozoan, 133; dating of, 131-132; of earth's mantle, 41; formation and disintegration cycle of, *diagram* 83; formations, 83-84; igneous, 82, 83, 84-85, 111, 112; metamorphic, 82, 83, 84-85; oldest known, 132; sedimentary, 82-83 84, 85, 111; specimens, *100-103*
Rotation, planetary, 37
Rotation of earth, 12, 13, *18;* as cause of winds, 60, 61, 63; future changes in, 164
Rubidium, 132
Ruby sphalerite, *101*
Runoff water, 106-108, 112, *114*

Salamanders, 134; early, 137, *144*
Salt deposits: Permian, 138; Silurian, 138
Salt dome, *84*
Salt water, desalinization of, 172
San Andreas fault, 38-39, 52
San Francisco earthquake, 39, 52, 53
Sand, 83, 107, 110, 111
Sandstone, 83, 85, 111
Satellites, man-made, 11, 12, 20-21, 28, 160, 161, 177, *179*, 182
Saturn, 11, 37, 38, 163, 165
Saturn booster, *182*

Scale trees, 138, *144*
Scandinavia, rise of, 87, 108
Scandinavian shield, 133
Scapolite, *102*
Scheelite, *102*
Scorpions, 134; Paleozoic, 137, *144*
Sea breeze, 62
Seasons, 12, *diagrams* 12-13, 18
Seaweed, early, 137, *144*
Sedimentary rock, 82-83, 84-85, 111
Sediments, 82-83, 107; ocean floor, 82, 110-111
Seed-ferns, 138; fossils, *130*, *135*, *144*
Seismograph, *39*, 40, *50*, 51; recording, *50-51*
Serapis, temple of, 106
Shale, 83, 85, 111
Sharks, early, 137, *144*
Shields, Cryptozoan, 133, 161
Shiogama, Japan, earthquake, *53*
Shock waves, earthquake, 39, 40, 41, 50; recording of, *50-51;* simulation, *48*
Siberia, 32, 33, 133, 163
Silicon, 83
Sills, magma, 84
Silurian period, 136-137
Single-celled organisms, 133, 135
Sinkholes, 109
Sirocco, 63
Slate, 83
Sleet, 64
Slime mold, 134, *152-153*
Smog, 73
Snails, 134; early, *144*
Snow, 64, 71
Sodium, 83
Soil-building, 110, 124
Solar eclipse, *24-25*
Solar power, *177*
Solar system, 9-10, 37; age of, 132; motions of, 13-14, *19;* origin of, 36-37, *45*, 89
South Pole, former location of, 162-163
Space: communication, *180-181*; travel, 182; views of earth from, 11-12. *See also* Satellites; Universe
Species, 134; average life span of, 165-166; differentiation and continuity of, 148
Spiders, 134; Paleozoic, 137, *144*
Squids, 134, 136
Stalactites, 109, *122-123*
Stalagmites, 109, *122-123*
Starfish, early, 137, *144*
Stegosaurs, 138
Storms, tropical, 63-64
Stratocumulus clouds, *70*, 71
Stratosphere, 58, 66, 67
Stratus clouds, 71
Summer solstice, 12, 13
Sun, 9, 36; distance of earth from, 12, 36, *table* 37; distances of planets from, 36, *table* 37; earth's orbit around, 12-13, 18, *19;* eclipse of, *24-25;* future of, *164*, 165; influence of, on motions of earth, 13-14, *18-19*, 164; light rays of, 60, 69; motion of, 13-14, 18, *19*, 37; nuclear reactions in, 37, 164, 165; origin of, 36-37; radiation of, *20-21*, 37, 44, 57, 58, 59, 60, 67; setting, *67-69;* size of, 160; surface temperature of, 42; theory of heat loss of, 162
Syene, Egypt, 10
Syncline, *84*

Taconite, 170, *171*
Tektites, *30*
Temperatures: atmospheric, 58, 59, 66; inside earth, 42, 46; ocean, fluctuation of, 162, 163; surface, 42, 164
Tertiary, *table* 137
Thorium, 42, 112, 132, 161
Thunder, 74
Thunderstorm, 61, *70-71*, *74-75*, 76
Tides: aerial, 160; continental, 23, 49, 160; effect of, on earth rotation, 164; land losses due to, 110, *125;* oceanic, 13, 23, 110
Tiros weather satellite, *179*
Titanium, 112
Toadstool Park, Neb., *118-119*
Tokyo earthquake (1923), 53
Tornado, 62, *76;* effects of, *76-77*
Trade winds, 12, 60, 63
Tree ferns: Devonian, 137; Permian, *144*
Trees: Carboniferous, 137, 138; Cretaceous, 137; Devonian, 137; Miocene, fossil, *143*
Triassic period, 136, 137
Trilobite, 136, 137, 138, *144*
Tristan da Cunha, 82
Tropopause, 58
Troposphere, 58, 60, 66, 67
Tungsten ore, *102*, 112
Typhoons, 63, 78
Tyrannosaurus, 139

Uintacyon fossil, *143*
Ultraviolet rays, 57, 58, 59, 60, 67
Unconformity, 85, 111
United States: coal deposits in, 93; earthquakes in, 38-39, *map* 40, *52-53;* fall of meteorites on, 30; loess deposits in, 109; mineral shortages in, 171; uranium deposits in, 98-99; water resources of, 172, *map* 174-175; weather features of, 61, 62, 75, 76, 175. *See also* North America
Universe, 14, 36, 160
Uranium, 42, 91, *99*, 161; dating, 132; energy yield of, *176;* prospecting, *98*, 102; refining, *99;* resources, 99, 112, 177
Uranus, 36, 37
Urey, Harold, 162
U.S. Weather Bureau, 62
Ussher, James, Archbishop, 35

Valleys, shaping of, 107-108
Van Allen, James, 20
Van Allen radiation belt, 12, *20-21. See also* Magnetosphere
Van Loon, Hendrik, 132
Vanadium, 112
Vanguard I satellite, 11
Variscite, *101*
Vatican Observatory, 68
Vega, 13, 14
Venus, *23*, 36, 37, *68*, 69; travel to, 182
Vertebrates, 134; first all-land, 137-138; first known, 136, 137; Mesozoic, 137, 138-139; Paleozoic, 136, 137
Victoria Island, Can., *128-129*
Viruses, *150-151*
Volcanic "ring of fire," 38, 161
Volcanic rock, 82, 83-84
Volcanoes, *46-47*, 64, 83, 85; in North America, *table* 136, 137
Vonnegut, Bernard, *178*

Index, *continued*

Waddenzee coast erosion, *125*
Warm front, *59*, 61
Water: precipitation and evaporation cycle, 64, 106; running, erosion by, 106-108; shortage of, 172; source of, 47; underground, 109
Water table, 109, 112
Water vapor in atmosphere, 57, 60, 64, 70

Waterman, Alan T., 42
Waterspout, *56*, 62, 76
Waves, ocean, 78, *79*, 110
Weather, 12, 60-64, 67; clouds, 61, 64, *70-71;* control, 160, *178,* 179; fog, *73;* fronts, *58-59,* 61-62; precipitation, 64, 70-71; prediction, 160, 179; thunderstorms, 61, *70-71, 74-75;* tropical storms, 63-64; winds, 60-61, 62-63, *76-78*

Weathering, 106, 110; chemical, 109-110, *122-123;* mechanical, 109. *See also* Erosion
Wegener, Alfred, 88, 89
Willamette, meteorite, *30*
Willemite, *102, 103*
Winds, 60-61, 62-63, *76-78,* 108-109; erosion by, 109, *118-119*
Winter solstice, 12

Wright brothers, 110
Wulfenite, yellow, *100*

Yellowstone National Park, *34,* 53, *121*
Yosemite Valley, *120*
Yugoslavia, 63

Zinc, 102, 171; mineral, *103*
Zion National Park, *115*

PRODUCTION STAFF FOR TIME INCORPORATED

Arthur R. Murphy (Vice President and Director of Production)
Robert E. Foy, James P. Menton and Caroline Ferri
Text photocomposed on Photon equipment under the direction of Albert J. Dunn and Arthur J. Dunn

✕

Printed by R. R. Donnelley & Sons Company, Crawfordsville, Indiana,
and Livermore and Knight Co., Providence, Rhode Island
Paper by The Mead Corporation, Dayton, Ohio
Bound by R. R. Donnelley & Sons Company, Crawfordsville, Indiana